Library of
Davidson College

Truman's Court

Recent Titles in
Contributions in Legal Studies
Series Editor: Paul L. Murphy

Corwin's Constitution: Essays and Insights of Edward S. Corwin
Kenneth D. Crews, editor

The Role of State Supreme Courts in the New Judicial Federalism
Susan P. Fino

State Relationships in America
Gerard V. Bradley

Rocky Mountain Constitution Making, 1850–1912
Gordon Morris Bakken

First Use of Nuclear Weapons: Under the Constitution, Who Decides?
Peter Raven-Hansen, editor

Judicial Selection: The Cross-Evolution of French and American Practices
Mary Volcansek and Jacqueline Lucienne Lafon

The Law School Papers of Benjamin F. Butler: New York University Law School in the 1830s
Ronald L. Brown, editor and compiler

The Civil Rights Revolution: The Old Court and Individual Rights
John Braemen

Whom Does the Constitution Command?
A Conceptual Analysis with Practical Implications
Larry Alexander and Paul Horton

Constitutionalism: The Philosophical Dimension
Alan S. Rosenbaum, editor

Human Rights in the States: New Directions in Constitutional Policymaking
Stanley H. Friedelbaum, editor

Death by Installments: The Ordeal of Willie Francis
Arthur S. Miller and Jeffrey H. Bowman

Truman's Court

A Study in Judicial Restraint

Frances Howell Rudko

Contributions in Legal Studies
Number 45

Greenwood Press
New York • Westport, Connecticut • London

Library of Congress Cataloging-in-Publication Data

Rudko, Frances Howell.
  Truman's Court : a study in judicial restraint / Frances Howell Rudko.
    p.   cm.—(Contributions in legal studies, ISSN 0147–1074 ; no. 45)
  Bibliography: p.
  Includes index.
  ISBN 0–313–26316–7 (lib. bdg. : alk. paper)
  1. United States. Supreme Court. 2. Judicial process—United States. 3. Political questions and judicial power—United States. I. Title. II. Series.
KF8742.R83 1988
347.73′26—dc19
[347.30735]   88–5664

British Library Cataloguing in Publication Data is available.

Copyright © 1988 by Frances Howell Rudko

All rights reserved. No portion of this book may be reproduced, by any process or technique, without the express written consent of the publisher.

Library of Congress Catalog Card Number: 88–5664
ISBN: 0–313–26316–7
ISSN: 0147–1074

First published in 1988

Greenwood Press, Inc.
88 Post Road West, Westport, Connecticut 06881

Printed in the United States of America

The paper used in this book complies with the Permanent Paper Standard issued by the National Information Standards Organization (Z39.48–1984).

10 9 8 7 6 5 4 3 2 1

Copyright Acknowledgments

The author and publisher gratefully acknowledge permission to use extracts from the following material:

Harold Hitz Burton Papers, Manuscript Division, Library of Congress, Washington D. C. Courtesy of William S. Burton.

Hugo La Fayette Black Papers, Manuscript Division, Library of Congress, Washington D. C. Courtesy of Hugo Black, Jr.

Hugo La Fayette Black. Personal Papers. Courtesy of Hugo Black, Jr.

Tom C. Clark Papers, Rare and Special Collection, Tarlton Law Library, University of Texas, Austin, Texas. Courtesy of the University of Texas.

Tom C. Clark. Personal Papers. Courtesy of Ramsey Clark.

Felix Frankfurter Papers, Manuscript Division, Harvard Law School Library, Cambridge, Massachusetts. Courtesy of Harvard Law School Library.

Sherman Minton Papers, Harry S. Truman Library, Independence, Missouri. Courtesy of the Harry S. Truman Library and Sherman A. Minton, M.D.

Sherman Minton. Personal Papers. Courtesy of Sherman A. Minton, M.D.

Edward F. Prichard, Jr. Oral History. Frederick Moore Vinson Papers, Special Collections of the Margaret I. King Library, University of Kentucky, Lexington, Kentucky. Courtesy of Lucy Prichard.

Truman Papers, Harry S. Truman Library, Independence, Missouri. Courtesy of the Harry S. Truman Library.

Frederick Moore Vinson Papers, Special Collections of the Margaret I. King Library, University of Kentucky, Lexington, Kentucky. Courtesy of the University of Kentucky Libraries.

Oral histories from W. E. Crutcher, Albert B. Maris, Newton N. Minow, William W. Oliver, Willard H. Pedrick, Howard J. Trienens, and Fred Vinson, Jr. are courtesy of the Oral History Program, Special Collections of the Margaret I. King Library, University of Kentucky Libraries.

Extracts from:
7 Harvard Law Review 129, 144, 156 © (1893) by the Harvard Law Review Association. Permission granted.
29 Harvard Law Review 683 © (1916) by the Harvard Law Review Association. Permission granted.
36 Harvard Law Review 909 © (1923) by the Harvard Law Review Association. Permission granted.

45 Harvard Law Review 33, 38, 80 © (1931) by the Harvard Law Review Association. Permission granted.
73 Harvard Law Review 1, 19 © (1959) by the Harvard Law Review Association. Permission granted.
76 Harvard Law Review 673, 675 © (1963) by the Harvard Law Review Association. Permission granted.
78 Harvard Law Review 1521 © (1965) by the Harvard Law Review Association. Permission granted.
100 Harvard Law Review 817, 840 © (1987) by the Harvard Law Review Association and Philip Elman. Permission granted.

To
James S. Chase, Historian,
A Dedicated Teacher
and Friend

CONTENTS

Preface		xi
Introduction		xvii
1.	Judicial Restraint versus Judicial Activism	1
2.	The Truman Legacy	25
3.	Burton's Tenure on the Court	45
4.	Vinson's Tenure on the Court	63
5.	Clark's Tenure on the Court	87
6.	Minton's Tenure on the Court	111
7.	Conclusion	129
Bibliography		137
Index		155

PREFACE

Supreme Court decisions are regularly scrutinized for their substantive impact on specific problems in society, and judges are usually categorized according to the perceived ideology of their particular decisions. Observers of the Court seldom question *how* particular decisions are made. And the impact of the Court's decisions, which comprises the policy-making power of the Court, commands not only the immediate attention of society but also the attention of most scholars who study the work of the Court as well. This concentration on the result, with its ideological trappings, often obscures the more profound judicial philosophy which formed the decision. A more fully informed response to a Court decision will encompass not only the decision and the political context in which it was made, but also the larger perspective of the judicial process leading to the decision. This study is primarily concerned not with the policy-making impact of the Court, but with the decision-making processes during a reasonably well-defined period of its history, specifically the Vinson era (1945–53), and within and beyond that period, with the judicial philosophy of Truman's four appointees to the Supreme Court.

Individual decisions of the Vinson Court have been previously analyzed by constitutional scholars for their substantive impact on the issues which they addressed. The political impact of the decisions has been amply and ably explored by John P. Frank and C. Herman Pritchett, among others. By addressing the question of how the four appointees made specific decisions, we not only better understand the decisions, we also enhance our understanding of the Supreme Court as an institution. There is a tendency to see the Supreme Court only as a political institution—its decisions as legislative rather than judicial. We need to remember that the Court, whatever may be the political impact of its decisions, functions by procedures that are distinctly judicial in nature. Looking at these decisions from the standpoint of judicial self-restraint or its absence reinforces this crucial institutional character that is usually ignored.

The Supreme Court serves as a check upon the other two branches of government, but does so within the restricted format imposed by its judicial nature and by well-understood, if oft-flouted, rules of judicial restraint. Ruling specifically and with apparent finality on political issues, the Court creates the impression of monolithic unity when, in fact, decisions are seldom unanimous and reasons supporting individual decisions of the Court are various. The observer, impressed with this sense of unity, seldom considers the function of the Court as a check on the other branches of government. Rather he tries to fit each decision into a preconceived policy scheme or to place it within an ideological spectrum. Frequently, a Supreme Court decision will either be attacked as a usurpation of the legislative function and labeled as an example of judicial activism, or be deplored as an abdication of the judicial function, when in both instances the real complaint is with the policy impact of the decision. The question of underlying philosophy—in a nutshell, judicial restraint versus judicial activism—is more important that its use as a handy rhetorical club suggests.

The tendency to confuse political ideology with judicial philosophy is intensified by claims from both liberals and conservatives to be advocates of judicial restraint, as is well illustrated by the controversy over President Reagan's nomination of Judge Robert H. Bork to the Supreme Court. Reagan made no secret of his desire to alter the political complexion of the Court, which he found too liberal, in order to overturn well-established precedents, especially those involving abortion, school prayer, and affirmative action. Yet in announcing Bork's nomination on July 1, 1987, Reagan extolled Bork as a "prominent advocate of judicial restraint," a principle he said which "recognizes that under the Constitution, it is the exclusive province of the legislatures to enact laws and the roles of the Court to interpret them."[1] Clearly the president believed that the philosophy of judicial restraint would serve the conservative political ends he desired.

One of Bork's leading liberal opponents, Senator Joseph R. Biden, Jr., Democrat from Delaware and chairman of the Senate Judiciary Committee, reached an opposite conclusion following a detailed analysis of Bork's judicial record. Biden found that Bork's decisions were invariably weighted politically toward the right, and he labelled him "a pillar of conservative activism."[2] Thus, both Bork's leading supporter and his most politically conspicuous adversary sought to obscure their differing political motivations by adopting a similar stance in favor of a politically neutral Court in which "restraint" carried positive implications while "activism" had negative connotations. "The fight over the nomination of Judge Robert H. Bork to a seat on the Supreme Court," *Washington Post* columnist David S. Broder concluded, "is a political battle."[3]

Politicians' and voters' concern with the impact of Supreme Court decisions and their perceived ideological orientation is understandable, yet these are not necessarily the determining factors among the justices themselves in reaching their decisions, as the behavior of the Vinson Court indicates. Politically, three of Truman's four appointees were liberal Democrats. Burton, a Republican, also endorsed the liberal programs advanced by the Democratic leadership under Presidents Franklin D. Roosevelt and Harry S. Truman. Political ideology, however, did not determine the decisions made while they were on the Supreme Court. Judicial philosophy played a greater role.

In order to delineate the judicial philosophies of Truman's appointees, I have focused on cases in the areas which raised the most significant issues of the post-war period, and which, therefore, cut closest to the heart of the matter. These are judicial procedure, loyalty-security, racial discrimination and alien rights. Each of these four areas involved the rights of individuals against the state and represented an important source of litigation in the beginning of the Cold War era. By its nature, moreover, litigation involving conflict of rights bears heavily upon policy and is highly controversial. A comprehensive look at opinions in these areas demonstrates that the application of judicial restraint or activism was not an abstract exercise, but rather an exercise in the judicial function of decision-making with attendant, far-reaching consequences.

The differing perspectives of the work of the Supreme Court are illustrated in the attitudes of President Harry S. Truman and Justice Tom Campbell Clark in the *Steel Seizure Case* (1952).[4] President Truman's reaction to the decision resulted from his expectation that the Court would uphold his seizing the industry and he denounced the Court's decision when validation was not forthcoming. The impact of the decision thwarted his plans to deal with the steel strike which occurred during the Korean War. Consequently, he considered the Court holding politically illiberal, even threatening to national security, and was personally offended by the votes of two of his appointees.

Clark's use of precedent in the case illustrated *how* the decision was made and indicated *why* the Court ruled as it did. Relying on an earlier decision by Chief Justice John Marshall in *Little v. Barreme* (1804)[5] which restricted President Thomas Jefferson's authority to the statutory provisions of the 1799 Non-Intercourse Act, Clark reasoned that Truman's authority was similarly restricted by the provisions of the 1947 Taft-Hartley amendments to the Wagner Act. President Jefferson issued orders authorizing seizure of vessels bound to and from France although the congressional act of 1799 only authorized seizure of vessels en route to France. The Court under Marshall held that Jefferson's orders were unauthorized. Clark reasoned that Congress had provided the exclusive method for presidential handling of strikes. Under the Taft-Hartley provision, the president was to appoint a board of inquiry before seeking an 80-day injunction. Clark's vote fitted

Truman's definition of judicial activism even though the decision was generally perceived as ideologically conservative. Relying on precedent was, however, an exercise of judicial restraint. Clark deferred to the legislative branch instead of to the executive branch as Truman would have preferred.

Properly understood, the restraint-activist dichotomy is a part of the judicial process. Exploring this process as implemented by Truman's appointees will assist in evaluating the work of the Court, placing it in greater historical perspective than that allowed by the usual liberal-conservative criterion, highlighting the nonpolitical nature of the Court.

No study of the Vinson era can begin or proceed without reliance on the unique scholarly work of John P. Frank and C. Herman Pritchett. I am deeply grateful to many people who have personally contributed to the development of this work. My greatest debt is to James S. Chase of the History Department at the University of Arkansas whose counsel, advice and encouragement have been immeasurable and constant. Drs. Willard B. Gatewood, Jr., Timothy P. Donovan and David Sloan also read, corrected and made valuable suggestions. John P. Frank and Daniel J. Meador graciously gave time and advice. The editorial staff of Greenwood Press made suggestions that added not only to the pleasure but also to the substance of the undertaking. I am especially indebted to Mildred Vasan and Alicia S. Merritt.

The library staffs of the Mullins Library of the University of Arkansas, the Harry S. Truman Library, and the law school libraries of the University of Arkansas, Southern Methodist University and Northwestern University offered much needed assistance. Especially helpful were the archivists of the Tom C. Clark Collection at the Tarlton Law Library, University of Texas, Austin, Texas; the Frederick Moore Vinson Collection at the Margaret I. King Library, University of Kentucky, Lexington, Kentucky; the Felix Frankfurter Collection at the Harvard Law School Library, Cambridge, Massachusetts; the Hugo La Fayette Black Collection, the Harold Hitz Burton Collection and the Felix Frankfurter Collection in the Manuscript Division of the Library of Congress, Washington, D.C. Louise Lindsey and George Skinner of the University of Arkansas Law Library were especially helpful. I wish to thank particularly Hugo Black, Jr., and Lucy Prichard for permission to review materials in the Black Papers and in the Oral History Section of the Vinson Papers, as well as Ramsey Clark, William S. Burton and Sherman Minton, Jr., for their cooperation.

Professors Morton Gitelman, Richard B. Atkinson and the late Robert E. Knowlton of the University of Arkansas Law School gave of their time and insight. Jeanie Wyant skillfully typed numerous drafts.

To these and others too numerous to mention, my gratitude. For errors, my apologies.

NOTES

1. *New York Times*, July 2, 1987, p. 23.
2. Ibid., September 3, 1987, p. 1.
3. *Richmond Times Dispatch*, September 13, 1987, p. 7.
4. *Youngstown Sheet and Tube Company v. Sawyer*, 343 U.S. 579 (1952).
5. 2 Cranch 170 (1804).

INTRODUCTION

Contemplating President Truman's nomination on June 6, 1946, of Frederick Moore Vinson as Chief Justice to the United States Supreme Court, Arthur M. Schlesinger, Jr. wrote, optimistically:

> The conflict on the Court, if it can be restrained from intellectual and personal extremes, may lead to a debate in the most fruitful tradition of American political thought. The tension between self-denial and activism is an historic element in our judicial system. Its wise resolution could easily make this Court, with its remarkable abilities and its agreement on a wide range of constitutional fundamentals, one of the great creative Courts of history.[1]

Schlesinger's remarks focused on the Court's long-standing and much publicized internal conflict over the decision-making process and, consequently, over the place of the Supreme Court in the larger political process, a conflict heightened by the presence on the Court of the two most formidable proponents of the opposing approaches to judicial review, Hugo La Fayette Black and Felix Frankfurter. Frankfurter advocated a restrained approach which respected time-honored, judge-made rules as guides to decision-making, whereas Black, disregarding judge-made rules—at times denouncing them—preferred to reason through each decision to the right conclusion. Frankfurter's method was an attempt to be more objective, more judicial, whereas Black's method was more subjective and result-oriented. Frankfurter's approach was predicated upon a restricted role for the judiciary in the political arena, whereas Black's approach rested on a concept of unlimited exercise of judicial review.

The Court which Vinson inherited in 1946 was not considered judicially active. The Roosevelt Court (1937–1946), operating during a period of national crisis, had functioned basically as a cooperating branch of government, validating New Deal legislation and endorsing executive action. The Vinson era, however, stood on the threshold of the Warren Court, a Court that was both active and liberal. Previously, activist Courts, most notoriously the Fuller Court of the 1890s and the Hughes Court of the 1930s, had been politically conservative.

Constitutional scholars have found that "the Court... never exercised its censorship of legislation, whether national or State, more energetically than during the half-century between 1887 and 1937, when its thinking was strongly colored by laissez faire concepts of the role of government."[2] In the late nineteenth century, a conservatively active Court, attacking major reform legislation, had emasculated the Interstate Commerce Act of 1887, declared the income tax provisions of 1894 unconstitutional and seriously impaired the Sherman Anti-Trust Act of 1890.[3] The aggressive invalidation of state as well as national laws prompted Professor James B. Thayer of Harvard Law School in 1893 to reassess the power of judicial review and to advocate its limitation by encouraging judges to exercise "narrow" control restricted by "rules of administration."[4] He "counseled a restricted and restrained role for the Court under what he regarded as a broadly permissive Constitution."[5]

The reform legislation in the early progressive era fared better than the measures passed in the decades following the Civil War. The Court upheld the Pure Food and Drug Act of 1906[6] and the Mann Act of 1910.[7] The Court also loosened earlier restrictions on the Interstate Commerce Commission by validating the Hepburn Act of 1906.[8] During this period, however, judicial attack on social legislation, although lessened, continued. Unpopular decisions invalidating the New York ten-hour bakeshop law[9] and the federal yellow dog statute[10] resulted in proposals by the Progressive Party in 1912 for judicial recall of unpopular decisions. In 1922, Wisconsin Senator Robert M. LaFollette, a leader in the progressive movement, assailed the Court's excessive invalidation of legislation in the preceding decade by proposing a constitutional amendment to reform the process of judicial review. Under the proposed amendment, Congress could check the Court's power of review by reenacting a statute held unconstitutional and lower federal courts were prohibited from deciding the constitutional validity of federal legislation.[11]

Renewed protests against judicial legislation surfaced in 1937. Between 1934 and 1936, the Court struck down an unprecedented number of national laws. New Deal regulatory measures addressing the problems caused by the Depression were particularly vulnerable. In 1935–36, the Court invalidated the Agriculture Adjustment Act of 1933, designed to stabilize prices by limiting production, the National Industrial Recovery Act of 1933, designed to provide presidentially approved price, wage and trade practice codes drafted basically by industry and labor groups, and the Federal Farm Bankruptcy Act of 1934, designed to allow a bankrupt farmer to repurchase his property at a currently appraised value on a deferred payment plan.[12]

Fearing further neutralization of his social legislation, President Franklin D. Roosevelt reacted to the Court's decisions in 1937 with a legislative proposal patterned on an earlier plan to revise the lower federal courts. The president's plan called for a new justice to be appointed for every justice seventy-and-one-half years old or older who preferred to remain on the Bench instead of retiring. This proposal would have allowed the president to appoint as many as six justices. If enacted, it would have enabled him to reorient the Court politically, and thus to save such crucial New Deal legislation as the Social Security Act of 1935 and the National Labor Relations Act of 1935.[13]

Public as well as Congressional sentiment was adverse and the measure as proposed by the president failed even to get out of the Senate Judiciary Committee. The Court, however, responded in 1937 by unexpectedly and dramatically upholding social regulation in four separate decisions delivered on the same day.[14] And when the Alabama Senator Hugo Black replaced Justice Willis Van Devanter on October 4, 1937, the direction of the Court changed permanently, beginning a "new phase in the history of the Court."[15] The justices responded positively to legislative programs during the next ten years, invalidating no major New Deal legislation, and reversing some previously restrictive decisions. From 1937 to Truman's accession in 1945, the Court consistently deferred to the legislative and executive branches. The distinguished constitutional historian Paul L. Murphy suggested that this shift resulted not only from World War II, which called for increased use of emergency powers by the executive, but also "stemmed in considerable part from the personal respect . . . of the majority of the justices [for] Franklin Roosevelt and not from any sudden doctrinal shift to judicial restraint."[16]

Between 1937 and 1943, Roosevelt appointed eight new justices to the Supreme Court.[17] The third justice, after Black and Stanley F. Reed, named January 5, 1939, was Frankfurter who left a teaching position at Harvard Law School to assume the vacancy created by the death of Justice Benjamin N. Cardozo. During the period of the Roosevelt Court, a strong philosophical division between Black and Frankfurter developed. Although the Court, under Chief Justice Charles Evans Hughes, changed its position on regulatory legislation and, during his last four years, broadly construed the constitutional sections, previously read narrowly, to endorse state and national economic and social measures, the internal conflict over judicial review grew. Harlan Fiske Stone's elevation to the Chief Justiceship replacing Hughes in 1941 did not stem the increasing division. Contrary to the widespread opinion that the division was an ideological split between liberals and conservatives, the differences (at times petty and personal) centered around the judicial approaches of the justices, not on their political biases. Justice Frankfurter assiduously followed the restraint approach, insisting that only legislative bodies should legislate, while Black, also politically liberal, aggressively sought to reach the desired result, disregarding the judge-made rule requiring deference to the legislative branch.

By the time Truman became president, the controversy on the Court was already fully developed, and had become the source of considerable unfavorable comment by those who followed the Court's decisions. After having been president only three months, Truman faced the problem of making his first appointment to the Supreme Court when Justice Owen J. Roberts retired. Less than a year later, Chief Justice Stone died. To the first vacancy, Truman appointed Harold Hitz Burton, an old friend and Republican Senator from Ohio. For Chief Justice, he chose his Secretary of the Treasury and former member of Congress, Frederick Moore Vinson. Two more vacancies occurred in 1949 and Truman appointed Tom Campbell Clark, his Attorney General, and Sherman Minton of Indiana, another old Senate cohort, then sitting on the Seventh Circuit Court of Appeals.

Truman's expectation from those he appointed to the Supreme Court was informed by his political orientation as well as by his varied experience in the law. He had been elected twice to the Senate from Missouri. During his first term which began in 1935, he supported Roosevelt's plan to restructure the Supreme Court. Although not a lawyer himself, Truman had attended law school at night from 1923 to 1925 while serving as an administrative judge for the eastern district of Jackson County, Missouri.

After going to Washington, he met Justice Louis D. Brandeis and became a regular guest at Brandeis' weekly "teas." He praised Justices Brandeis and Oliver Wendell Holmes, Jr., (who had retired from the Court in 1932) as liberal dissenters, describing them as his favorite justices. He endorsed Brandeis' legal philosophy while sharing his views on the dangers of big business.

As president, he wanted cooperation between the executive and the legislative and judicial branches. He had resented the problems the New Deal had encountered with the Court, denouncing the decisions as judicial legislation. In a poll of Congressmen taken by the *New York Times*, reported immediately after Roosevelt's message announcing his proposal to reorganize the judiciary, Truman had cautiously expressed his support: "I am not in favor of packing any court to obtain any special set of decisions any more than I am in favor of jury-fixing, . . . I am . . . of the opinion that the Supreme Court cannot be packed and that when a man becomes a member of it . . . he becomes what he should be—judicially independent."[18] As the fight intensified, however, Truman's support increased. He charged that the Court "ha[d] been [packed] for fifty years, against progressive legislation," and that the justices had "in late years . . . taken unto themselves the right to declare acts of Congress unconstitutional."[19]

Truman's assessment of Brandeis is revealing: "I think I've read every one of his decisions . . . I'm sure whatever he said was right. Because he was a man who always thought his way through to the right conclusions."[20] Truman expected his appointees to *find* the law. He assumed that if they did so, they would always come to a right conclusion. For Truman, the role of the Court in interpreting the Constitution should be essentially passive. The men he appointed gave him basically what he wanted, although their specific decisions were not always to his liking.

The Vinson era ended when President Dwight D. Eisenhower nominated on October 5, 1953 California Governor Earl Warren to fill the vacancy created by Vinson's death. The judicial activism of the Warren Court would, of course, elicit numerous charges of judicial legislation because "[i]ts most significant pronouncements... decreed change in the status quo."[21] In decisions on reapportionment, segregation and criminal procedure, the Court construed the equal protection clause affirmatively in an attempt to bring practice into conformity with the ideal.[22] Although the Court's majority opinions were activist and liberal, the conflict over approach continued unabated. In dissenting opinions until his resignation on August 28, 1962, Frankfurter echoed Thayer's plea for judicial restraint. Black, on the other hand, now found himself more often on the side of the majority.

Schlesinger's hope for a wise resolution of the conflict between judicial self-restraint and activism was not realized during the Vinson era. Given the subjective nature of decision making, the hope may have been unrealistic, then as now. Not only did each justice bring a host of individual predilections—personal and political as well as philosophical—to bear upon his decisions, the collegial nature of the Court immensely complicated the process as Court members interacted with each other, seeking support for their respective positions. Some compromise was inevitable. With equal inevitability, personality and personal relations entered into the final product, although to what degree is uncertain. Responding to this variety of influences, the Truman appointees, as their decisions reveal, adopted an eclectic approach, picking and choosing from the established judge-made rules formulated over the years to assist judges in reaching their decisions. Only occasionally did each make what Professor Herbert Wechsler called a "principled decision which rest[ed] on... reasons that in their generality and their neutrality transcend[ed] the immediate result that [was] involved."[23] But if the Vinson Court did not resolve the perpetual tension between judicial self-denial and activism, their disagreements did at least result in a lively debate about the nature and limits of judicial power.

NOTES

1. Arthur M. Schlesinger, Jr., "The Supreme Court: 1947," *Fortune* 35, no. 1 (January 1947):212.

2. Edward S. Corwin, *The Constitution and What It Means Today*, revised by Harold W. Chase and Craig R. Ducat (Princeton, N.J.: Princeton University Press, 1978), p. 223.

3. Through a series of decisions, the court had stripped authority away

from the Interstate Commerce Commission by 1897. In *Pollock v. Farmers' Loan & Trust Co.*, 158 U.S. 601 (1895), the Court declared the income tax unconstitutional. And in *United States v. E.C. Knight Co.*, 156 U.S. 1 (1895), the Court restricted application of the Sherman Anti-Trust Act to transportation (excluding manufacturing).

4. James B. Thayer, "The Origin and Scope of the American Doctrine of Constitutional Law," 7 *Harvard Law Review* 129, 144 (1893).

5. Alexander M. Bickel and Benno C. Schmidt, Jr., *The Oliver Wendell Holmes Devise History of the Supreme Court of the United States, The Judiciary and Responsible Government, 1910–21*, vol. 9 (New York: Macmillan Publishing Company, 1984), p. 18.

6. *Hipolite Egg Co. v. United States*, 220 U.S. 45 (1911).

7. *Hoke v. United States*, 227 U.S. 308 (1913).

8. The Court endorsed the Hepburn Act of 1906 which restricted the scope of Court review to the rulings of the Interstate Commerce Commission, thereby breathing new life into the Interstate Commerce Act. The Court under the Hepburn Act could only review the regularity of an order. In *The Minnesota Rate Cases*, 230 U.S. 352 (1913), the Court recognized state authority to regulate rail rates and in *The Shreveport Rate Cases*, 234 U.S. 342 (1914), the Court recognized the authority of the Interstate Commerce Commission to regulate interstate rail rates.

9. *Lochner v. New York*, 198 U.S. 45 (1905).

10. *Adair v. United States*, 208 U.S. 161 (1908).

11. William F. Swindler, *Court and Constitution in the Twentieth Century, The Old Legality, 1889–1932* (New York: The Bobbs-Merrill Company, 1969), pp. 283–84.

12. In a decision on January 6, 1936 by a 6 to 3 majority, the Court invalidated the Agricultural Adjustment Act of 1933, *United States v. Butler*, 297 U.S. 1 (1936). In the 1935 "hot oil" decision, the Court invalidated a portion of the National Industrial Recovery Act, *Panama Refining Co. v. Ryan*, 293 U.S. 388 (1935), and completed the job in a case heard six months later, *Schechter Poultry Corp. v. United States*, 295 U.S. 495 (1935). The Court invalidated the first Frazier-Lempke Federal Farm Bankruptcy Act in *Louisville Joint Stock Land Bank v. Radford*, 295 U.S. 555 (1935).

13. The Court later upheld the Social Security Act in two cases. In *Stewart Machine Co. v. Davis*, 301 U.S. 548 (1937), the Court upheld the tax on employers and federal unemployment grants to states, and in *Helvering v. Davis*, 301 U.S. 619 (1937), the Court upheld the old age tax and benefit provisions. The National Labor Relations Act was found constitutional in *NLRB v. Jones and Laughlin Steel Corporation*, 301 U.S. 1 (1937), thus reversing the Court's favorable stand on yellow dog contracts in 1908.

14. On March 29, 1937, the Court upheld a Washington state law regulating minimum wages for women and minors, *West Coast Hotel Co. v. Parrish*

et al., 300 U.S. 379 (1937); validated the revised Frazier-Lemke Federal Farm Bankruptcy Act offering farmers mortgage relief, *Wright v. Vinton Branch*, 300 U.S. 440 (1937); sustained a Federal firearms tax in *Sonzinsky v. United States*, 300 U.S. 506 (1937); and sustained railroad labor legislation passed in 1934 which amended the Railway Labor Act of 1926, *Virginia Railroad Co. v. System Federation*, 300 U.S. 515 (1937).

15. Page Smith, *The Constitution, A Documentary and Narrative History* (New York: William Morrow and Co., Inc., 1980), p. 496.

16. Paul L. Murphy, *The Constitution in Crisis Times, 1918-1969* (Evanston, Ill.: Harper and Row Publishers, 1972), p. 246.

17. Roosevelt nominated Hugo La Fayette Black on August 12, 1937 to replace Justice Willis Van Devanter, Stanley Forman Reed on January 15, 1938 to replace Justice George Sutherland, Felix Frankfurther on January 5, 1939 to replace Justice Benjamin N. Cardozo, William Orville Douglas on March 20, 1939 to replace Justice Louis Dembitz Brandeis, Frank Murphy on January 4, 1940 to replace Justice Pierce Butler, James Francis Byrnes on June 12, 1941 to replace Justice James Clark McReynolds, Robert Houghwout Jackson on June 12, 1941 to replace Justice Harlan Fiske Stone whom he elevated on the same day to Chief Justice, and Wiley Blount Rutledge on January 11, 1943 to replace James Francis Brynes.

18. *New York Times*, February 10, 1937, p. 15.

19. From Senatorial Papers quoted by Richard Kirkendall, "Fred M. Vinson," Leon Friedman and Fred L. Israel, eds., *The Justices of the Supreme Court, 1789-1978*, vol. 4 (New York: Chelsea House, 1980), pp. 2640, 2641.

20. Merle Miller, *Plain Speaking, An Oral Biography of Harry S. Truman* (New York: Berkley Publishing Corporation, 1974), p. 412. See also Robert J. Donovan, *Conflict and Crisis, The Presidency of Harry S. Truman, 1945-1948* (New York: W.W. Norton and Company, 1977).

21. J. Skelly Wright, "The Role of the Supreme Court in a Democratic Society—Judicial Activism or Restraint?" 54 *Cornell Law Review* 1, 2 (1968).

22. Ibid. On reapportionment, see *Baker v. Carr*, 369 U.S. 186 (1962), and its progeny culminating in the one-man, one-vote, one-value requirement, *Gray v. Sanders*, 372 U.S. 368 (1963), *Wesberry V. Sanders*, 376 U.S. 1 (1964), *Reynolds v. Sims*, 377 U.S. 533 (1964), *WMCA, Inc. v. Lomenzo*, 377 U.S. 633 (1964), *Maryland Comm. for Fair Representation v. Tawes*, 377 U.S. 656 (1964), *Davis v. Mann*, 377 U.S. 678 (1964), *Roman v. Sincock*, 377 U.S. 695 (1964) and *Lucas v. Forty-Fourth Gen'l Ass'y.*, 377 U.S. 713 (1964). On segregation, see *Brown v. Board of Education*, 347 U.S. 483 (1954), and its progeny, *Johnson v. Virginia*, 373 U.S. 61 (1963), *State Athl. Comm'n v. Dorsey*, 359 U.S. 533 (1959), *Gayle v. Browder*, 352 U.S. 903 (1956), *Holmes v. City of Atlanta*, 350 U.S. 879 (1955), *Mayor of Baltimore v. Dawson*, 350 U.S. 877 (1955), and *Muir v. Louisville Park Theatrical Ass'n.*, 347 U.S. 971 (1954). On criminal procedure, see *inter alia*, *Griffin v. Illinois*, 351 U.S. 12 (1956), *Gideon*

v. Wainwright, 372 U.S. 335 (1963), *Mapp v. Ohio*, 367 U.S. 642 (1961) and *Miranda v. Arizona*, 384 U.S. 436 (1966).

23. Herbert Wechsler, "Toward Neutral Principles of Constitutional Law," 73 *Harvard Law Review* 1, 19 (1959).

Truman's Court

ONE

JUDICIAL RESTRAINT VERSUS JUDICIAL ACTIVISM

BACKGROUND

The two approaches of judicial self-restraint and judicial activism to constitutional adjudication have been operative since the inception of judicial review and have been utilized in varying degrees by each justice who sat on the Supreme Court. Judicial self-restraint is an attitude toward legislative or official acts under review which presumes the validity of such acts and requires a thorough showing of contradiction with some constitutional precept in order to void the government action. Judicial activism is a less hesitant approach to constitutional adjudication which does not value traditional rules governing review.

Two cases decided in the 1790s concerning debts existing at the time of the Revolutionary War involved the Court initially in judicial review, albeit of state rather than national legislation. In *Chisholm v. Georgia* (1793),[1] which also raised a question of jurisdiction, the Court broadly affirmed the right of two citizens of South Carolina, acting as executors for a British creditor, to sue the state of Georgia for return of property confiscated during the Revolution. In reaction, Congress immediately approved and sent to the states a constitutional amendment to disallow federal court jurisdiction in suits by citizens against states. Before the Eleventh Amendment was ratified in January of 1798 the Court had ruled in *Ware v. Hylton* (1796)[2] that the Treaty of Paris of 1783 ending the Revolution, which provided that no legal impediment would be placed on creditors' rights to collect debts, invalidated a Virginia state act of 1777 which effectively defeated British creditors' claims. These cases clearly indicated that the Court early assumed well before the advent of John Marshall in 1801 the right of judicial review. They also indicate that Congress bridled at this use of judicial authority and was prepared to chide it.

Before 1801, in *Hylton v. United States* (1796),[3] the Court implicitly extended its right of judicial review to encompass national legislation when it upheld a congressionally imposed tax on carriages as constitutional. But it was, of course, not until *Marbury v. Madison* (1803)[4] that Marshall firmly established the doctrine of judicial review by explicitly engrafting upon the Constitution the key premise that the Constitution is the fundamental law of the land:

> all those who have framed written constitutions contemplate them as forming the fundamental and paramount law of the nation, and consequently the theory of every such government must be, that an act of the legislature repugnant to the constitution is void.[5]

This case unmistakably enunciated, and more importantly exercised, the power of the Court to declare congressional acts void. But at the same time, in holding a portion of the Judiciary Act of 1789 void, Marshall found that the Court's power of original jurisdiction could not be augmented beyond constitutional authorization by acts of Congress. In this sense, the case stands as an example of the Court's refusal to extend jurisdiction beyond constitutional limits, which is in itself an act of judicial self-restraint.

In *Fletcher v. Peck* (1810),[6] Marshall's language forcefully and finally asserted the power of judicial review over state legislative acts, but at the same time illustrated the restraint inherent in Marshall's concept of judicial review:

> The question, whether a law be void for its repugnancy to the constitution, is at all times, a question of much delicacy, which ought seldom, if ever, to be decided in the affirmative, in a doubtful case.... [I]t is not on slight implication and vague conjecture that the legislature is to be pronounced to have transcended its powers, ... the opposition between the constitution and the law should be such that the judge feels a clear and strong conviction of their incompatibility with each other.[7]

This quotation contained the seeds of the Court's self-imposed maxim that a legislative act will be overturned only in *clear* cases and only when the constitutional issue cannot be avoided. In *Fletcher v. Peck*, the Court struck down the state law because it conflicted with a previous state statute under which rights had vested and thus violated the sanctity of contract, protected *either* by general principles *or* by particular provisions of the Constitution.

The restrained attitude of the Court in dealing with national legislation is attested by the fact that after *Marbury v. Madison* in 1803, it did not declare a congressional act void until the *Dred Scott* case (1857).[8] The Court formulated over the years various rules of judicial restraint, although these have not been vigorously followed in every instance. Professor Henry J. Abraham, in his work on the judicial process, enumerated sixteen such rules, which included the *refusal* to: (1) grant advisory opinions; (2) decide political questions; (3) decide a case on constitutional grounds if there are other grounds for deciding it; (4) impute illegal motives to the lawmakers; (5) substitute the Court's wisdom for that of the legislature or executive; (6) "serve as a check against inept, unwise, emotional, unrepresentative legislators"; (7) decide questions of fact; (8) decide a question unless all remedies in the lower courts have been exhausted; and (9) decide an issue unless all proper procedures have been followed before an appeal has been taken. Other maxims require that: (10) an actual "case" or "controversy" be present; (11) the person invoking the Constitution have standing; (12) the person invoke specifically that portion of the Constitution on which he relies; (13) the person suffer actual detriment from that of which he complains; and (14) the federal question be substantial. The Court (15) will also presume the validity of the statute or act in question and (16) will look to precedent for help in deciding the case.[9]

The earlier period is in sharp contrast with the years from 1887 through 1937, which saw active judicial censorship of legislation under the two concepts of liberty of contract and the laissez faire role of government. The constitutional scholar, Alexander M. Bickel, called these, "the bad years, the Middle Ages, when men were beknighted, and nearly brought the institution [of the Court] to ruin."[10] In the latter part of this period, Justices Holmes and Brandeis were frequent dissenters and they often called for a restrained approach in judicial review. Brandeis declared that the Court "had converted judicial review into the power of a 'super legislature,' " while Holmes complained that he could discover "hardly any limit but the sky" to the power claimed by the Court to disallow state acts "which may happen to strike a majority of its members for any reason undesirable."[11]

Justice Harlan F. Stone also lent his voice to the outcry against judicial activism, "[T]he only check upon our own exercise of power is our sense of self-restraint."[12] Alpheus T. Mason described Justice Stone's tenure on the Court as one in which he resisted the conservatives' judicial activism in the economic realm during his first years on the Court and the liberals' judicial activism in the civil liberties area during his later years on the Court. The idea of preferred freedom for the pre-New Deal conservative court had been economic, whereas the preferred freedom for the post–1937 liberal court was civil liberties.[13]

The assault on the judiciary by the executive and legislative branches, whose programs were being defeated by judicial activism, peaked in 1937. A recognition that the judiciary should restrain its veto over legislation in order to preserve itself was prompted by the so-called Court-packing plan advanced by President Roosevelt. In *West Coast Hotel Co. v. Parrish et al.* (1937),[14] Justice Owen Roberts changed his vote to support the New Deal legislation before the Court. The Senate at that time was debating passage of Roosevelt's

Court legislation. The political need for the legislative reform was satisfied by this and other contemporaneous decisions and Roosevelt's subsequent appointments to the Court created a new judicial era. Yet the debate over the proper role of the Court continued as one of his appointees was the most ardent practitioner of judicial activism, Hugo Black, and another the most articulate proponent of judicial restraint, Felix Frankfurter.

Both men served on the court during the tenures of Truman's appointees. Hugo Black sat on the Court from 1937 to 1971. All of President Truman's appointees served their full terms within those years. Felix Frankfurter sat on the Court from 1939 to 1962. Only one of Truman's appointees, Tom Clark, remained on the Bench after Frankfurter's retirement, serving until June of 1967. The conflict between Black and Frankfurter developed soon after Frankfurter's appointment and lasted throughout the Chief Justiceships of Hughes, Stone, and Vinson and virtually all of Warren's term. Each profoundly influenced the ultimate performance of the Court by the force of his individual opinions, but even more because their sharp differences helped to establish the framework within which the entire Court operated.

Because the conflict between Black and Frankfurter is evident not only in their divergent approaches to constitutional decision making, but also in their judicial philosophies, an attempt will be made to show how each justice's approach was complemented and reinforced by his judicial philosophy, and to ascertain in what manner and to what extent their approaches and philosophies were reflected in the judicial performances of the Truman appointees.

THE ROOSEVELT LEGACY

Justice Hugo La Fayette Black

President Roosevelt appointed Hugo Black, age fifty-one, to the Supreme Court in 1937, when the resignation of Justice Willis Van Devanter provided a vacancy. When Roosevelt offered the justiceship, Black is reported to have said, "Mr. President, are you sure that I'll be more useful in the Court than in the Senate?"[15] Black, a devoted New Dealer, had championed the administration's programs since Roosevelt's election in 1932.

He had been born in Clay County in Alabama, the eighth and last child born to a postmistress, Martha Toland Black, and a general storekeeper, William La Fayette Black. He attended grade school in Ashland, and later enrolled in an "enlarged high school," Ashland College. He immediately entered medical school, but quickly dropped out in order to enter the University of Alabama in preparation for becoming a lawyer. When the University refused to admit him as a sophomore, he skipped the general education of an undergraduate degree and went directly to law school. Black's education in the liberal arts was, therefore, mostly informal. During his first term in a predominantly Republican Senate, he "spent a great deal of time remedying the defects in his education"[16] by "assigning himself extensive reading in history and economics."[17]

As a practicing attorney, Black became the champion of the underdog. In one early case, for example, he pleaded the cause of a black prisoner illegally imprisoned after his sentence term had expired. After becoming a judge, he was noted for his quickness in disposing of cases, a great aid to those unable to make bail. His most extensive private practice was on behalf of personal injury litigants, an expression of his sympathy for the victim.[18] Expeditiousness and sympathy for the oppressed and, some said, political expediency were destined to be trademarks of his justiceship.

He was first elected to the U.S. Senate in 1926, and reelected in 1932. He continued to manifest an interest in the plight of the "little man," a concern clearly dictated both by his personal inclinations and the desperate economic plight of most of his constituents. His position also reflected a regional bias. As a first-term Senator, he introduced a bill to close America to immigration for a five-year period, a bill no doubt popular among the white Anglo-Saxon Protestants of Alabama. He fought for using Muscle Shoals Dam for the production of cheap fertilizer which would benefit the farmers in the Tennessee River Valley. Like most southerners he strongly supported Prohibition.[19] And when retiring Senator Tom Heflin asked for a federal investigation into alleged election irregularities, Black voted against the investigation, denying in true southern style, "the right of the federal Government to go down into the state of Alabama, sir, and tell the people who shall vote and who shall not vote."[20]

Black's affiliation with the Ku Klux Klan was an example of his alleged political expediency. He had joined the Klan in 1923, but resigned his membership July 9, 1925 in the Robert E. Lee Klan No. 1 in Birmingham (membership approximately 10,000) one month after announcing his candidacy for the Senate on June 10th. The resignation was a "friendly" one, made at the "beginning of his senatorial campaign."[21] Without doubt, the Alabama Klan, claiming control of 85,000 votes, helped elect him to his first term. Black's reputation for political expediency was such that Frankfurter would later accuse him of checking the newspapers for indicators of which way the prevailing political winds were blowing before voting on a particular case.[22]

When Black began his second term as a member of the majority party, his service was notable for his avid support of the New Deal and his inspired investigative work. He fought especially hard for an employment bill he sponsored that included provisions for a thirty-hour work week and a prohibition on child labor.[23] He led investigations into subsidies for the Merchant Marines and airlines, and took particular interest in the lobbying activities of business groups, especially those of the utility companies. His investigative methods as chairman of the Senate Special Committee to Investigate

Lobbying Activities were later described as ruthless, and he was "condemned as a zealot who disregarded constitutional and personal right."[24] His use of the "dragnet subpoena" in order to document the misuse of Western Union telegrams by lobbyists was singled out for special condemnation, and the subpoena successfully enjoined by a Chicago law firm.[25] During these years, Black began a life-long friendship with Sherman Minton who served with him in the Senate on the investigating committee. Partly as a result of these investigative activities and his previous membership in the Klan, Black's nomination to the Supreme Court caused an uproar. His confirmation by a vote of 63 to 16 placed Roosevelt's first judicial activist on the Court.

Late in his judicial career, Black summarized his philosophy in three separate extra-judicial statements. At age seventy-four, he delivered the first James Madison Lecture at New York University School of Law on February 17, 1960, after twenty-three years on the Bench.[26] Two years later, he gave an extensive interview with Professor Edmond Cahn of the New York University School of Law at the biennial convention of the American Jewish Congress.[27] At age eighty-one, he delivered the James S. Carpentier lectures at Columbia University School of Law in 1968, entitled *A Constitutional Faith*.[28]

In the Madison Lecture,[29] Black discussed the first ten amendments to the Constitution. He rejected the notion that the "Bill of Rights' guarantees ... must, if outweighed by the public interest, be subordinated to the Government's competing interest" as one of many formulations of the *faulty* premise that "all constitutional problems are questions of reasonableness, proximity and degree." Black approached the Constitution with a different premise:

> It is my belief that there are "absolutes" in our Bill of Rights, and that they were put there on purpose by men who knew what words meant, and meant their prohibitions to be "absolutes." The whole history and background of the constitution and Bill of Rights, as I understand it, belies the assumption or conclusion that our ultimate constitutional freedoms are no more than our English ancestors had when they came to this new land to get new freedoms.[30]

Black then discussed the absolute nature of each amendment, emphasizing the "plain words, easily understood" which secured to the people rights "beyond the reach of government."[31] Black reasoned that the primary purpose of the Constitution was to "withdraw from the Government all power to act in certain areas" and he found "no justification whatever for the 'balancing' of a particular right against some expressly granted power of Congress."[32] He feared the result of the balancing approach, that "in times of emergency and stress, it gave Government the right to do what it thought necessary to protect itself, regardless of the rights of individuals."[33] Black expounded his view that the Constitution was written to create a limited government, to prevent legislative supremacy, and to provide an independent judiciary. He believed that the Bill of Rights was a document securing absolute rights to the people and that the First Amendment was "truly the heart of the Bill of Rights."[34]

Black reiterated his beliefs two years later in an interview with Professor Edmond Cahn that reflected the enthusiasm of the advocate, not the dispassionate reason of a judge weighing conflicting rights:

> I am for the First Amendment from the first word to the last. I believe it means what it says, and it says to me, "Government shall keep its hands off religion. Government shall not attempt to control the ideas a man has. Government shall not attempt to establish a religion of any kind. Government shall not abridge freedom of the press or speech." It shall let anybody talk in this country.[35]

When asked about the government's right to preserve itself, Black agreed that the government had such a right. But he added, "I think it can be preserved only by leaving people with the utmost freedom. . . . I do not think this Government must look to force."[36]

A Constitutional Faith presented a more subdued expression of Black's views. Nevertheless he reemphasized his belief in the absolute nature of the First Amendment, pointing out that he voted in *New York Times Co. v. Sullivan* (1964)[37] to reverse the libel judgment against the *Times* and other defendants on the basis that "a state has no power to use a civil libel law or any other law to impose damages for merely discussing public affairs and criticizing public officers."[38]

Black's views on due process must be viewed in connection with his emphasis on the Bill of Rights. He interpreted the Fourteenth Amendment as a wholesale incorporation of the due process guarantees contained in the Bill of Rights. The first ten amendments defined due process for Black and all of these provisions were applicable, in his view, to both the federal and state governments. This reasoning provided an objective guide to due process problems. Applying judicial interpretation involving substantive due process to cases to determine if the law or procedure was unreasonable, capricious, arbitrary, contrary to a fundamental system of justice, shocked the conscience or offended the community's sense of fair play and decency was totally rejected by Black. The interpretive process was too elusive and was subject to abuse as evidenced by the "many 5 to 4 decisions . . . rendered in which the majority of justices interpret[ed] the Due Process Clause in line with their own economic predelictions."[39] Black's literalness in limiting due process to the specific contents of the Bill of Rights even led him in 1942 to find that wiretapping did not fall within the prohibitions of illegal search and seizure and did not, therefore, violate due process.[40]

In these 1968 lectures, Black answered his critics who labeled him a judicial activist. He defined the label to mean two things: (1) that he was willing or anxious to settle constitutional questions that could have been avoided; and (2) that he was willing to determine constitutional and other legal questions on what he believed the law should be.[41]

In discussing the first part of this definition, Black refuted the wisdom of the "judge-created doctrine that it is inherently good to avoid constitutional questions."[42] He believed that some issues needed to be decided, although they could be avoided in resolution of a particular case. He cited with conviction those cases in which he dissented because the majority opinion adhered to the tenets of judicial self-restraint.[43] The proper and only restraint which the Justice recognized was constitutional restraint. He believed that the failure to answer or consider all constitutional questions in a given case was an abdication of the Court's responsibility.

In discussing the second part of the definition, Black flatly denied that he decided questions according to his beliefs. Indeed, he heartily denounced the practice. He described a justice as "one who should 'interpret' the Constitution and laws, which mean[t] to explain and expound, not to alter, amend or remake."[44] Black thus defined "interpret" to mean explain and expound. He did not discuss the possibility that before one can do this, one must understand the Constitution or law, and that one's understanding of the Constitution or law *may be* an alteration, amendment, or partial or total remake of the *meaning* of that which is being interpreted. The amendment process was, for Black, the only means whereby the Constitution was to be made current. Interpretation could not be used to adapt the Constitution to changing times. In the Epilogue to the lectures, he eloquently expressed his personal constitutional faith:

> I cannot close without saying a few words to express my deepest respect and boundless admiration and love for our Constitution and the men who drafted it.... I am a typical example of this highly successful experiment in government.... [The] Constitution is my legal bible, its plan of government is my plan and its destiny my destiny. I cherish every word of it, from the first to the last, and I personally deplore even the slighest deviation from its least important commands.[45]

Such a personal and emotional testimony epitomized Black's performance on the Court. He was not a disinterested judge interpreting the inanimate law. Black had very fixed, fundamental ideas on the meaning of the Constitution which led him to seek an active role for the judiciary.

Of the three schools of American jurisprudence, natural law, positive law and sociological law, Black's philosophy has been denoted as belonging in the positive law tradition. Legal positivism which was advanced in England by John Austin and Jeremy Bentham in the late eighteenth and early nineteenth centuries contained the notion that "the only law relevant to a legal system is 'positive law' [consisting] of a command made and enforced by the sovereign."[46] A Supreme Court justice in reviewing law under this theory would merely negate the weaker positive law when finding a contradictory command within "the four corners of the Constitution."[47] Tinsley E. Yarbrough concluded that Black believed in the basic principles of positivism:

1. that lawmaking belongs to the legislatures, not to the judges;
2. that to interpret laws, judges must look to the original *literal meaning* of the legislator, and if more than one interpretation is valid, weight should go to the construction "with greater merit";
3. that law and morals are separate entities; and
4. that clarity and consistency are necessary as definite standards of law.[48]

Black's performance on the bench and his pronouncements indicated that he did indeed adopt the positivist's philosophy in constitutional adjudication. His literal interpretation of the Constitution in each instance was followed by an unreluctant application of the force of the positive law of the land. He did not feel himself bound by judge-made rules of self-restraint. Frankfurter once, in vain, attempted to convince Black to change an opinion by cautioning him that Bentham often threw out the baby with the bath.[49] Strict reliance on the letter of the positive law could result in generalizations with implications beyond the issue at hand.

Justice Felix Frankfurter

Felix Frankfurter, age fifty-seven, was appointed by Roosevelt to the Supreme Court chair vacated by Benjamin Cardozo, "the Scholar's Seat,"[50] also held by Holmes. Before his appointment, Frankfurter had served extensively as Roosevelt's private advisor on a wide range of problems, and he had placed many of his brightest Harvard law students in key positions in the administration. With Brandeis, he was viewed as the intellectual architect of the second New Deal.[51] Frankfurter had earlier turned down Roosevelt's offer to make him Attorney General, preferring to work behind the scenes, and while he feigned surprise at the Supreme Court nomination, he had long hoped for it as the culmination of a distinguished career of public service. As he wrote appreciatively to Roosevelt: "I am given the gift of opportunity for service to the nation which in any circumstance would be owing, but which I would rather have had at your hands than at those of any other President, barring Lincoln."[52]

Frankfurter was the third of eight children born to a Jewish businessman,

Leopold Frankfurter, and his wife Emma, in Vienna, Austria in 1882. He spoke German as his first tongue and Hungarian as his second.[53] After immigrating to America at age twelve, he attended school at P.S. 25 on New York's East Side. He was graduated at age nineteen with a B.A. from City College of New York. He worked his way through Harvard Law School graduating in 1906 with highest honors. He joined the faculty in 1914, teaching courses in administrative law, public utilities and jurisdiction until his resignation to accept the Supreme Court appointment. In 1933–34, he had taken a year's leave to serve as a visiting professor at Oxford University, where he met John Maynard Keynes and other British economists with whom he discussed Roosevelt's recovery program.[54]

Before joining the faculty at Harvard, Frankfurter served on the staff of Henry L. Stimson, United States Attorney for the Southern District of New York. In 1911, he went to Washington when Stimson became Secretary of War to serve as Law Officer of the Bureau of Insular Affairs, dealing with overseas possessions. Ideologically, Frankfurter was attuned to the more advanced wing of the progressive movement. Like many intellectuals, he was not clearly identified with any political party. Indeed, over the years, he supported presidential candidates nominated by three different parties— Theodore Roosevelt as Republican (1904) and Progressive (1912), Robert LaFollette as Progressive (1924), Al Smith (1928) and Franklin D. Roosevelt as Democrats (1932, 1936).

Frankfurter's association with attorney Louis D. Brandeis began while he worked at the Bureau of Insular Affairs. It was a personal and professional association based initially on common interests and mutual respect which quickly developed into a confidential partnership in support of a variety of public causes. Although the two men supported different presidential candidates in 1912 (Brandeis being the inspiration for Wilson's "New Freedom"), their basic interests remained virtually identical. In 1913, Brandeis used his influence to secure Frankfurter's appointment to the Harvard Law School faculty. When Brandeis was appointed to the Supreme Court by President Woodrow Wilson in 1916, he enlisted Frankfurter's help to promote legislative programs and various social causes including Zionism. Secretly until 1938, Brandeis financially supported Frankfurter's efforts, providing him initially with $1,000 per year and increasing the amount in 1926 to $3,500.[55]

Over the years, Frankfurter adopted liberal and unpopular causes. He was a founder of the American Civil Liberties Union, a Zionist activist and a legal advisor to the National Association for the Advancement of Colored People. He vigorously championed the cause of Sacco and Vanzetti. He defended, in true Brandeisian fashion, social legislation before the Supreme Court. After 1932 Frankfurter became an unofficial advisor to the Roosevelt administration, helping to draft the Securities Act of 1933 and the Public Utilities Holding Act of 1935.[56] His political activities prior to his Supreme

Court appointment gained him a reputation as a liberal, if not a radical, crusader.

Frankfurter was also a prolific writer and filled the *Harvard Law Review* with articles on numerous legal topics. Not surprisingly, he had a well-articulated judicial philosophy which was vividly revealed in articles extolling the virtues of John Marshall, Louis Brandeis and Oliver Wendell Holmes, Jr.

In a 1955 speech on "John Marshall and the Judicial Function," delivered at the Harvard Law School, commemorating the 200th anniversary of John Marshall's birth, he enunciated his ideas on the difficulties involved in adjusting claims under the Fourteenth Amendment, "the largest source of the Court's business," calling for an "invincible disinterestedness rooted in temperament and confirmed by discipline"[57] in deciding such issues. He stated:

> The Due Process Clauses extend to triune interests—life, liberty, and property—and "property" cannot be deleted by judicial fiat rendering it nugatory regarding legislation touching property.... [P]rotection of property interests may ... quite fairly be deemed, in appropriate circumstances, an aspect of liberty.[58]

He emphasized the need to have "sturdy doubt that one ha[d] found the proper standard for exercising the judicial function," noting that "yesterday, the active area in this field was concerned with 'property.' Today, it is 'civil liberties.'"[59] Frankfurter's insistence on the judicial restraint tenet of not passing on constitutional issues unless necessary was based on his belief "that most of the occasions when the Supreme Court has come into virulent conflict with public opinion were those in which the Court disregarded its settled tradition against needlessly pronouncing on constitutional issues."[60] He cited, among others, the *Dred Scott Case* (1857)[61] as a potent example of the damage done to the Court by judicial activism. According to Frankfurter, Marshall was concerned with:

> the Constitution as an instrument predominantly regulating the machinery of government, and more particularly, distributing powers between the central government and the States. The Constitution was not thought of as the repository of the supreme law limiting all government, with a court wielding the deepest-cutting power of deciding whether there is any authority in government at all to do what is sought to be done.[62]

Just as Frankfurter incorporated his conception of Marshall's jurisprudence into his own philosophy of judicial function, he also borrowed from Brandeis. Praising Brandeis on the occasion of his seventy-fifth birthday, Frankfurter expressed what he saw as their common belief:

> The Constitution provided for the future partly by not forecasting it and partly by the generality of its language.... [T]he ambiguities and lacunae of the document left ample scope for the unfolding of life.... [T]he Constitution is flexible enough to meet the demands of modern society.[63]

This general view of the Constitution had led "Mr. Justice Brandeis to give free play to the States and the Nation within their respective spheres," believing that "adequate opportunity for experimentation should not... be denied to them by a static conception of the Constitution."[64] Brandeis' battle was against narrow interpretation of the due process clause in economic issues, whereas Frankfurter's battle was against narrow interpretation of the due process clause in the civil liberties area particularly; but the concept of judicial restraint with deference to legislation was the same for both justices.

Frankfurter applauded Brandeis for his exercise of restraint, declaring that the Court had "no greater duty than the duty not to decide, or not to decide beyond its circumscribed authority."[65] He quoted from a Brandeis opinion: "When the record does present a case and judgment must be rendered, constitutional determination must be avoided if a nonconstitutional ground [would dispose] of the immediate litigation."[66] Frankfurter concluded that "[t]o forego judgment under such circumstances [was] not abdication of judicial power, but recognition of rational limits to [the Court's] competence."[67] He found in Brandeis' opinions "a consciousness of a world for which no absolute is adequate... a world of more or less, of give and take, of live and let live. Interests clash but no single one must yield.... And even liberty has its bounds."[68] Frankfurter's relativism stands obviously in sharp contrast to the absolutism espoused by Black.

Inevitably, Frankfurter greatly admired Justice Oliver Wendell Holmes, Jr. In a 1916 article written for the *Harvard Law Review*, Frankfurter analyzed Holmes' opinions in two specific areas, the commerce clause and the Fourteenth Amendment.[69] In the first of these areas, Frankfurter approved Holmes' interpretation of the commerce clause which favored practical legislative assistance of interstate commerce. In the second area, which consumed most of Frankfurter's attention, he approved Holmes' famous dissent in the *Lochner* case as the true meaning of the Fourteenth Amendment. For the proposition that rights are not absolute, but *must* be balanced, he found support in Holmes' words:

> All rights tend to declare themselves absolute to their logical extreme. Yet all in fact are limited by the neighborhood of principles or policy which are other than those on which the particular right is founded, and which become strong enough to hold their own when a particular point is reached.[70]

Informing Justice Holmes' judicial performance was a respect for the Constitution as a means of "ordering the life of a young nation" which left to the individual justice a latitude in judgment to be exercised with caution lest "the Constitution become the partisan of a particular set of ethical or economic opinions."[71] In describing Holmes' understanding of the functioning of government, Frankfurter announced his own understanding that "government means experimentation" and "deference to local knowledge." And Frankfurter answered the question of why there is a limited authority in institutions by quoting Santayana, "... because there is no absolute imperative, ... and finally because life is a compromise."[72] Both statements are portents of his disagreement with Black, who insisted on constitutional absolutes and denied the necessity of compromise inherent in the balancing of interests concept.

In a second article on Holmes,[73] Frankfurter articulated more fully his conception of the Court's role in constitutional adjudication:

> The Supreme Court is the final authority in adjusting the relationship of the individual to the separate States, of the individual to the United States, of the forty-eight States to one another, and of each, some or all of the States to the United States.... But though the Court thus exercises a political function, it escapes the rough and tumble of politics partly through the restraints of the traditional mental habits and the scrutiny of professional judgment, intermittently effective; but largely because it does not directly exercise its powers to promote or deny affirmative ends of the state.... These are delicate and tremendous questions, not to be answered by mechanical magic distilled from the four corners of the Constitution, nor self revealed in the Constitution "by taking the words and a dictionary."[74]

Frankfurter praised Holmes' opinions which repelled "efforts to spell pedantic perfection into the Fourteenth Amendment," and which recognized "the necessity for allowing play to the joints of the crude machine of government."[75]

Frankfurter attributed his basic attitude of judicial self-restraint to Professor James Bradley Thayer. Thayer left Harvard one year before Frankfurter arrived but his influence still permeated the school and lived on through Holmes, Brandeis and Frankfurter. Frankfurter recognized Thayer's influential article, "The Origin and Scope of the American Doctrine of Constitutional Law," published in 1893, as the "great guide for judges."[76] He placed the highest value on Thayer's theory that legislative acts must be allowed to stand unless "those who have the right to make laws have not merely made a mistake, but have made a very clear one—so clear that it is not open to rational questioning."[77] Frankfurter's deference to legislative acts attested to his belief that the legislature was the lawmaking body, an experimental laboratory to devise a workable democracy and that "[t]he judicial function [was] merely that of fixing the outside border of reasonable legislative action."[78] Frankfurter knew that his was an unpopular approach, noting "many of my friends want me to save them from the effort to prevent bad legislation from being passed, and if it is passed, even more effort to get it repealed."[79] Frankfurter thought that a restrained judicial approach would aid in making democracy work.

Of the three schools of legal jurisprudence previously mentioned, Frankfurter's philosophy approximated that of the sociological school. His lifetime interest in social progress through social programs and legislation pointed in that direction. Although his exercise of the judicial function was tempered by a restraint not shared by all adherents to this philosophy, he agreed that law was "essentially a part of the culture of society—man-made, fallible rules designed to resolve conflict among competing societal interests. The judge is neither a discoverer of eternal verities nor *a logician mechanically applying sovereign commands to individual controversies.*[80]

CONFLICT OF JUDICIAL ACTIVISM AND JUDICIAL RESTRAINT AS SEEN IN *YOUNGSTOWN SHEET AND TUBE COMPANY V. SAWYER AND DENNIS ET AL. V. UNITED STATES*

A comparison of the opinions of Justices Black and Frankfurter in *Youngstown Sheet and Tube Company v. Sawyer* (1952)[81] and in *Dennis et al. v. United States* (1951)[82] will highlight the differences in their judicial approaches.

In the *Steel Seizure Case*, Justice Black wrote the majority opinion. President Truman's Executive Order 10340 directing the Secretary of Commerce, Charles Sawyer, to seize control of the steel plants to avert a strike had been enjoined by the United States District Court Judge in Washington, D.C. The Supreme Court affirmed and Justice Black delivered the opinion for the Court. Black's opinion of two and one-half pages dealt primarily with the authority of the executive to issue such an order. Black found no legislative authorization for the order, noting in the legislative history of the Taft-Hartley Act that Congress specifically "rejected an amendment which would have authorized such governmental seizures in cases of emergency."[83]

He then turned to the Constitution for authorization of presidential power "implied from the aggregate of his powers under the Constitution." Black found no such implication from the grant of executive power or military power. He analyzed the order and found it was cast in legislative form, "like a statute,"[84] and was legislative in substance. The order, thus deemed legislative, constitutionally could not be authorized as only Congress could legislate. The order could not stand as an exercise of constitutionally granted power.

Black's method was to look directly to the Constitution for authorization for the order. It was a direct and simple approach to determine if there was constitutional authority for the Executive Order. The result was a head-on collision between the two branches. The judiciary said "no" to the executive and the judiciary prevailed. This was judicial activism in motion.

Frankfurter wrote a concurring opinion of approximately thirty-nine pages with appendices. He began with an historical review of the powers of the judiciary and found that "[t]he Framers did not make the judiciary the overseer of our government."[85] He described the Court's duty to exercise "due regard for the implications of the distribution of powers," noted the restraint rule of constitutional interpretation—"not to pass on a constitutional issue at all . . . if the case may be decided without considering delicate problems of power under the Constitution," and concluded that the issue in the case could be and should be resolved without an inquiry into the powers of the Presidency.[86] Frankfurter chided the majority:

> To start with a consideration of the relation between the President's powers and those of Congress, a most delicate matter that has occupied the thoughts of statesmen and judges since the Nation was founded and will continue to occupy their thoughts as long as our democracy lasts—is to start at the wrong end.[87]

Frankfurter reviewed the history of presidential use of seizure power.[88] He deemed it "an inadmissibly narrow conception of American Constitutional law to confine it to the words of the Constitution and to disregard the gloss which life ha[d] written upon them."[89] Although he concurred in the holding, Justice Frankfurter expressed reluctance: "The judiciary may, as this case proves, have to intervene . . . but in doing so, we should be wary and humble."[90] The task was an unpleasant duty for him. He compared President Truman to President Washington in a similar situation, quoting Chief Justice John Jay's letter to Washington expressing regret for the Court's inability to give advisory opinions.

Frankfurter emphasized the need to decide the case on narrow review and agreed with the limited scope of *certiorari* by which the case was brought before the Court. *Certiorari*, the writ issued to the lower court to send up the record, was one method by which the Court could limit review. The Court, in granting the writ, either limited the review to particular issues or agreed to determine all issues. Frankfurter thought that only the decisive constitutional issues should be considered.

Frankfurter's opinion was judicial self-restraint in action. He tried to confine the holding, looked for precedents to justify the opinion, deprecated the jugular approach and found the job unpleasant. In this case, both Black and Frankfurter reached the same conclusion, but the reasoning in each opinion revealed their irreconcilable approaches.

In the *Dennis* case, the two justices disagreed. Frankfurter wrote a separate opinion concurring with the majority which held that the Smith Act of 1940 did not violate the First and Fifth Amendments or other provisions of the Bill of Rights. The Act proscribed advocating or teaching the overthrow or destruction of government and organizing or being a member of any group involved in similar activity. The Court affirmed the conviction of the petitioners for violating the conspiracy provisions of the Smith Act.

Justice Black's dissent was brief, consisting of one page. His main disagreement with the majority opinion was in constitutional approach. He noted that the prisoners were charged with conspiring to organize the Communist party and with agreeing to circulate information. He declared that the conviction was a prior censorship of speech and press forbidden by the First Amendment. He repeated his views on the absolute right of free speech and noted that the Framers considered free expression worth the risk. He denounced the clear and present danger test as a "minimum compulsion of the Bill of Rights," as a limitation on the true meaning of free speech guarantees, and looked to a calmer time when the Court would "restore the First Amendment liberties to the high preferred place where they belong in a free society."[91]

Black also expressed his disagreement with the limited grant of *certiorari*.[92] The case was heard only on objection that the Smith Act violated the First and Fifth Amendments. Black contended that the record showed also a discriminatory selection of jurors and open hostility of one jury member toward the accused.

In his opinion, Justice Frankfurter was content to grant a limited review to the case. He addressed the issue of whether Congress had constitutional power to "enact a statute making it a crime to conspire to do what [the accused] have been found to have conspired to do."[93] He cited historical precedents beginning with Madison to affirm that the government has the power of self-preservation, subject to limitation by the restrictions of the First Amendment. He discussed the Bill of Rights as an embodiment of certain guarantees and immunities inherited from England subject to "certain well recognized exceptions arising from the necessities of the case."[94] He reviewed precedents to further the process of "shaping the law."

Frankfurter contended that deference to the legislature was to be exercised if the statute was a reasonable expression of legislative judgment, and he found that the Smith Act was reasonable legislation. He deplored the automatic use of tests like Holmes' "clear and present danger" formula, contending that such tests prevented a reasoned approach to judicial questions. He discussed the value scale of different forms of speech. He weighed the government's interest in self-preservation against the defendant's right to free speech and found the scale tipped in favor of the government. His basic reason for upholding the conviction was his determination that the legislation was not unreasonable.

These cases dealt with the division of powers within the federal government and with the interpretation of the civil rights of citizens under a federal statute. Black's activism led him to repudiate boldly the authority of the executive, having found no expressed or implied constitutional or legislative grant of power. His dependence on the absolutism of the First Amendment led him to repudiate boldly the exercise of legislative power by Congress. Frankfurter's judicial self-restraint led him reluctantly to negate executive power when compelled by conscience after an analytical appraisal of facts and a review of the applicable precedents. His deference to legislative authority and his reliance on the reasonableness of the statute prompted him to affirm the exercise of legislative power by Congress.

The divergent approaches of judicial activism and judicial restraint were pronounced during the years that Frankfurter and Black served on the Court and are most vividly seen in the constitutional feud between the two justices. G. Edward White defined Frankfurter's philosophy as "process liberalism" contrasted with the "substantive liberalism" which he ascribed to Black. Process liberalism translated into a cautious approach to judging with deference to law-making agencies. Substantive liberalism was characterized by the more active "humanitarian impulse of modern liberalism."[95]

Philosophical hostilities, it should be noted, existed also among other members of the Court, and the disagreement between Black and Frankfurter had also acquired by the time of Chief Justice Stone's death in 1946 a petty personal dimension.[96] In order to avoid intensifying these philosophical and personal hostilities, Truman rejected the idea of elevating a sitting member of the Court to the Chief Justiceship even though several members were amply qualified to serve. He chose instead an old friend, his close associate Fred Vinson, a man valued in large measure because of proven capacity as a conciliator.

Black and Frankfurter would continue their verbal war through dissents and separate concurring opinions, and Truman's purposes in choosing Vinson were not fulfilled. Black, however, in paying tribute to Frankfurter after his death, noted: "Our differences in the main were far less about the ultimate aims of our Constitution than they were about the most appropriate way for our Court to aid in achieving those aims."[97]

When Harold Burton, Fred Vinson, Tom Clark and Sherman Minton were appointed to the bench, they fell heir to the continuing disagreement between Black and Frankfurter over approaches and philosophies. How each new justice responded will be examined in the chapters which follow.

NOTES

1. 2 Dallas 419 (1793).
2. 3 Dallas 199 (1796).
3. 3 Dallas 171 (1796).

4. 1 Cranch 137 (1803). For a general discussion of this case, see Albert J. Beveridge, *The Life of John Marshall*, vol. 3 (Dunwoody, Ga.: Norman S. Berg, Publishers, 1974). See generally the Federalist No. 78 (Hamilton), Roy P. Fairfield, ed. *The Federalist Papers* (Garden City, N.Y.: Doubleday and Company, Inc., 1966), pp. 226–33. See also Alexander M. Bickel, *The Least Dangerous Branch* (New York: Bobbs-Merrill Company, Inc., 1962), pp. 114–15. Alexander Bickel traced the self-restraint maxims requiring a "case" or "controversy" and "standing" to the reasoning in *Marbury v. Madison*.

5. 1 Cranch 137, 177 (1803).

6. 6 Cranch 87 (1810).

7. 6 Cranch 87, 128 (1810). Allan B. Magruder, *John Marshall, American Statesman* (Cambridge: The Riverside Press, 1885). Leonard Baker, *John Marshall, A Life in Law* (New York: Macmillan and Company, 1974), p. 568. Baker described Marshall's comments as a "model of judicial restraint."

8. 19 Howard 393 (1857).

9. Henry J. Abraham, *The Judicial Process* (New York: Oxford University Press, 1980), pp. 373–96. See also Edward S. Corwin, *The Constitution and What it Means Today* (Princeton, N.J.: Princeton University Press, 1978), pp. 212–44; and Justice Brandeis' dissent in *Ashwander v. T.V.A.*, 297 U.S. 288 (1936).

10. Alexander M. Bickel, *The Supreme Court and the Idea of Progress* (New York: Harper and Row, 1970), p. 41.

11. Edward S. Corwin, *The Constitution and What It Means Today* (Princeton, N.J.: Princeton University Press, 1978), quoted at p. 223.

12. See Stone's opinion in *United States v. Butler*, 297 U.S. 1 at 79 (1936).

13. Alpheus T. Mason, *The Supreme Court from Taft to Burger* (Baton Rouge: Louisiana State University Press, 1979), p. 133.

14. 300 U.S. 379 (1937).

15. Quoted in John P. Frank, "Hugo L. Black," Leon Friedman and Fred L. Israel, eds. *The Justices of the Supreme Court, 1789–1956, Their Lives and Major Opinions*, vol. 3 (New York: Chelsea House, 1969), p. 2322. Frank also reported that "[i]n 1937, it was widely believed that F.D.R.'s first appointment would go to his Senate majority leader, Joseph T. Robinson of Arkansas... but Robinson died before the question could be put to the test." John P. Frank, *The Marble Palace* (New York: Alfred A. Knopf, 1968), p. 57.

16. Daniel M. Berman, "The Political Philosophy of Hugo L. Black" (unpublished Ph.D. dissertation, Rutgers University, 1957), p. 24.

17. Charles A. Reich, "Mr. Justice Black and the Living Constitution," 76 *Harvard Law Review* 673, 675 (1963).

18. Berman, "The Political Philosophy of Hugo L. Black," pp. 4–13.

19. Black's position opposing Prohibition has been attributed to his strict Baptist background reinforced by the death of an older brother, who, while

inebriated, drowned. See Gerald T. Dunne, *Hugo Black and the Judicial Revolution* (New York: Simon and Schuster, 1977), pp. 106–7. See also John P. Frank, *Mr. Justice Black: The Man and His Opinions* (New York: Alfred A. Knopf, Inc., 1949), p. 41.

20. Berman, "The Political Philosophy of Hugo Black," p. 28.
21. Frank, *Mr. Justice Black*, p. 38.
22. H. N. Hirsch, *The Enigma of Felix Frankfurter* (New York: Basic Books, Inc., 1981), pp. 152–53.
23. This bill eventually emerged in 1938 as the Fair Labor Standards Act. The Act which passed contained a forty-hour week and minimum wage provisions. See John P. Frank, "Hugo L. Black," p. 2327.
24. Reich, "Mr. Justice Black and the Living Constitution," p. 675.
25. Berman, "The Political Philosophy of Hugo L. Black," p. 40. See also Frank, *Mr. Justice Black*, p. 84.
26. Hugo L. Black, "The Bill of Rights," 35 *New York University Law Review*, 865 (1960).
27. Edmond Cahn, "Justice Black and First Amendment 'Absolutes': A Public Interview," 37 *New York University Law Review* 549 (1962).
28. Hugo L. Black, *A Constitutional Faith* (New York: Alfred A. Knopf, 1969).
29. Samuel Krislov, Associate Professor of Political Science at Michigan State University, pointed out that Black seldom made off-the-bench pronouncements and attributed this rare departure from the tradition of "judicial lockjaw" to his "desire to make sure that his doctrines had firm roots" and received "full view of broad public attention." Krislov discussed four approaches to First Amendment rights, of which Black's absolutism was one, Frankfurter's balancing of interests another. See Samuel Krislov, "Mr. Justice Black Reopens the Free Speech Debate," 11 *UCLA Law Review* 189, 190 (1964).
30. Hugo Black, "The Bill of Rights," p. 867.
31. Ibid., p. 874.
32. Ibid., p. 875.
33. Ibid., p. 878.
34. Ibid., p. 881. For support of Black's doctrine of absolutes, see generally Alexander Meiklejohn, "The First Amendment in an Absolute," 1961 *Supreme Court Review* at 245. For contrary views about the incorporation theory of the Fourteenth Amendment and historical conclusions differing from Black's, see Charles Fairman, "Does the Fourteenth Amendment Incorporate the Bill of Rights?" 6 *Stanford Law Review* 5 (1949), and Charles Fairman, "The Supreme Court and the Constitutional Limitations on State Governmental Authority," 21 *University of Chicago Law Review* 40, (1953). Louis Henkin also refuted Black's wholesale incorporation theory in " 'Selective Incorporation' in the Fourteenth Amendment," 73 *The Yale Law Journal* 74 (1963). An enthusiastic response to Fairman is contained in 22

University of Chicago Law Review 1 (1954), "Charles Fairman, 'Legislative History,' and the Constitutional Limitations of State Authority" by William Winslow Crosskey.

35. Cahn, "Justice Black and First Amendment 'Absolutes,' " p. 563.
36. Ibid., p. 555.
37. 376 U.S. 254, 293 (1964).
38. Black, *A Constitutional Faith*, pp. 48–49.
39. Ibid., p. 41.
40. *Goldstein v. United States*, 316 U.S. 114 (1942). See also *Goldman v. United States*, 316 U.S. 129 (1942). The court held that attachment of a detectaphone outside a room to eavesdrop was, like wiretapping, permissible. See also John P. Frank, "The United States Supreme Court: 1951–52," 20 *University of Chicago Law Review* 1, 36 (1952).
41. Black, *A Constitutional Faith*, p. 563.
42. Ibid., p. 18.
43. Ibid., pp. 15–18.
44. Ibid., p. 20.
45. Ibid., pp. 65–66.
46. Tinsley E. Yarbrough, "Mr. Justice Black and Legal Positivism," 57 *Virginia Law Review* 375, 378 (1971). See also M. P. Golding, ed. *The Nature of Law: Readings in Legal Philosophy* (New York: Random House, 1966).
47. The term "four corners of the Constitution" was used by Justice Frankfurter to denote literal and mechanical interpretation of the Constitution. See also Justice Owen Roberts' opinion in *United States v. Butler*, 297 U.S. 1, 62 (1936), where he described the duty of the Court as one of laying "the article of the Constitution which is invoked beside the statute which is challenged and . . . [deciding] whether the latter squares with the former." Because there is disagreement about what is contained within "the four corners of the Constitution," the term is not widely used. An example of the meaning as used here is Justice Black's dissent in *Griswold v. Connecticut*, 381 U.S. 479 (1965), in which he refused to find a right to privacy emanating from the Constitution saying, "I like my privacy as well as the next one, but I am nevertheless compelled to admit that government has a right to invade it unless prohibited by some specific constitutional provision." 381 U.S. at 510. In a later case, *Trimble et al. v. Gordon et al.*, 430 U.S. 762, 779–80 (1977), Justice William H. Rehnquist in his dissent acknowledged the restrictive nature of the term.
48. Yarbrough, "Mr. Justice Black and Legal Positivism," pp. 383–406.
49. H. N. Hirsch, *The Enigma of Felix Frankfurter* (New York: Basic Books, Inc., 1981), p. 146.
50. Helen Shirley Thomas, *Felix Frankfurter, Scholar on the Bench* (Baltimore: The Johns Hopkins Press, 1960), p. vii.
51. The so-called second New Deal began in April of 1935 with four major

legislative projects: the Works Progress Administration (WPA), the Soil Conservation Act, the National Labor Relations Act (Wagner-Connery) and the Social Security Act, all passed by the fall of 1935. Other legislation in this second phase of the New Deal included welfare-oriented programs and a re-invigorated anti-trust program. For an extensive discussion of the Brandeis-Frankfurter influence on Roosevelt and his programs, see Bruce Allen Murphy, *The Brandeis-Frankfurter Connection* (New York: Oxford University Press, 1982), pp. 152–85.

52. Albert M. Sacks, "Felix Frankfurter," Leon Friedman and Fred L. Israel, eds. *The Justices of the Supreme Court, 1789–1956, Their Lives and Major Opinions*, vol. 3 (New York: Chelsea House, 1969), p. 2405.

53. E. F. Prichard and Archibald MacLeish, eds., *Law and Politics, Occasional Papers of Felix Frankfurter, 1913–1938* (New York: Capricorn Books, 1962), p. x.

54. Michael E. Parrish, *Felix Frankfurter and His Times: The Reform Years* (New York: The Free Press, Macmillan Publishing Co., Inc., 1982), pp. 238–42.

55. Bruce Allen Murphy detailed their collaboration, describing it as mutually beneficial. Murphy, *The Brandeis-Frankfurter Connection*, pp. 37–45. Their relationship became strained when the two men disagreed over Roosevelt's plan to enlarge the Court. Brandeis opposed the plan and was critical of the initial New Deal programs. Frankfurter, secretly supportive and less critical, was placed in an "uncomfortable position between a prophet and a president." See Parrish, *Felix Frankfurter and His Times: The Reform Years*, p. 261.

56. H. N. Hirsch, *The Enigma of Felix Frankfurter*, p. 111.

57. Felix Frankfurter, "John Marshall and the Judicial Function," Arthur E. Sutherland, ed., *Government Under Law* (New York: Da Capo Press, 1968), p. 21.

58. Ibid., p. 22.

59. Ibid., p. 21.

60. Ibid., p. 27.

61. 19 Howard 393 (1857).

62. Sutherland, ed., *Government Under Law*, p. 16.

63. Felix Frankfurter, "Mr. Justice Brandeis and the Constitution," 45 *Harvard Law Review* 33–111, 38 (1931).

64. Ibid., p. 39, 44.

65. Ibid., p. 79. See also Alexander M. Bickel, *The Least Dangerous Branch*, pp. 128–98, where Bickel discussed "The Passive Virtues" as "devices for disposing of a case while avoiding judgment on the constitutional issue it raises," p. 169.

66. 45 *Harvard Law Review* 33, 80.

67. Ibid.

68. Ibid., p. 99.
69. Felix Frankfurter, "The Constitutional Opinions of Mr. Justice Holmes," 29 *Harvard Law Review* 683 (1916).
70. Ibid., p. 687.
71. Ibid., p. 686.
72. Ibid., p. 699.
73. Felix Frankfurter, "Twenty Years of Mr. Justice Holmes' Constitutional Opinions," 36 *Harvard Law Review* 909 (1923).
74. Ibid., pp. 910–11.
75. Ibid., p. 927.
76. Harlan B. Phillips, ed., *Felix Frankfurter Reminisces* (New York: Reynal and Company, 1960), pp. 299–300.
77. James Bradley Thayer, "The Origin and Scope of the American Doctrine of Constitutional Law," 7 *Harvard Law Review* 129, 144 (1893).
78. Ibid., p. 149.
79. Phillips, ed., *Felix Frankfurter Reminisces*, p. 300.
80. Tinsley E. Yarbrough, "Mr. Justice Black and Legal Positivism," p. 278.
81. 343 U.S. 579 (1952), hereinafter referred to as the *Steel Seizure Case*.
82. 341 U.S. 494 (1951).
83. 343 U.S. at 586.
84. 343 U.S. at 588.
85. 343 U.S. at 594.
86. 343 U.S. at 597.
87. 343 U.S. at 595.
88. 343 U.S. at 611–13.
89. 343 U.S. at 610.
90. 343 U.S. at 597.
91. 341 U.S. at 581.
92. Under the Rule of Four, at least four of the Justices had to vote to grant the review. The Court could also limit the scope of review. The Act of 1925 gave the "Supreme Court almost unlimited jurisdiction to decide for itself what cases it would hear." John P. Frank, *The Marble Palace*, p. 15.
93. 341 U.S. at 518.
94. 341 U.S. at 524.
95. G. Edward White, *The American Judicial Tradition, Profiles of Leading American Judges* (New York: Oxford University Press, 1976), pp. 324–25.
96. Gerald T. Dunne, "Justice Hugo Black and Robert Jackson: The Great Feud," 19 *Saint Louis University Law Journal* 465 (1975). Mr. Dunne described in detail the ideological disunity between Justices Black, Frankfurter and Jackson. The article was published before Mr. Dunne's book. A more complete treatment can be found in Gerald T. Dunne, *Hugo Black and the Judicial Revolution* (New York: Simon and Schuster, 1977).

97. Hugo L. Black, "Mr. Justice Frankfurter," 78 *Harvard Law Review* 1521 (1965). Black and Frankfurter have been studied comparatively by various scholars. For an earlier work, see Wallace Mendelson's *Justices Black and Frankfurter: Conflict on the Court* (Chicago: University of Chicago Press, 1966). More recently, Mark Silverstein explored the role that different political values played in the Black and Frankfurter decisions. Mark Silverstein, *Constitutional Faiths: Felix Frankfurter, Hugo Black and the Process of Judicial Decision Making* (Ithaca, N.Y.: Cornell University Press, 1984).

TWO

THE TRUMAN LEGACY

TRUMAN'S MOTIVATIONS FOR THE APPOINTMENTS

President Harry S. Truman appointed one hundred and twenty judges to the federal courts, including the four he nominated for the Supreme Court. These appointments, in addition to President Franklin Roosevelt's approximately one hundred and eighty (including eight Associate Justices of the Supreme Court and one Chief Justice) combined to alter permanently the political composition of the federal judiciary, thereby closing the books on the judicial history of the past.[1] Truman's motivations for selecting his four Supreme Court appointees were both political and personal. He worked closely as either senator or president with all four. Burton, Vinson and Minton had served with him in Congress. Clark and Vinson were members of Truman's cabinet at the time of their appointments, and had previously served in Roosevelt's administration. Each of them shared Truman's disdain for the pre–1937 activist Court.

In his study of American presidents and their appointments to the Supreme Court, Professor Abraham identified four criteria which were used in selecting Supreme Court justices: (1) objective merit, (2) personal friendship, (3) balancing "representation" or "representativeness" on the Court, and (4) "real" political and ideological compatibility.[2] While all of these factors, in varying degrees, played a part in determining Truman's appointments, personal friendship and political considerations were probably predominant. All of his appointees met his "criteria for the post: they had all held public office; they were his political, professional and personal friends; he understood them, he liked them; he liked their politics."[3]

Clark, Truman's third appointee, subsequently described the part that he, as Attorney General, played in Truman's selection process:

> I had the practice of sending Mr. Truman three names whenever a vacancy occurred.... I would usually select as one of my three candidates one person out of the Senate or the House, one sitting judge from either the federal or the state system, and one practicing attorney.... For example, on the first vacancy which happened on the Supreme Court, one of my three candidates was Harold Burton.... The second appointment to the Supreme Court was Chief Justice Vinson.... The president suggested that I talk to retired Chief Justice [Charles Evans] Hughes... [who suggested the name of] Fred Vinson.... I was the President's third appointment.... The story goes that the first name was Tom Clark, the second name was Tom C. Clark, and the third name was Brother Clark. But the president moved on my appointment before there was any list.[4]

Truman made his first appointments, as noted, during a period of great conflict among the Court members. The first vacancy was occasioned by the resignation of Justice Owen Roberts in July of 1945. Roberts had dissented fifty-three times during his last session on the Court and the period preceding his resignation had been marked by his bitter protest against the Court's disregard for precedent which he felt "left the [trial] courts... on an uncharted sea of doubt and difficulty."[5] So intense were the feelings on the Court that the justices could not agree on a text for a farewell letter.

The fracas over the farewell letter to Roberts epitomized the personal conflicts on the Court at the start of Truman's presidency. Justice Black suggested two seemingly minor deletions in the draft which Chief Justice Stone had circulated, the dropping of the phrase "that our association with you in the daily work of the Court must now come to an end" and of the sentence, "You have made fidelity to principle your guide to decision."[6] Stone requested Black to recirculate his letter with the two deletions, but he also sent out a memorandum by Frankfurter refusing to accede to the deletion of the sentence. Black responded by withdrawing his proposed letter from further consideration:

> The memorandum sent at Frankfurter's request indicates that the members of the Court should pass upon two conflicting drafts. I am still of the opinion that the matter should be postponed until the Court reconvenes, and I therefore request that you do not mail any letter, as a Court letter, until the whole matter can be discussed in Conference.[7]

Douglas, writing to Black from Oregon a week later characterized the matter as a "goddam tempest in a teapot. FF is looking for trouble—some opening so R can let go a blast. I hope we can manage it so that does not happen."[8] No letter was sent.

Chief Justice Harlan Fiske Stone's death on April 22, 1946 provided the second opening on the Court. The "iconoclastic" Stone Court had declared nineteen state laws unconstitutional (only five unanimously) and had overruled twenty-five earlier Court decisions.[9] This intense judicial activity had been accompanied by major disagreements among Court members which received national publicity at the time of the appointment of Stone's successor.

Following Stone's death, newspaper exposure of the tension on the Supreme Court accompanied intense speculation about the possible elevation of a member on the Court to the vacant position. On May 16, 1946, before Truman had selected Stone's replacement, the *Washington Star* printed an article exposing a Court memorandum penned by Justices Frankfurter and Jackson critical of Black's participation in *Jewell Ridge Coal Corp. v. United Mine Workers* (1945).[10] The internecine feud between Black and Jackson climaxed over Black's failure to disqualify himself in the case, a disqualification necessitated, Jackson argued, by Black's former partnership (some twenty years earlier) with counsel for the mine workers. In the 5 to 4 decision, Black cast the deciding vote which favored the mine workers' bid for portal-to-portal pay. Jackson voted with the opposition.

The publication of the memorandum in effect precluded the possibility that either Black or Jackson would be named to the vacancy. The memorandum not only focused public attention on the immediate cause of the dispute, but it also triggered Jackson's vitriolic attack on Black. Jackson explained the details of the disagreement surrounding the issue of Black's disqualification in a cablegram sent from Nuremburg, where he was serving as special prosecutor during the trial of war criminals, to both the Senate and House Judiciary committees considering Vinson's confirmation. The cablegram, received by Congress on June 10th, four days after Vinson's nomination, revealed the depth of the bitterness among members of the Court, although it did not affect the confirmation proceedings for the Chief Justiceship.[11]

Truman, on September 18, 1945, announced the appointment of Republican Senator Harold Burton to fill the Roberts vacancy. In offering the job to Burton, Truman told him, "I want someone who will do a thoroughly judicial job and not legislate. You are fitted for the court, you have a judicial temperament."[12] In addition to their personal friendship which began years earlier when Burton was "the workhorse" on the Committee to Investigate the National Defense Program,[13] there were two political advantages in Truman's selection. He replaced one Republican justice with another, thus maintaining the bipartisan complexion of the Court, and the appointment allowed the Democratic governor of Ohio to appoint a Democrat to the Senate to complete Burton's unexpired term.[14] Tom Clark as Attorney General was consulted on the appointment and, although Clark preferred the appointment of Robert P. Patterson, Assistant Secretary of War, Truman chose Burton.

Clark denied that political considerations motivated Truman's selection. He attributed the choice to three factors: first, "[Burton] was on the [Truman Investigating] Committee; [second,] he had judicial [posts] before, and [third,] . . . he would make a good justice."[15] Clark incorrectly attributed judicial experience to Burton, who had not been a judge, although Clark may have been referring to his experience on the Senate Judiciary Committee.

Minton evidently felt that political considerations were the determining factor, and he disapproved of the appointment. On September 20, 1945, from his seat on the Seventh Circuit Court of Appeals, he wrote his old Senate colleague, Hugo Black:

> I thought the [Democratic] gang had sold him off the idea of appointing a Republican. . . . It is alright [sic]—while I don't agree with him as to the wisdom of appointing a Republican or [with] his choice of Republican. I cheerfully accept his judgment. . . . The politics of it just doesn't make sense to me. . . . I never knew Burton well but my observation of him would not lead me to conclude that he could fill the assignment he has given himself . . . to restore the Court's prestige and restore its decency and dignity from fellows like you and Bill Douglass. [sic][16]

Truman's friendship with Burton originated in the Senate. Wesley McCune found that "[i]t was love at first sight. Truman often told friends praiseworthy things about Burton's fair mindedness, teamwork, and conscientious approach to the investigating power."[17] Truman was the first president to attend the induction ceremonies for a Supreme Court justice and Burton expressed his gratitude in a note to the President on October 4, 1945.

> Dear Harry,
> It was thoughtful and generous of you to come to the session of the Court on October 1st which included my induction into the office to which you appointed me. . . . I only hope that I can justify the trust reposed in me.[18]

Truman maintained a close friendship with most of his appointees during their tenures on the Court. This was especially true of Chief Justice Fred Vinson, his second appointment, announced June 6, 1946.[19] Vinson held various positions in the Roosevelt administration after his resignation from the Court of Appeals in May of 1943, and had been Director of the Office of War Mobilization and Reconversion for only ten days when Truman became president on April 12, 1945. In July, Truman named him Secretary of the Treasury. Truman's diary entry of June 17, 1945 summed up his lasting assessment of Judge Fred Vinson as a "straight shooter, knows Congress and how [Congressmen] think, a man to trust."[20] It was an easy-going relationship. On the day he left office in 1953, Truman wrote, "Inauguration Day—a beautiful day . . . Ceremony came off as scheduled. . . . It was a grand luncheon. The Chief Justice was there and received a good ribbing for alleged disrespect to the former President."[21] Truman, in fact, had hoped that Vinson would succeed him in the White House, so great was his regard for him, but Vinson declined to become a candidate.[22] He died only eight and one-half months after Truman left office.

Clark described the appointment of Vinson as an attempt to "figure out just who would be the best peacemaker."[23] The Stone years had indicated the need for a strong Chief Justice to bring order to the Court. Truman, in an unmailed letter drafted May 6, 1950 to Merlo J. Pusey of the *Washington Post*, described his method of selection. He first had surveyed the roster of federal judges in order to weigh their possible elevation to the Chief Justiceship. He then consulted former Chief Justice Charles Evans Hughes who, according to Truman, said "that in his opinion, the best man for the place would be [the] Secretary of the Treasury."[24] A conversation with former Justice Roberts elicited the same response.[25] Vinson's appointment followed.

Truman consistently maintained that Hughes recommended Vinson as his first choice. Pusey, author of an authoritative biography of Hughes, said however that Hughes told him that he had recommended Jackson, although Truman disputed this three years later when Pusey "took the matter up at the White House."[26] Clark indicated that Hughes suggested in an interview with him "three or four names" before naming Vinson. Clark concluded: "I, of course, knew of the warmth that Mr. Truman felt for Fred Vinson and so it was a simple matter after that: he appointed Vinson chief justice."[27]

Truman's other two appointments were made in 1949. Justice Frank Murphy died July 10, 1949, and Justice Wiley Rutledge died approximately two months later in September. The third appointment, replacing Murphy, went to Tom Clark, Truman's Attorney General for four years. Truman appointed Clark "at the urging of Chief Justice Vinson who wanted a colleague who would support his point of view."[28] Clark, a native of Texas and a protegé of Speaker of the House of Representatives Sam Rayburn and Senator Tom Connally, had worked with the Truman Committee in 1944 while Assistant Attorney General. Over the years, he and Truman had exchanged gifts and shared good times. The personal nature of their relationship surfaced in a letter Truman wrote to Clark on April 14, 1952, three years after his appointment:

> I certainly appreciate your note of the 12th and I'll set aside Thursday, May 8th, for the purpose of a celebration at your house. I don't know what I'd do for a birthday celebration if you didn't take care of it.
>
> Harry[29]

While on the Court, Clark and Vinson continued to play poker with Truman. The poker parties began on Saturday evening to accommodate the Court's schedule. Clark and Chief Justice Vinson would go down together to the presidential yacht, the "Williamsburg," "about 5:00 p.m. after the Court adjourned."[30] Conversations, Clark remembered, would be about:

> current news . . . not often . . . serious. . . . We would eat dinner. We would usually start before dinner, and then we would have dinner, and then we would play until about 2 o'clock. The President and I used to go up and just lay down right on the deck, wouldn't have any headrest or anything. You know this was summertime—it was good boating time. In the winter we'd play at our respective houses. He would just—sometimes we'd get to talking and he would tell me about, how when he was growing up—about the discrimination against the blacks, and how they couldn't get to first base, and everybody used them and things of that kind, you know. He was going to try do something about it, that's what he told me.[31]

Truman and Clark continued a friendly correspondence until Truman's death. Clark fondly remembered his personal association with Truman, expressing his gratitude "for the opportunity to have been . . . his friend over the years . . . and [for] the privilege of . . . knowing him intimately."[32] Truman undoubtedly reciprocated these warm feelings although in 1952, Clark's vote in the *Steel Seizure Case* infuriated him.

Shortly after Clark went on the bench, Truman, replying to a letter from Clark, told him ". . . That writing looks just as well on Court stationery as it did on the Attorney General['s]." He also noted, "You have a new colleague on the Court and I want to say to you that he is one of the finest fellows who ever came over the pike—in fact I think he came of the same piece of cloth that you and the Chief Justice did."[33]

Truman expected the new appointee, Sherman Minton, to be one of his best contributions to the Court. He had the judicial experience which Truman believed was a strong asset although clearly not a prerequisite. The Supreme Court appointment elevated Minton from the Seventh Circuit Court of Appeals to which Roosevelt had appointed him in 1941. He was an old friend of Truman's. They had entered the Senate in the same year, 1935, and had been associated with each other politically since that time.[34] Minton had strongly supported Truman's nomination as vice-president in 1944 against the incumbent, Henry A. Wallace.[35] Clark attributed Minton's appointment to the fact that Truman and he were "close friends and Minton was on the Truman Committee." He also thought Minton's "experience as a judge from '41 to '49 was very strong—had emphasis in Truman's mind."[36] Clark evidently confused Minton's work on Black's investigating committee with the Truman Committee.

While on the Circuit Bench, Minton, in 1946, wrote to his friend, the President, concerning the appointment of a new Chief Justice. The letter revealed Minton's partisanship and his intimate friendship with Truman as well as indicating his own judicial and political philosophy:

> My dear Harry:
> Many of our friends are disturbed because they fear you might appoint a Chief Justice who is a Republican. I am sorry if Chief Justice Hughes unsettled your determination to promote someone on the Court. . . . I am firmly convinced that the Court must be kept liberal. Don't let us be responsible for another Court controlled by the moneybags of the country. . . .
> Now "I make bold" to suggest Justice Black as Chief and [Lewis B.] Schwellenbach as Associate. Even by his former enemies, Justice Black is admitted to be the ablest man on the bench. He is capable of doing and does the bulk of the work. He is liberal, and is to that Court a breath of fresh air in a musty, damp cellar.[37]

Responding to Minton's "good advice," Truman replied jovially but noncommittally: "I often wish you and I were again sitting beside each other in the back row of the Senate. There are a lot of things going on there now that I believe the two of us could remedy."[38] Minton expressed his disappointment directly to Black, "I am keenly disappointed at the president's action concerning the Court, not because I don't like Vinson, because I do, and I think he'll be a good chief, but I like you so much better, and I told the President so, but his letter back to me . . . brought no mention of your name."[39]

TRUMAN'S EXPECTATIONS AND DISAPPOINTMENTS

Truman's conception of the judicial function created the expectation that his appointees' performances would be "judicial," which to Truman meant deferential and *non-active*. He expressed this conception in his admonition to Burton to "find the law" and to "stop making the law up there."[40] The assumption that judges do not make law, but are only oracles who find the law was characteristic of earlier concepts of the judicial function. The idea of the judge as oracle was largely replaced by the twentieth century by widespread acknowledgment that judges are indeed lawmakers.[41] The fact that Truman's idea of the oracular judicial function was held in the 1940s showed a continuity and overlapping of the two concepts. It also represented his reaction to the pre–1937 Court which actively thwarted legislation which he favored. Even among those who admit to a legitimate ingredient of lawmaking in the judicial function, there is often the understanding that it should be restrained. Truman expressed his concern that his appointees should not be legislative. He believed in a limited judiciary and he expected his appointees to defer to the legislative and executive branches.

Although they shared friendship and a common belief in the limited function of the judiciary, the appointees' decisions on particular cases sometimes disappointed Truman and he was, more generally, frustrated by their inability to unify the Court. In a 1949 letter to Richard M. Duncan, United States District Judge, he expressed his general concerns, "It looks as if the Supreme Court has really made a mess of itself... you can't run an organization if everyone dissents."[42] His greatest disappointment resulted from the decision in the *Steel Seizure Case*. In an unmailed letter to Justice William O. Douglas, shortly after that decision, he unburdened his anger:

> I am sorry that I didn't have an opportunity to discuss precedents with you before you came to the conclusion you did on that crazy decision that has tied up the country.... There was no decision by the majority although there were seven opinions against what was best for the country. I don't see how a Court made up of so-called liberals could do what the Court did to me.[43]

Years later, in a lecture given at Columbia University, Truman wryly observed that "packing the Supreme Court simply can't be done... I've tried and it won't work... Whenever you put a man on the Supreme Court, he ceases to be your friend. I'm sure of that."[44]

The Truman appointees split evenly in the *Steel Seizure Case*. Burton and Clark voted against the president's power to seize the industry. Vinson and Minton voted in his favor. Truman thought he could depend on the votes of Clark and Vinson because he had relied on their advice before issuing Executive Order 10340. Truman relied heavily on a memorandum written by Clark in February 1949, when as Attorney General he had advised Truman that injunctive authority to halt strikes in vital industries need not be written into legislation because the president's inherent powers were sufficient to deal with such emergencies even in peacetime.[45] In addition to this memorandum, Truman relied on Vinson who as Chief Justice had "privately advised the president to go ahead with the seizure, basing the recommendation on legal grounds."[46]

Although deeply disappointed by the majority opinion, Truman was pleased that Vinson and Minton stood by him. He was convinced that Vinson's "dissenting opinion hit the nail right on the head," and was "sure that some day his view [would] come to be recognized as the correct one."[47]

On the other hand, Truman expressed bitterness toward Tom Clark. In an interview with Merle Miller, published two years after Truman's death and never reviewed by the former president, he said:

Tom Clark was my biggest mistake... He was no damn good as Attorney General, and on the Supreme Court... he has been even worse. He hasn't made one right decision that I can think of... it isn't so much that he's a *bad* man. It's just that he's such a dumb son of a bitch. He's about the dumbest man I think I've ever run across... Being dumb's just about the worst thing there is when it comes to holding high office, and that's especially true when it's on the Supreme Court of the United States.[48]

It is difficult to reconcile these harsh words with the fact that Truman and Clark continued a warm, friendly correspondence after Truman left Washington. They regularly exchanged Christmas and birthday greetings and, occasionally, gifts.[49] Truman characterized a 1961 luncheon with the Supreme Court hosted by Clark as "one of the most pleasant luncheons and meetings that I had while back East."[50] He used the luncheon as an opportunity to defend his opinion that the *Steel Seizure Case* decision was "in line with the *Dred Scott Decision*."[51] Truman also expressed regret about Clark's decision to retire from the Court,[52] and later noted that he had "observed with deep satisfaction" Clark's devotion to his responsibilities.[53] Close friend and personal attorney to Truman, Rufus Burrus, insisted that Truman thought highly of Clark and that the Miller quotation was "somehow a mistake." Very emphatically, Burrus discounted Miller's report, noting that the book contained many inaccuracies, including a reference to him by the wrong name, Luther Burrus.[54]

Whether the quotation reflected Truman's considered opinion of Clark is at least doubtful, although it probably reflected his pique over Clark's opinion in the *Steel Seizure Case*.[55] Others have critically assessed Clark's value as a Supreme Court justice more favorably. In June of 1970, sixty-five legal scholars evaluated the ninety-six justices who served between 1789 and 1969. Of the seven degrees of performance, Clark's name was listed as one of fifty-five in the middle group considered "average." On the other hand, Minton, Vinson and Burton were listed among the eight in the lowest group considered "failures."[56]

PUBLIC REACTION

Varying degrees of approval accompanied the announcements of the four appointments. Burton was unanimously confirmed on the same day the nomination reached the Senate, as "the Senate almost invariably treats as a *cas d'honneur* the Presidential designation of a sitting member."[57] Some labor leaders were strongly opposed, but they addressed Truman directly rather than make a public fight. Newspaper response to the nomination was generally complimentary.[58]

The Senate Judiciary Committee examined only two minor reports against

Vinson, moving favorably on his nomination with only one dissenting vote from Senator E. H. Moore, an Oklahoman who did not oppose the nomination on the Senate floor. The Senate confirmed Vinson's nomination by a voice vote with no debate.[59] Press reaction to Vinson's nomination, however, was unenthusiastic. Newspapers after Stone's death had been filled with speculation that Black, Jackson or Douglas would be appointed.[60] When the May 16th article in the *Washington Star* openly exposed the quarreling between Jackson and Black,[61] and precipitated Jackson's cablegram condemning Black, speculation began to include the possibility that an outside appointment might be wise.[62] Vinson's appointment was regarded as a prescription for easing tension on a personally and ideologically divided court.

Minton, although a former Senator, had some difficulty during confirmation proceedings. He refused the Senate Judiciary Committee's invitation to testify, citing Frankfurter's previous refusal as authority and questioning the propriety of a prospective justice testifying on issues that might come before the Court. He answered the major objection to his nomination—his support for Roosevelt's Court bill—in a letter published in the *New York Times* on October 4, 1949 asserting that he had supported the bill because, as assistant majority whip, he felt obliged to support his president.[63] The Senate Judiciary Committee inquired into Minton's health about which some questions were raised, reviewed a quarrel with the *St. Louis Globe-Democrat*, and questioned some of his public policy stands.[64] After meeting for one-half day on September 17, 1949, the committee reported favorably, and Minton was confirmed by a vote of 48 to 16.[65]

The nomination of Tom Clark occasioned a bitter confirmation hearing and was the most heatedly opposed of all four appointments. The Senate Judiciary Committee met for three days (August 9, 10, and 11, 1949), and heard objections from civil libertarians, representatives of the Communist party and black groups.[66] The opposition to Clark's appointment attacked his "anti-libertarian posture" and other aspects of his performance as Attorney General. Press comment on his selection was largely unfavorable.[67] Nevertheless, he was overwhelmingly confirmed 73 to 8 by the Senate.

The appointment of Vinson as Chief Justice brought with it the hope that his political moderation and soothing personality would end the era of multiple opinions which had produced constitutional uncertainty as well as personal animosity among the justices. Fred Rodell reported that this hope was doomed to failure because "... the Black-and-Douglas against Jackson-and-Frankfurter row ... was intellectual, not personal, and all four of the participants were Vinson's intellectual superiors."[68] Arthur M. Schlesinger, Jr., in the January, 1947 article for *Fortune*, describing the Court inherited by Vinson, predicted, "It will be hard for [Vinson] to cope intellectually with men like Black and Frankfurter: his mind does not move fast in the same way ... Vinson will have ... to influence the Court by a certain massive instinct for practicality."[69]

ASSESSMENT

Historical treatment of the Vinson era, that period from June 1946 to September, 1953 when Truman's appointees served together and decisively influenced the cases before the Court, has not been favorable. Vinson served seven years on the bench. An assessment made the year following Vinson's death in 1953 by John P. Frank found that the volume of cases declined constantly during the Vinson years, reaching in 1951 and 1952 the "lowest level in a century."[70] This low productivity was partly attributable to the increased use of the discretionary power to deny *certiorari*, a practice urged by adherents of judicial restraint, thus reflecting, in part, the judicial philosophy of the Truman appointees.

Frank found also that despite Vinson's efforts, he was not successful in reducing the number of multiple decisions; the number of decided cases declined, but dissension continued. Although this may be explained by the inherent nature of the Court, as Frankfurter would insist, questions about Vinson's ability to marshall the Court behind him have persisted.

Speculation has centered particularly around the case of *Brown v. Board of Education* (1954)[71] which was accepted by the Court for arguments on December 8, 1952, but was held over for decision to the term following Vinson's death. Burton noted in his diary on May 8, 1954 that Warren had done "a magnificent job that may win a unanimous Court. (This would have been impossible a year ago, probably 6–3 with the Chief Justice at the time one of the dissenters)."[72]

Yet Vinson's clerk, Newton N. Minow, believed that *Brown* would have been decided the same way "and with the same unanimity" had Vinson lived.[73] Discussion of Vinson's possible vote in *Brown* has been a method of disparaging the quality of Vinson's leadership. To some extent, perhaps inadvertently, the discussion is an outgrowth of the enmity of Frankfurter for Vinson. William W. Oliver, former law clerk to both Vinson and Warren, explained that "Frankfurter became anti-Vinson and certainly was talking against him in the academic circles that Frankfurter had contact with... I think that helped damage Vinson's reputation and place in history."[74]

Frankfurter had initially shamelessly flattered the Chief Justice in an attempt to influence him, but Vinson was not receptive and the two men, who were temperamental and intellectual opposites, became increasingly hostile. Edward F. Prichard, Jr., Frankfurter's law clerk in 1939–40, a native Kentuckian and one of the New Deal Harvard lawyers, described the problem thusly:

> Justice Frankfurter, I'm sure, did not have a high regard for Judge Vinson's judicial capabilities and I think he was not very adept at concealing his views on things of that sort, and... there developed really some personal rancor between them. [Mr. Vinson's] was a

very rough-hewn kind of mind. In many ways, he was not philosophically inclined, not a man widely read, not a man of widely ranging intellectual interests. He was a practical day-to-day kind of person, he didn't spin out and articulate philosophical positions—just the opposite of Frankfurter. Frankfurter was quick and nimble, impetuous. Both could be impetuous at times. Vinson was a man who, despite his affable nature, could take offense if he were affronted and Frankfurter was a good affronter.[75]

Philip Elman, Frankfurter's law clerk in 1941 and 1942, later on the staff of the Solicitor General's office, recounted how he met Frankfurter at Union Station when he returned to Washington for Vinson's funeral:

He was in high spirits. Frankfurter said to me, "I'm in mourning," sarcastically. What he meant was that Vinson's departure from the Court was going to remove the roadblock in *Brown* . . . and looking me straight in the eye said, "Phil, this is the first solid piece of evidence I've ever had that there really is a God."[76]

Vinson's poor relationship with Frankfurter may have interfered with the work of the Court as well as tainting its image. Clark recalled a conference in which Vinson "was sort of making towards Felix," an advance which was broken by Clark's pushing his chair back.[77] More importantly, however, the voting pattern of the two men was opposed. Howard J. Trienens, Vinson's former law clerk, remembered a period when "Frankfurter wouldn't sign a Vinson opinion no matter what it said."[78]

Frank, in his assessment of the Vinson era, described a basic "Vinson block" composed of Reed, Vinson, Burton, Clark and Minton which indicated that the Truman appointees voted together in at least some areas. The percentage figures of their individual votes on civil liberties showed a correlation of votes in that area. Over the period 1946–1953, Vinson voted 83 percent of the time to deny a claimed right, Burton voted 74 percent for denial, Clark 75 percent for denial and Minton 87 percent for denial.[79] In this area where government interests conflicted with those of the individual, Truman's appointees, by percentage, supported the state. Frank, writing in 1954, thought the Court's performance indicated a "turning of the course of American jurisprudence."[80]

William F. Swindler, however, writing in 1970, reduced this period to the "Vinson Interlude":

Truman, by his four appointments, had reduced the former rapid pace of the new constitutionalism to a walk . . . Vinson's death terminated the interlude between the constitutional reforms of the late thirties and the renewed effort to articulate the constitutional requirements of the mid-century.[81]

The new constitutionalism was an acceptance, beginning in 1937, of a more positive role for the Court in fashioning a welfare state. Truman referred to this when he told a group of students at Columbia University that it took the Supreme Court a hundred and fifty years to find the word "welfare" in the Constitution.[82] The Vinson Court, with its prodding, deliberative approach to judicial decision making, enjoyed a period in which philosophy and ideology on the Court were emphasized less and process emphasized more. Although the political results announced by the Vinson Court were mixed, that is both liberal and conservative, the Truman appointees, given the fewer number of cases, had more time for deliberation. They were not intellectual giants, but holdovers on the Court made certain that the debate would be shaped by more formidable minds than theirs.

Truman's concept of the role of the Supreme Court did not encompass opinions about the judicial process. He did not separate his political expectations from his perception of the Court's function. He denied the charge that his appointments were basically political, insisting that they were based on "judicial ability." He was, however, quick to complain about certain decisions with which he disagreed. He felt that in matters before the Court where the "welfare of the country was at stake ... all those fellows [he] appointed voted against [him]."[83] Truman, in all simplicity, expressed the "greatest respect" for the Court. However, he wanted Court decisions endorsing his political aims. When the Court ruled as he desired, they had "found" the law. When they ruled against his wishes, they "went crossways."[84]

From his discussion of the duties of the three branches of government, it is clear that Truman favored strong legislative and executive roles and a less positive role for the judicial branch. As president, Truman exercised broad implied powers and felt that it was necessary at times to "stretch" the Constitution a little bit. The implied powers doctrine was, he asserted, the "real strength" of the Constitution, "not the words exactly as they are set down in the document."[85] Robert H. Ferrell concluded that, in Truman's mind, "the Court stood apart from the hurly-burly of government and Congress and the President did the work."[86] To the extent that the Court exercised deference to the executive and legislative branches, Truman's appointees served him well.

Prichard, expressing great respect for Truman, nevertheless considered his Supreme Court appointments his "most disastrous legacy," contending that the Court in the Vinson era allowed "gross inroads to be made by the executive and legislative branches on the individual liberties of the people."[87] This had remained the prevailing view among scholars who have studied the impact of the Court's decisions on civil liberties. The Vinson Court, however, sat during the aftermath of World War II and the birth of the Cold War. The inroads made on personal liberties which were a part of the war effort came to a Court staffed with men who felt the immediacy of wartime. Their decisions reflected those concerns. But more importantly, the factionalization on the Court occasioned the lengthy discussion and examination of basic rights necessary for change.

Pragmatically, the Court decided each issue on the merits, failing to accept either the wholesale incorporation of the Fourteenth Amendment encouraged by Black's dissent in *Adamson v. California* (1948)[88] or the constitutional thesis encouraged by Frankfurter that some of the Bill of Rights were applicable to the states by virtue of their inherent worth, while others, those dealing with procedural rights, were dated and not subject to incorporation. Truman's appointees listened, deliberated and voted. They carried on the quiet business of deciding issues in a nonflamboyant manner.

Schlesinger had stated in 1947 that "the debate between self-denial and activism [could] continue endlessly."[89] During the terms served by Burton, Vinson, Clark and Minton, the debate continued with changing alliances on voting discernible in the plethora of multiple opinions. The men appointed by Truman did not always vote together. They, too, were influenced by the two opposing judicial approaches of self-restraint and activism.

As Schlesinger correctly viewed it, the debate was not between liberals and conservatives, but between two fundamentally different views of the role of the judiciary:

> In brief, the Black-Douglas wing appear[ed] to be more concerned with settling particular cases in accordance with their own social preconceptions; the Frankfurter-Jackson wing with preserving the judiciary in its established but limited place in the American system.[90]

The Black-Douglas wing, judicially active, was a result-oriented jurisprudence, whereas the Frankfurter-Jackson wing, practicing judicial restraint with less regard for result, concentrated upon what they conceived to be the proper objectives and limited function of the judiciary. Each of Truman's appointees served on the Court at a time when "the tension between self-denial and activism" was especially acute, and each had to accommodate himself within that framework.[91]

NOTES

1. William F. Swindler, *Court and Constitution in the 20th Century, The New Legality, 1932–1968* (Kansas City: Bobbs-Merrill Co., Inc., 1970), p. 95.

2. Henry J. Abraham, *Justices and Presidents, A Political History of Ap-*

pointments to the Supreme Court (New York: Oxford University Press, 1985), p. 65.

3. Ibid., p. 238.

4. Francis H. Heller, *The Truman White House: The Administration of the Presidency, 1945-1953* (Lawrence: The Regents Press of Kansas, 1980), pp. 29-31.

5. Swindler, *Court and Constitution in the 20th Century*, pp. 132-33.

6. Memorandum circulated by Chief Justice Stone, August 31, 1945, Black Papers, file "Chief Justice," Manuscript Division, Library of Congress, Washington, D. C.

7. Letter, Black to Chief Justice Stone, August 31, 1945, Black Papers, file "Chief Justice," Manuscript Division, Library of Congress, Washington, D.C.

8. Letter, Douglas to Black, September 13, 1945, Black Papers, file "Chief Justice," Manuscript Division, Library of Congress, Washington, D. C.

9. Swindler, *Court and Constitution in the 20th Century*, p. 137.

10. 325 U.S. 161 (1945).

11. James Bolner, "Mr. Chief Justice Vinson" (Ph.D. dissertation, University of Virginia, 1962), pp. 69-75; see also John P. Frank, *Mr. Justice Black: The Man and His Opinions* (New York: Alfred A. Knopf, 1949), pp. 123-31.

12. Ronald Gene Marquardt, "The Judicial Justice: Mr. Justice Burton and the Supreme Court" (Ph.D. dissertation, University of Missouri, 1973), quoting Burton's diary entry of September 17, 1945, p. 55. See also: Arthur Krock, *Memoirs, Sixty Years in the Firing Line* (New York: Funk and Wagnalls, 1968), pp. 302-3.

13. Harold F. Gosnell, *Truman's Crises, A Political Biography of Harry S. Truman* (Westport, Conn.: Greenwood Press, 1980), quoting William O. Douglas, p. 543.

14. Marquardt, "The Judicial Justice: Mr. Justice Burton and the Supreme Court," p. 59.

15. Tom C. Clark, Oral History Interview, October 17, 1971 and February 8, 1973, Harry S. Truman Library, Independence, Missouri, p. 48.

16. Letter, Minton to Black, September 20, 1945, Black Papers, file "Minton," Manuscript Division, Library of Congress, Washington, D. C.

17. Wesley McCune, *The Nine Young Men* (New York: Harper & Brothers, 1947), p. 234.

18. Letter, Truman to Burton, October 4, 1945, Truman Papers, file "Presidential Secretary's," Harry S. Truman Library, Independence, Missouri.

19. Approximately two years after the appointment of Vinson, Truman wrote to Ernest M. Tipton, Chief Justice of the Supreme Court of Missouri, for help in selecting a Missouri tree from which to make Vinson a gavel,

adding that he personally would meet any expenses involved. The gavel was eventually made from the Jefferson tree at Fulton, Missouri, and presented to the Chief Justice by his friend from Missouri. Letter, Truman to Tipton, August 10, 1948, Truman Papers, file "Presidential Secretary's," Harry S. Truman Library, Independence, Missouri.

20. Robert H. Ferrell, ed., *Off the Record, the Private Papers of Harry S. Truman* (New York: Harper and Row, 1980), p. 46.

21. Ibid., pp. 287–88.

22. Ibid., p. 213. See also Gosnell, *Truman's Crises*, p. 508.

23. Clark, Oral History Interview, Truman Papers, p. 54.

24. Monte M. Poen, ed., *Strictly Personal and Confidential, The Letters Harry Truman Never Mailed* (Boston: Little, Brown and Company, 1982), p. 68.

25. Ibid., p. 69.

26. Merlo J. Pusey, *Charles Evans Hughes* (New York: Macmillan, 1951), vol. 2, p. 802.

27. In this discussion between former Truman cabinet members Charles F. Brannan, former Secretary of Agriculture; W. Averell Harriman, former Secretary of Commerce; John W. Snyder, former Secretary of the Treasury; and Tom Clark, Clark quoted Hughes as saying, "I designated [Vinson] as head of the OPA Court [the] Emergency Court of Appeals." Clark continued,

> The chief justice could designate sitting judges—and Fred, at that time, was on the Court of Appeals—to any court and so Hughes had designated Vinson to the OPA Court, which was an expediting court. Hughes said Vinson had done a wonderful job there.

Heller, *The Truman White House: The Administration of the Presidency, 1945–53*, p. 30. Clark's memory was incorrect. Stone, in fact, was Chief Justice and appointed Vinson in 1942 to the Emergency Court of Appeals set up to hear disputes arising in the Office of Price Administration. Hughes retired as Chief Justice on July 1, 1941.

28. Gosnell, *Truman's Crises*, p. 419.

29. Letter, Truman to Clark, April 14, 1952. Truman Papers, file "Presidential Secretary's," Harry S. Truman Library, Independence, Missouri.

30. Clark, Oral History Interview, Truman Papers, p. 138.

31. Ibid., p. 140.

32. Ibid., p. 229.

33. Letter, Truman to Clark, September 17, 1949, Truman Papers, file "Presidential Secretary's," Harry S. Truman Library, Independence, Missouri.

34. David N. Atkinson, "Mr. Justice Minton and the Supreme Court (1949–1956)" (Ph.D. dissertation, University of Iowa, 1969), p. 58.

35. Ibid., pp. 64–65.

36. Clark, Oral History Interview, Truman Papers, p. 51.

37. Letter, Minton to Truman, May 22, 1946, Truman Papers, file "Presidential Secretary's," Harry S. Truman Library, Independence, Missouri.
38. Letter, Truman to Minton, May 25, 1946, Truman Papers, file "Presidential Secretary's," Harry S. Truman Library, Independence, Missouri.
39. Letter, Minton to Black, June 7, 1946, Black Papers, file "Minton," Manuscript Division, Library of Congress, Washington, D. C.
40. Marquardt, "The Judicial Justice: Mr. Justice Burton and the Supreme Court," pp. 58-59.
41. G. Edward White, *The American Judicial Tradition, Profiles of Leading American Judges* (New York: Oxford University Press, 1976), p. 2. See also Grant Gilmore, *The Ages of American Law* (New Haven, Conn.: Yale University, 1977). See Morton J. Horwitz, *The Transformation of American Law, 1780-1860* (Cambridge, Mass.: Harvard University Press, 1977), for a discussion of the period (1780-1820) when "judges began to conceive of themselves as legislators," p. 23.
42. Ferrell, ed., *Off the Record*, p. 90.
43. Poen, ed., *Strictly Personal and Confidential*, pp. 81-82.
44. Abraham, *Justices and Presidents*, quoting Truman, p. 70.
45. Robert J. Donovan, *The Tumultuous Years, The Presidency of Harry S. Truman, 1949-1953* (New York: W. W. Norton and Company, 1982), pp. 382-86; p. 417, n. 26. For Tom Clark's advice, see the Department of Justice memorandum, "Inherent Executive Power to Deal with Emergencies Resulting from Labor Disputes in Vital Industries Affecting the Health, Safety, and Welfare of the Entire Nation," February 7, 1949. Holmes Baldridge Papers, Box 1, Inherent Executive Power Folder. Harry S. Truman Library, Independence, Missouri.
46. Donovan, *The Tumultuous Years, the Presidency of Harry S. Truman, 1949-1953* (New York: W. W. Norton and Company, 1982), p. 386.
47. Harry S. Truman, *Memoirs*, vol. 2 (Garden City, N.Y.: Doubleday and Company, 1956), p. 476.
48. Merle Miller, *Plain Speaking, An Oral History of Harry S. Truman* (New York: Berkeley Publishing Corporation, G. Putnam's Sons, 1974), pp. 225-6.
49. After Truman left Washington, Clark often served as a contact through which people reached Truman. In 1963, Clark arranged for Truman to speak at the American Bar Association's annual meeting, an engagement which had to be cancelled because of Truman's ill health. Letter, Clark to Truman, March 4, 1963; Letter, Ivan Lee Holt to Rufus Burrus, August 6, 1963, Clark Papers, file "Truman Correspondence," Rare and Special Collections, Tarlton Law Library, University of Texas, Austin, Texas. In 1965, Clark persuaded Truman to serve as honorary chairman of the Joint Committee on Civic Education sponsored by the American Heritage Foundation. Letter, Clark to Truman, January 5, 1965, Clark Papers, file "Truman Correspondence," Rare and Special Collections, Tarlton Law Library, University of

Texas, Austin, Texas. In 1968, Truman agreed to serve as Honorary President of the Twenty-Third National Conference on Citizenship. Letter, Truman to Clark, May 1, 1968, Clark Papers, file "Truman Correspondence," Rare and Special Collections, Tarlton Law Library, University of Texas, Austin, Texas. In 1965, when Truman intervened, Clark agreed to reverse his decision not to speak at the Richards-Gebaur Air Base. Letter, Clark to Truman, March 23, 1965, Truman Papers, file "Post Presidential Correspondence," Harry S. Truman Library, Independence, Missouri. Truman also expressed his delight that Clark had agreed to place some of his papers at the Truman Library. Letter, Truman to Clark, October 13, 1962, Truman Papers, file "Post Presidential Correspondence," Harry S. Truman Library, Independence, Missouri.

50. Letter, Truman to Clark, November 10, 1961, Clark Papers, file "Truman Correspondence," Rare and Special Collections, Tarlton Law Library, University of Texas, Austin, Texas. See also letters exchanged between Truman and Clark, October 5, 13, 18, 20, 23, 24, 1961.

51. Letter, Truman to Clark, November 10, 1961, Clark Papers, file "Truman Correspondence," Rare and Special Collections, Tarlton Law Library, University of Texas, Austin, Texas.

52. Letter, Truman to Clark, March 30, 1967, Clark Papers, file "Truman Correspondence," Rare and Special Collections, Tarlton Law Library, University of Texas, Austin, Texas.

53. Telegram, Truman to Clark, c/o American Bar Association, June 12, 1967, Clark Papers, file "Truman Correspondence," Rare and Special Collections, Tarlton Law Library, University of Texas, Austin, Texas.

54. Interview with Rufus Burrus, Independence, Missouri, September 21, 1987.

55. A thorough discussion of Truman's comments about Tom Clark and Truman's relationship with Clark can be found in Dennis D. Dorin's "Truman's 'Biggest Mistake': Tom Clark's Appointment to the Supreme Court," in William F. Levantrosser, ed., *Harry S. Truman, The Man from Independence* (Westport, Conn.: Greenwood Press, 1986), pp. 323–55.

56. Abraham, *Justices and Presidents*, pp. 377–79.

57. Ibid., pp. 38–39.

58. Marquaradt, "The Judicial Justice: Mr. Justice Burton and the Supreme Court," pp. 64–68.

59. James J. Bolner, "Mr. Chief Justice Vinson" (Ph.D. dissertation, University of Virginia, 1962), p. 54.

60. Ibid., pp. 52–77.

61. Jackson referred to this newspaper article in the famous cablegram which he sent to the Senate and House Judiciary Committees considering Vinson's nomination. The cablegram was published in the *New York Times*, June 11, 1946, p. 2.

62. Bolner, "Mr. Chief Justice Vinson," pp. 71–74.

63. *New York Times*, Tuesday, October 4, 1949, p. 25.
64. Atkinson, "Mr. Justice Minton and the Supreme Court (1949–1956)," pp. 68–72.
65. Roy M. Mersky and J. Myron Jacobstein, *The Supreme Court of the United States: Hearings and Reports on Successful and Unsuccessful Nominations of Supreme Court Justices by the Senate Judiciary Committee, 1916–1972*, vol. 5 (Buffalo, N.Y.: Wm. S. Hein and Company, 1975), pp. 1–23, Nomination of Sherman Minton.
66. Ibid., pp. 1–359, Nomination of Tom C. Clark.
67. Abraham, *Justices and Presidents*, p. 243. See also Alonzo L. Hamby, *Beyond the New Deal, Harry S. Truman and American Liberalism* (New York: Columbia University Press, 1973), p. 337.
68. Fred Rodell, *Nine Men, A Political History of the Supreme Court from 1790–1955* (New York: Random House, 1955), p. 305.
69. Arthur M. Schlesinger, Jr., "The Supreme Court: 1947," *Fortune* 35, no. 1 (January 1947), p. 212.
70. John P. Frank, "Fred Vinson and the Chief Justiceship," 21 *University of Chicago Law Review*, 212, 289 (1954).
71. 347 U.S. 483 (1954).
72. Diary entry of May 8, 1954, Burton Papers, Manuscript Division, Library of Congress, Washington, D.C.
73. Newton N. Minow, Oral History Interview, February 27, 1975, Vinson Papers, Special Collections of the Margaret I. King Library, University of Kentucky, Lexington, Kentucky.
74. William W. Oliver, Oral History Interview, Vinson Papers, Special Collections of the Margaret I. King Library, University of Kentucky, Lexington, Kentucky.
75. Edward F. Prichard, Jr., Oral History Interview, October 11, 1974, Vinson Papers, Special Collections of the Margaret I. King Library, University of Kentucky, Lexington, Kentucky.
76. Philip Elman, "The Solicitor General's Office, Justice Frankfurter and Civil Rights Legislation, 1946–1960: An Oral History," 100 *Harvard Law Review*, 817, 840 (1987). Elman also expressed in a note written to Frankfurter sentiments which were shared by some lawyers who argued before the Supreme Court while Vinson was Chief Justice, "The Chief Justice seems to have a lot in common with Pat McCarran. What a mean little despot he is. Has there ever been a member of the Court who was deficient in so many respects, as a man and as a judge. Even that s.o.b. McReynolds, despite his defects of character, stands by comparison as a towering figure and powerful intellect. McReynolds was strong—this man is a pygmy—morally and mentally. And so uncouth." Note from Elman to Frankfurter on Solicitor General memorandum paper, September, undated, Felix Frankfurter Papers, file "Vinson Correspondence," Manuscript Division, Library of Congress, Washington, D. C.

77. Tom C. Clark, Oral History Interview, August 20, 1973, Vinson Papers, Special Collections of the Margaret I. King Library, University of Kentucky, Lexington, Kentucky.

78. Howard J. Trienens, Oral History Interview, February 27, 1975, Vinson Papers, Special Collections of the Margaret I. King Library, University of Kentucky, Lexington, Kentucky.

79. Frank, "Fred Vinson and the Chief Justiceship," pp. 229, 243.

80. Ibid., p. 212.

81. Swindler, *Court and Constitution in the 20th Century*, p. 182.

82. Harry S. Truman, *Truman Speaks* (New York: Columbia University Press, 1960), p. 39.

83. Ibid., p. 62.

84. Ibid., p. 58.

85. Ibid., p. 53.

86. Robert H. Ferrell, *Harry S. Truman and the Modern American Presidency* (Boston: Little, Brown and Company, 1983), p. 164.

87. Prichard, Oral History Interview, Vinson Papers.

88. 332 U.S. 46 (1948).

89. Schlesinger, "The Supreme Court: 1947," p. 208.

90. Ibid., p. 201.

91. Ibid., p. 212.

THREE

BURTON'S TENURE ON THE COURT

> To you... and to many others, I have often expressed my admiration [of] you as a member of the Supreme Court, for no other member of the Supreme Court deserves admiration more than you for exercising with exquisite and unqualified fidelity the judicial power entrusted to members of the Court.[1]
> Justice Felix Frankfurter to Harold Hitz Burton, April 22, 1964

BACKGROUND

Harold Hitz Burton, Truman's first appointee, was fifty-seven when appointed to the Supreme Court on September 18, 1945. He was confirmed the following day. On taking the oath of office, he became the fifty-fourth justice and began a thirteen-year tenure on the Court. Burton sat under three Chief Justices, serving under Chief Justice Harlan Stone for seven months, under Chief Justice Fred Vinson for his entire term, and under Chief Justice Earl Warren for five years. Although personally friendly with both Truman and Eisenhower, he was closer politically to Eisenhower than to the president who appointed him. Eisenhower actively sought Burton's advice on appointments to the lower court vacancies,[2] and when Burton discussed his retirement with Eisenhower on July 17, 1958, he was asked to advise both Eisenhower and Attorney General William Rogers concerning his successor.[3] The announcement of Burton's retirement was made on October 13, 1958.[4] His retirement from the Supreme Court was prompted by an increasingly severe case of Parkinson's disease, although subsequently, he was able to preside over cases in the Circuit Court of Appeals for the District of Columbia through early 1962. He died October 28, 1964 at the age of seventy-six, approximately six years after his retirement from the Supreme Court.

Born June 22, 1888, in Jamaica Plain, Massachusetts, the son of Alfred Edgar Burton, a professor of civil engineering at the Massachusetts Institute of Technology, Burton spent the first seven years of his life in Switzerland where his mother, Gertrude Hitz Burton, in ill health, was convalescing. He began school in Leysin, Switzerland, transferring after his mother's death to the Allen Boarding School in West Newton, Massachusetts. He graduated from Newton High School, received degrees from Bowdoin College (1909) and Harvard Law School (1912). An excellent student, he graduated from Bowdoin summa cum laude with a Phi Beta Kappa key. After law school, he moved to Cleveland, Ohio to begin the practice of corporate law with his wife's uncle, Rollin A. Wilbur. He followed Wilbur to Salt Lake City in 1914 when he was made counsel to the Utah Power and Light Company. With this experience, Burton soon became head counsel to the Idaho Power Company in Boise, Idaho in 1915. His career was interrupted by military duty in France and Belgium with the 361st Infantry division during World War I where he compiled a distinguished record, attested by many decorations.

After the war, he returned to Cleveland rather than Boise and became increasingly involved in politics. A Republican, he served in the Ohio House of Representatives, as chief legal officer for the City of Cleveland, as interim mayor of and as associate counsel for the City, before his election in 1935 as mayor of Cleveland, a post he held until his election to the United States Senate in 1940.[5]

Burton's law practice of approximately twenty-one years combined with his political activities to provide him ample practical experience in both law and government. By the time of his Court appointment, he had worked at every level of government, from the local school board to the United States Senate. His academic experience was limited to teaching a course in corporate law at Western Reserve University. Like Frankfurter, he spent his early years abroad, went to Harvard Law School and had a sustained interest in public service. Unlike Frankfurter, Burton's activities were in the elective, and somewhat parochial, side of politics rather than in the advancement of noble causes. He did, however, represent the "good government" element in the state GOP arrayed against the so-called party bosses. As mayor, he worked closely with the Roosevelt administration. He joined with other big city mayors including Fiorello LaGuardia of New York City and Edward J. Kelly of Chicago to urge Roosevelt and Congress to enact relief measures for the unemployed.[6]

Like Black he had served in the Senate. While there, and at the suggestion of his colleague from Missouri, Burton co-sponsored a resolution drafted by Senator Joseph Ball of Minnesota, a leading Republican internationalist, calling for the formation of an international peace-keeping organization. The resolution, known as the Ball-Burton-Hill-Hatch resolution,[7] called for the United States to assume leadership in the formation of what eventually became the United Nations organization. When the resolution failed in the Foreign Relations Committee, Burton co-sponsored the Connally resolution, named after Tom Connally, Chairman of the Foreign Relations Committee, as a substitute for the B_2H_2 resolution. The Connally resolution, although amended to conform with the final agreement worked out between the State Department and Russia, "set the stage" for the adoption of the United Nations agreement. Burton actively supported all steps leading to the final adoption of the United Nations treaty in 1945.[8] Domestically, he supported the Hill-Burton Hospital Act which was "the basis for most hospital construction in communities throughout the nation in the 1950s and 1960s."[9] He served on the Senate Judiciary Committee and on the special Truman committee to investigate the national defense procurement program, popularly known as the Truman Committee. Burton's legislative experience proved helpful to him on the Court as he used it in cases involving statutory construction for which he developed a reputation for expertise, an area in which his penchant for deliberate and thorough analysis also stood him in good stead.

Statutory construction requires that the justice be able to ascertain from relevant sources how the statute was intended to operate and to determine how the factual aspects of the case being decided are controlled by the statute. This was especially important in cases involving construction of the Internal Revenue Code. These internal revenue decisions revealed both Burton's method of reaching a decision and his specialized role as a member of the Court. John P. Frank described Burton's tax opinions as "of more than casual difficulty and breadth, . . . of high standard in construction, clarity, and utilization of relevant material."[10]

In one of the tax cases, Burton, voting with Black, was able to influence Frankfurter to change his vote. In *Commissioner of Internal Revenue v. Estate of Louis Sternberger* (1955),[11] Burton, at Black's suggestion, wrote the dissent which, when circulated, won majority approval by a 6 to 2 vote, Justices Stanley Reed and William O. Douglas dissenting. In the opinion, Burton cited regulations as well as precedents to support his interpretation of the law and noted that the regulations were intended to prevent abuses of the legislation.

In another case in which Burton and Frankfurter disagreed, Burton wrote the majority opinion and Frankfurter the dissent. Burton, writing for the majority in *Commissioner of Internal Revenue v. Wodehouse* (1949),[12] held that the payments received by P.G. Wodehouse, a nonresident alien author, for serial rights, were royalties and taxable. Frankfurter wrote a dissent arguing that Wodehouse had made an absolute transfer and that such funds were not taxable to a nonresident alien.

Burton's persuasiveness was such that he succeeded in converting the Court to his position when a previous dissent became the majority opinion, although both Frankfurter and Black dissented. In *Commissioner of Internal*

Revenue v. Wilcox et al. (1946),[13] Burton, as the lone dissenter, argued that embezzled funds should be taxed but the majority voted against taxing gains unlawfully held and subject to return. Six years later, in *Rutkin v. United States* (1952),[14] Burton wrote the majority opinion taxing funds obtained by extortion and holding that unlawful as well as lawful gains were taxable. Black's vigorous dissent argued that the ill-gotten gains were not legally the property of the extortioner or the embezzler and were therefore not taxable to the criminal. Black, in conference, complained, "By overruling... you step out of your way to send a man to the penitentiary who depended on *Wilcox*... I don't stand on *stare decisis* but why do those who do—overrule the case in order to send a man to the penitentiary?"[15]

JUDICIAL PERFORMANCE

Burton's performance on the Supreme Court was severely criticized during his tenure. Drew Pearson, a columnist in the muckraking tradition, writing for the *Washington Post* on June 23, 1947, criticized not only his meager output but also his life-style, characterizing him as an inveterate party-goer, implying that his social life hampered his performance. Pearson complained that Burton seemed "to think that being on the Supreme Court is not for the purpose of handing down opinions but to enjoy a continued round of parties."[16] Frankfurter responded to this by assuring Burton:

> I am outraged by Drew Pearson's column to which my attention has just been called. I have known every man who sat on this Court since 1906—many of them well and half a dozen intimately. It is on that basis that I can say to you what I have said behind your back, that this Court never had a Justice who was harder working or more conscientious.[17]

John P. Frank called Pearson's allegations "grossly unfair," and attributed Burton's low output to "elaborate preparation."[18] Fred Rodell found his production rate poor: Burton "managed, despite hard work, to turn out only 5 to 6 majority opinions a year (the figure was precisely 6 in one term when Black wrote 29 and Douglas 27)."[19]

The significance of this low output was not readily apparent. The Chief Justice assigned opinions if he stood with the majority, the senior justice assigned cases when the Chief Justice was with the minority. Vinson's practice was to assign the majority opinion in divided cases to one who was wavering in order to solidify that person's vote.[20] Burton could only write those majority opinions assigned to him. Also, Burton's method of opinion writing was so deliberate that it limited his output. Mary Frances Berry, who interviewed Burton's clerks, reported that he, unlike other justices, wrote his own opinions in longhand many times, using his clerks for this purpose only during his first year, and later only in *United States v. E. I. Dupont de Nemours and Co.* (1957).[21] Burton's tendency to vote with the majority and his reluctance to express separate opinions was a pattern basically consistent with a conservative approach to problem solving. Of the total opinions written by Burton, approximately 63 percent were majority, a bare 8 percent were concurring and only 29 percent were dissenting.[22]

Burton's opinion writing was statistically evaluated by Albert P. Blaustein and Roy M. Mersky in their analysis of the judicial output of the first one hundred justices. They reported on a total of 166 opinions for Burton, which included 96 majority, 50 dissenting and 15 concurring opinions. Burton averaged 12.77 opinions per year, contrasting with the 27.13 average for Black and 30.30 for Frankfurter, neither of whom was ever faulted for low output. Burton's production compared less unfavorably with the Truman appointees' averages, but it was still the lowest yearly average reported for any justice since that of the thirty-second justice, Benjamin R. Curtis (1851–1857) who averaged only 10.50 opinions per year. Of the Truman appointees, Vinson averaged 13 opinions per year, Clark 19.67 and Minton 15.57.[23]

The productivity of the entire Vinson Court was relatively low. Under the Judiciary Act of 1925 allowing discretionary jurisdiction, the Court was granting *certiorari* on the Rule of Four, which required agreement of at least four justices to grant review.[24] In 1948, the Court delivered 114 opinions and did not hear 948 cases. In 1949, the Court wrote 94 opinions and did not hear 1,033 cases. To dispose of these cases, the Court either dismissed the appeal or denied *certiorari*.[25] Doris Marie Provine, in her statistical analysis of the case selection process, found that Burton's propensity to grant review ranked tenth in a study of fifteen justices during the ten year period, 1947–57. Frankfurter ranked eleventh and the three other Truman appointees followed: Clark was twelfth, Vinson was thirteenth, and Minton was fifteenth.[26]

Burton's reasons for denying *certiorari* also reflected his judicial restraint. More often than other justices, he agreed with Frankfurter who began the session each year by decrying the lack of sufficient time devoted to the cases which were taken under consideration.[27] Burton echoed this view in the memorandum filed with the grant of *certiorari* in the *Dennis* case. He and Frankfurter voted to deny the petition and Frankfurter concurred in the memorandum. Burton objected to hearing the case directly from the trial court, bypassing the Court of Appeals:

> The constitutional issue which is the subject of the appeal deserves for its solution all of the wisdom that our judicial process makes available. The need for soundness in the result outweighs the need for speed in reaching it. The Nation is entitled to the substantial value inherent in an intermediate consideration of the issue by the Court of Appeals.[28]

USE OF JUDICIAL RESTRAINT

Burton utilized the tenets of judical restraint in his opinions in the three areas of criminal procedure, loyalty-security and racial discrimination.

Criminal Procedure Cases

In the area of criminal procedure, Burton emphasized the rights of the state against the individual, deferring to the state authority most often when confronted with a constitutional question.

In *Bute v. People of State of Illinois* (1948),[29] Burton wrote the majority opinion which upheld the 1938 conviction of Roy Bute. Bute appeared in his own defense and pleaded guilty to two indictments charging indecent liberties with children. The record was silent on whether the defendant had been offered counsel by the court. The due process question was whether the State of Illinois through the Fourteenth Amendment or by state law should be held to federal due process procedure which required assignment of counsel.

Burton related the history of the federal court requirement that counsel be appointed unless the defendant knowingly had waived his right. This requirement, prior to 1938, was limited to cases of treason and other capital crimes. One month before Bute's trial, the Supreme Court held in *Johnson v. Zerbst* (1938)[30] that counsel *must* be appointed for the defendant in any federal criminal case unless the right was knowingly waived. This federal procedure practice was dictated by the rights contained in Amendment Six and stated in Rule 44 of the Federal Rules of Criminal Procedure which became effective March 21, 1946. Burton reasoned that federal criminal procedure was not required of the states. He traced the state procedural practice in Illinois and examined the Illinois constitution and bill of rights to determine the due process climate in that state. Illinois state law required appointment of counsel only in capital cases. Although Burton recognized the trend among the states toward the federal practice, as recommended by the American Law Institute, he concluded that "the states have discretion to determine in the light of their respective histories and needs many practices in their criminal procedure, including this practice."[31] Burton thereby deferred to the state practice, finding no special circumstances warranting an inference of lack of due process or a requirement for an affirmative waiver. Burton did not find a denial of due process, as did the dissenters, Douglas and Black. In the dissent, Douglas argued for applicability to the states of the Sixth Amendment requirements through the due process clause of the Fourteenth Amendment. He insisted that the guarantee of a fair trial necessarily included the appointment of counsel in cases where the alleged crime was a difficult one to defend.

Burton's approach was tempered by two attitudes—respect for the state's ability to handle its police activities and concern for stability. He believed that "doubts should be resolved in favor of the integrity, competence and proper performance of their official duties by the judge and the state's attorney,"[32] reasoning that government stability depended upon the giving of full faith and credit to the functioning of governmental units.[33] He thus employed the self-restraint maxim of refusing to impute illegal motives to executive officers.

Burton used similar logic in deciding one of the two last cases for which he wrote the majority opinion ten years later. In *Ashdown v. State of Utah* (1958),[34] Burton upheld the conviction of the defendant, a Mrs. Ashdown, who had confessed to having poisoned her husband. The confession was made after five and one-half hours of interrogation conducted immediately after the husband's funeral and without counsel present. After relating the facts surrounding the confession, Burton concluded that "the interview with [the] petitioner was temperate and courteous. The sheriff proceeded cautiously and acted with consideration for the feelings of the petitioner."[35] Again, Black and Douglas dissented. But Frankfurter, voting with the majority expressed his agreement to Burton:

> I like this very much and not least because you cite no case and indulge in no rhetoric. Everyone agrees on the relevant principles in these cases and they turn on, and should be treated entirely on, the facts of the particular case.[36]

Burton wrote two dissents in search and seizure cases which demonstrated that he did recognize some limits to government authority. In *McDonald et al. v. United States* (1948),[37] Burton dissented from the majority holding which excluded evidence obtained incident to an arrest. No arrest or search warrant was obtained by the officers who had had the defendant under surveillance for two months. In order to catch the lottery operation in progress, the officers surprised the defendant, arrested him and confiscated the evidence. Burton reasoned that in such an arrest, there was no search. Officers, with sufficient suspicions, moved to arrest a suspect while the crime was in progress and merely seized the "articles then in plain sight."[38] His opinion stressed the difficulty involved in apprehending suspects in this type of crime, and again he deferred to executive authority.

In the other case, *On Lee v. United States* (1952),[39] Burton's dissent was joined by Justice Frankfurter, who told him later that his opinion "surprised and delighted" him.[40] Frankfurter suggested only one change in the phrasing of a sentence, while expressing his pleasure in joining,[41] although previously he had felt compelled by the "tone" of Jackson's opinion to circulate also his own "piece" asking Burton to join him.[42] The majority upheld the narcotics conviction of On Lee whose friend, Chin Poy, "wired for sound," had cooperated with narcotics agents. By wearing a small microphone during a visit to On Lee's premises, Chin Poy allowed an agent to hear incriminating evidence. The majority considered that this action did not violate the Fourth Amendment and found no trespass because Chin Poy was an invited guest. Burton's dissent argued that the Fourth Amendment extended to seizure of intangible as well as tangible evidence.[43] He reasoned that Chin Poy's presence was surreptitious and resulted in a warrantless search and seizure of words. The presence of the transmitter "was the presence of [the agent's] ear," and the evidence thereby obtained should have been excluded.[44] Frankfurter worried about the effect of the majority opinion: "When this Court sanctions *On Lees*, the law-enforcing agencies will be lazily lawless."[45]

Burton's respect for state procedural practices was decisive in the jury selection case, *Ballard v. United States* (1946).[46] The majority dismissed a grand jury indictment for fraudulent procurement of money against members of the I Am sect because women were excluded from the grand jury panel issuing the indictment. Burton, in his dissent, argued that federal jury selection had been predicated on the method of jury selection in the state wherein the court sat reaching a result which would have obtained in 40 percent of the states. This federal deference to state methods of jury selection indicated that state practice, however diverse, should be followed. Under the facts of the case, California law allowed women to serve on juries, but as a matter of practice, they were not called for duty. Burton defined the failure to call women a "substantial exemption," but found it no more offensive than the existing state laws which excluded women from jury duty.[47] He reasoned that congressional acts merely deferred to state practice and that state practice should be honored in this case. Yet, despite his conclusion in the *Ballard* case, Burton, at least tentatively, cast doubt on the validity of this type of sexual discrimination:

> The general and increasing absence of sound reasons for distinctions between men and women in matters of suffrage, office holding, education, economic status, civil liberties, church membership, cultural activities, and even war service, [emphasized] the lack of reason for making a point of the presence or absence of either sex, as such, on either grand or petit juries.[48]

Although Frankfurter also wrote a dissenting opinion in the *Ballard* case, he commended Burton on his work: "I have not the slightest doubt that Holmes, Brandeis and Cardozo would say 'amen' to your refutation of the claim that the exclusion of women . . . was fatal to the indictment and the verdict."[49]

One of Burton's most interesting opinions in the area of criminal procedure was his dissent in *State of Louisiana ex rel. Francis v. Resweber, Sheriff et al.* (1947),[50] a case in which both Black and Frankfurter agreed with the majority. The attempt to execute Willie Francis for murder failed because of a mechanical malfunction of the electric chair. The majority held that a second attempt at execution would not constitute double jeopardy or cruel and unusual punishment. The case illustrated the nebulous aspect of the substantive due process "shock the conscience" test embraced by Frankfurter. Frankfurter's conscience was not sufficiently shocked by this punishment. In his concurring opinion, Frankfurter, practicing self-restraint, acknowledged a sense of revulsion and a personal inclination to Burton's view but denied this reaction as a private response to be judicially quashed. Frankfurter began a two-page letter to Burton by saying, "I have to hold on to myself not to reach your result."[51] He explained, however, that the "disciplined thinking of a lifetime" about the "extremely limited nullifying power of the court vis-à-vis state action" compelled him to defer to the state court's decision.[52]

Burton reasoned that taking human life by "unnecessarily cruel means [shocked] the most fundamental instincts of civilized man."[53] He interpreted the Louisiana law as strictly requiring that an electric current sufficient to produce death be *continuously* applied until death resulted. He thought the means for producing death, *if humane*, should be instantaneous and painless or it violated the Eighth Amendment. Burton pointed out that repeated attempts to electrocute, if intentional, would be obviously cruel and unusual punishment and concluded that unintentional attempts were no less so. Accordingly, Burton would have remanded the case, with orders to the lower court not to release Francis and not to allow another attempt at electrocution. In this case, both Frankfurter and Burton showed deference to the state authority. Frankfurter deferred to the state court's interpretation of the state legislative act, Burton to the legislative act as he construed it. Although Frankfurter expressed his views in at least three written expositions and two letters to Burton as well as in a memorandum to the Court, he was unable to convince him.

Loyalty-Security Cases

The Burton opinions in the loyalty-security cases further evidenced his pro-government orientation. In *Dennis* (1951),[54] he joined in the majority opinion written by Chief Justice Vinson upholding the Smith Act as nonviolative of the First Amendment and finding a clear and present danger presented by the "conspiracy to organize the Communist Party and to teach and advocate the overthrow" of the government.[55] His vote in *Yates v. United States* (1957),[56] however, was an addendum to the *Dennis* decision. In the *Yates* case, John Marshall Harlan wrote the majority opinion overturning the conviction of fourteen defendants under the Smith Act. His decision made convictions under the Act more difficult. Burton's vote was a result of a change of mind during consideration of the case.[57] During the initial conferences, he had expressed an intention to affirm the convictions, but was influenced by Harlan's rationale that the Smith Act did not "prohibit advocacy and teaching of forcible overthrow as an abstract principle."[58] In both cases, Burton deferred to the legislation, but in *Yates* he construed the statute more leniently.

Burton wrote the majority opinion in *Joint Anti-Fascist Refugee Committee v. McGrath* (1951).[59] Executive Order 9835 authorized the Attorney General to supply a list of organizations deemed "totalitarian, fascist, communist or subversive" to the Loyalty Review Board of the United States Civil Service Commission.[60] Burton's opinion narrowly found the use of the list an arbitrary exercise of power. He did not deny the validity of such a list if properly drawn and defendable. He therefore remanded the case for a hearing on the merits, asserting that the summary dismissal of the complainant's case was evidence of arbitrariness and a denial of due process. Burton, insisting on strict procedural regularity, ordered the Attorney General to answer the petitioners' allegations that they did not in fact belong on such a list.

One of the last two opinions written by Burton involved dismissal of a teacher for failure to answer questions about past affiliations with the Communist Party. In *Beilan v. Board of Education, School District of Philadelphia* (1958),[61] Burton wrote the majority opinion, assigned to him by Frankfurter. Herman A. Beilan lost his teaching job of twenty-one years after refusing to answer school officials' questions posed some thirteen months before dismissal. Only five days before he was discharged, he asserted his privilege against self-incrimination under the Fifth Amendment when questioned by a subcommittee of the House Committee on UnAmerican Activities.[62] Burton followed the restraint tenet of avoiding constitutional issues if possible and decided the cases narrowly, finding support to affirm the teacher's dismissal on a failure to cooperate with the Board of Education which had based the dismissal on the charge of incompetency, not disloyalty. Frankfurter agreed with Burton, noting in the margin of the circulated copy, "Yes. This opinion vindicates my assignment of the case to you."[63] He wrote a concurring opinion, emphasizing the duty of local administrations to take care of their own affairs, concluding, "I am not charged with administering the school system of Pennsylvania."[64] Warren, Douglas, Black and Brennan dissented, approached the constitutional issues boldly, and found a violation of the teacher's First and Fourteenth Amendment rights.

Burton's votes in the 1957 bar admission cases, *Schware v. Board of Bar Examiners* (1957)[65] and *Konigsberg v. State Bar* (1957),[66] appeared to be capitulations in which he agreed with the majority opinions written by Black. In both cases, he voted to reverse the lower state court rulings which denied each applicant entry into the legal profession on the basis of failure to establish a good moral character. Both Konigsberg and Schware had histories of Communist affiliations. Frankfurter sought to influence Burton's vote and "simply could not understand, philosophically, how Burton could uncharacteristically vote to override state control" when a reasonable basis supported the state action.[67] In this instance, Mary Frances Berry postulated that Burton's "concern over the defendants' exclusion from their chosen occupation[s] overrode his usual support of states' rights and judicial self-restraint."[68]

Racial Discrimination Cases

Burton's opinions in the segregation cases revealed his basic independence. His performance was consistently in opposition to legally mandated discrimination, with the exception of the first case decided on this issue after he reached the Court. C. Herman Pritchett's study disclosed that Burton voted against claimed individual liberties more often than not.[69] Mary Frances Berry found that there was no conscious effort on Burton's part to be anti- or pro-civil libertarian, describing his overall performance as an effort to take seriously the task of judging.

In *Morgan v. Commonwealth of Virginia* (1948),[70] Burton was the lone dissenter. The majority invalidated a Virginia statute requiring public motor carriers to segregate passengers according to color, reasoning that the requirement placed an undue burden on interstate commerce. Burton's dissent attacked the lack of evidence to support the majority finding of undue burden. Burton deferred to the state legislation, considering the problem basically a local matter, and argued that the states had been free to formulate rules governing segregation on public motor cars. Burton reviewed state practice to show that the various state requirements were divergent: 18 states prohibited segregation by public motor carriers, 20 made no provision, and 10 contiguous states required segregation.[71] He then disputed the need for a court-imposed uniform rule, while recognizing that the prohibition of segregation in eighteen states was "important progress in the direction of uniformity."[72]

In a subsequent common carrier case, Burton wrote the majority opinion. In *Henderson v. United States et al.* (1950),[73] Burton based the holding on Section 3(1) of the Interstate Commerce Act which proscribed any practice by a common carrier which made, gave or caused "any undue or unreasonable preference or advantage to any particular person" or subjected any "particular person ... to any undue or unreasonable prejudice or disadvantage in any respect."[74] Elmer Henderson, a black traveling on a Southern Railway Company train, had vainly sought service in the dining car in May of 1942. He filed a complaint with the Interstate Commerce Commission in October and the Commission devised a plan whereby ten tables for whites and one table for blacks would be provided in all dining cars with provisions to draw the curtains when both sections were in use. Henderson sued the United States and the Commission, alleging that the administrative ruling was a violation of the non-discriminatory provisions contained in the Commerce Act. Burton found that the plan was patently discriminatory and invalid under the Interstate Commerce Act. He was able to confine the holding and not reach the constitutional issue.

The *Henderson* case was decided on the same day with two other racial cases, June 5, 1950, for which Chief Justice Vinson wrote the majority opinions. Burton voted with the majority in each case and the opinion in each did address the constitutional issue.

In *Sweatt v. Painter et al.* (1950),[75] Herman Sweatt was denied admission to the University of Texas Law School. He alleged violation of the equal protection clause of the Fourteenth Amendment. The state court continued the case to allow for separate and equal facilities to be readied. In his opinion, Vinson compared the separate facilities with those at the University of Texas and found them unequal. In order for Sweatt to "claim his full constitutional right," Vinson reasoned, "the Fourteenth Amendment require[d] that [he] be admitted to the University of Texas Law School."[76]

In *McLaurin v. Oklahoma State Regents for Higher Education et al.* (1950),[77] the Court used the equal protection clause of the Fourteenth Amendment to assure G. W. McLaurin, a black graduate student at the University of Oklahoma, equal rights. After a previous legal battle, McLaurin had been admitted to the graduate school at the University. The laws under which he had been excluded had been amended by the Oklahoma legislature to allow blacks to attend classes not offered elsewhere. McLaurin was admitted as a doctoral candidate in education, but his admission was conditioned upon rules designated by the president of the University. McLaurin was to "sit apart at a designated desk in an adjoining classroom; to sit at a designated desk on the mezzanine floor of the library, . . . not to use the desks in the regular meeting room; and to sit at a designated table and to eat at a different time from the other students in the school cafeteria."[78] The unanimous Court held that any student admitted to a state-supported school must receive equal treatment under the Fourteenth Amendment equal protection clause.

In the historic *Brown v. Board of Education* (1954)[79] case, Burton voted with a unanimous Court to overrule the separate-but-equal doctrine derived from *Plessy v. Ferguson* (1896).[80] Burton enthusiastically embraced the rationale behind *Brown* and early stood with Black and Douglas in favor of overruling *Plessy*[81] in the Court discussions preceding the decision.

ASSESSMENT

Burton's judicial approach from the beginning of his tenure was one of judicial restraint. In temperament, he was deliberate, cautious, even slow. Although he consulted Black immediately for help in his new job, he was probably prompted to do so because of their mutual experience as Senators, rather than as an expression of kindred devotion to judicial activism. It was to Frankfurter that Burton ultimately turned for instruction in his new job, and it was with him that he formed the closest judicial relationship. On May

5, 1946, Frankfurter recommended books on jurisdiction, procedure and constitutional law.[82] Of the twelve titles suggested, Frankfurter authored six, Thayer two. Burton regularly made diary notations about reading these titles and other material that Frankfurter later suggested. He also quoted, in full, complimentary remarks made by other justices about his opinions. The predominant number were penned by Frankfurter, and the recurring sentiment was best captured in this remark: "I am glad to join this. The outcome of this case is a good illustration of the difference between starting with a problem to be solved instead of a predetermined conclusion to be justified."[83]

Burton's biographer, Mary Frances Berry, pointed out that Burton's judicial approach closely coincided with the sixteen tenets of judicial self-restraint enumerated by Henry J. Abraham.[84] Berry postulated that Burton's judicial performance was the result of the molding influences in his background which produced a "generally conservative mind-set." She described Burton as a "lawyer's judge" who attempted to decide cases objectively and dispassionately.[85]

Burton's opinions and votes indicated clearly that he was not a result-oriented justice. He saw both sides of a legal problem, carefully weighed the issues and played the game of making judicial decisions by the self-imposed rules of judicial restraint. He insisted on procedural regularity, deferred to both states and federal legislation and avoided constitutional issues when possible. How much of his final product was predetermined by a conservative mind-set cannot, obviously, be determined precisely, but Berry believed it decisive. The important role that mind-set or frame of reference plays in the judicial process had been recognized earlier by Benjamin Cardozo:

> There is in each of us a stream of tendency . . . which gives coherence and direction to thought and action. Judges cannot escape that current any more than other mortals. All their lives, forces which they do not recognize and cannot name, have been tugging at them—inherited instincts, traditional beliefs, acquired convictions; and the resultant is an outlook on life, a conception of social needs, a sense in James's phrase of 'the total push and pressure of the cosmos,' which, when reasons are nicely balanced, must determine where choice shall fall.[86]

In the push and pull between the adherents of restraint and the apostles of activism, Burton remained fundamentally independent of both, deciding cases in his own particular way. His concurrences with Black and Frankfurter in different decisions at various times were expressions of mutual agreement on particular cases. There is some significance to the fact that Burton's last vote in the Senate was a vote cast against an administration bill.[87] He demonstrated the same independence during his Court career. His opinions were conditioned by his adherence to judicial restraint but, above all, they were a reasoned effort at problem solving which avoided the larger philosophical issues.

NOTES

1. Letter, Frankfurter to Burton, April 22, 1964, Burton Papers, file "Frankfurter Correspondence," Manuscript Division, Library of Congress, Washington, D. C.
2. Ronald Gene Marquardt, "The Judicial Justice: Mr. Justice Burton and the Supreme Court" (Ph.D. dissertation, University of Missouri, 1973), pp. 181–83.
3. Mary Frances Berry, *Stability, Security and Continuity, Mr. Justice Burton and Decision-Making in the Supreme Court (1945–1958)* (Westport, Conn.: Greenwood Press, 1978), p. 225.
4. Ibid., pp. 227–28.
5. Marquardt, "The Judicial Justice: Mr. Justice Burton and the Supreme Court," pp. 31–95.
6. Ibid., p. 34.
7. U.S. Congressional Record, 78th Cong., 1st Session, vol. 89, part 2, A 3786.
8. Berry, *Stability, Security and Continuity*, pp. 14–17.
9. Ibid., p. 13.
10. John P. Frank, "The United States Supreme Court: 1951–52," 20 *University of Chicago Law Review* 1, 66 (1952).
11. 348 U.S. 187 (1955).
12. 337 U.S. 369 (1949).
13. 327 U.S. 404 (1946).
14. 343 U.S. 130 (1952).
15. Conference notes by Clark, Clark Papers, file "Supreme Court," Rare and Special Collections, Tarlton Law Library, University of Texas, Austin, Texas.
16. Drew Pearson, "The Washington Merry-Go-Round," *Washington Post*, June 23, 1947, p. 15, col. 5.
17. Letter, Frankfurter to Burton, June 23, 1947, Burton Papers, file "Frankfurter Correspondence," Manuscript Division, Library of Congress, Washington, D. C.
18. John P. Frank, "The United States Supreme Court: 1946–47," 5 *The University of Chicago Law Review* 1, 48 (1947).
19. Fred Rodell, *Nine Men, A Political History of the Supreme Court from 1790 to 1955* (New York: Random House, 1955), p. 310.
20. Berry, *Stability, Security and Continuity*, p. 149.
21. 335 U.S. 586 (1957).

22. Marquardt, "The Judicial Justice: Mr. Justice Burton and the Supreme Court," p. 259.

23. Albert P. Blaustein and Roy M. Mersky, *The First One Hundred Justices* (Hamden, Conn.: The Shoe String Press, Inc., 1978), pp. 147–49.

24. 28 U.S.C. §§ 1251, 1257; Marquardt, "The Judicial Justice: Mr. Justice Burton and the Supreme Court," p. 294. See also Berry, *Stability, Security and Continuity*, p. 147, for an appraisal of the "full dress discussion" given each case before denial of *certiorari*.

25. Fowler V. Harper and Alan S. Rosenthal, "What the Supreme Court Did Not Do in the 1949 Term—An Appraisal of *Certiorari*," 99 *University of Pennsylvania Law Review*, 293, pp. 293–94.

26. Doris Marie Provine, *Case Selection in the United States Supreme Court* (Chicago: The University of Chicago Press, 1980), pp. 114–15.

27. Berry, *Stability, Security and Continuity*, pp. 179–80.

28. U.S. Congress, House of Representatives, *The Steel Seizure Case*. H. Doc. 534, Part II, Petitions for Certiorari and Briefs in the Supreme Court. 82nd Congress, 2nd Session, 1952, p. 458 (1672).

29. 333 U.S. 640 (1948).

30. 304 U.S. 458 (1938).

31. 333 U.S. at 675.

32. 333 U.S. at 671.

33. 333 U.S. at 672.

34. 357 U.S. 426 (1958).

35. 357 U.S. at 430.

36. Marginal note from Frankfurter to Burton, May 28, 1958, Burton Papers, file "Supreme Court," Manuscript Division, Library of Congress, Washington, D. C.

37. 335 U.S. 451 (1948).

38. 335 U.S. at 463.

39. 343 U.S. 747 (1952).

40. Letter, Frankfurter to Burton, February 14, 1956, Burton Papers, file "Supreme Court," Manuscript Division, Library of Congress, Washington, D. C.

41. Memorandum from Frankfurter to Burton, May 6, 1953, Burton Papers, file "Supreme Court," Manuscript Division, Library of Congress, Washington, D. C.

42. Memorandum from Frankfurter to Burton, undated, noted on opinion circulated May 19, 1952, Burton Papers, file "Supreme Court," Manuscript Division, Library of Congress, Washington, D. C.

43. 343 U.S. at 765.

44. 343 U.S. at 767.

45. Letter, Frankfurter to Burton, February 20, 1953, Burton Papers, file "Frankfurter Correspondence," Manuscript Division, Library of Congress, Washington, D. C.

46. 329 U.S. 187 (1946).
47. 329 U.S. at 203, 204.
48. 329 U.S. at 205.
49. Letter, Frankfurter to Burton, December 5, 1946, Burton Papers, file "Frankfurter Correspondence," Manuscript Division, Library of Congress, Washington, D. C.
50. 329 U.S. 459 (1947).
51. Letter, Frankfurter to Burton, December 13, 1946, Burton Papers, file "Frankfurter Correspondence," Manuscript Division, Library of Congress, Washington, D. C.
52. Ibid.
53. 329 U.S. at 473.
54. 341 U.S. 494 (1951).
55. 341 U.S. at 517.
56. 354 US. 298 (1957).
57. Berry, *Stability, Security and Continuity*, p. 203–4.
58. 354 U.S. at 300.
59. 341 U.S. 123 (1951).
60. 341 U.S. at 125.
61. 357 U.S. 399 (1958).
62. 357 U.S. at 424.
63. Marginal note from Frankfurter to Burton, Burton Papers, file "Supreme Court," Manuscript Division, Library of Congress, Washington, D. C.
64. 357 U.S. at 411.
65. 353 U.S. 232 (1957).
66. 353 U.S. 252 (1957).
67. Frankfurter quoted at Berry, *Stability, Security and Continuity*, p. 202.
68. Ibid., p. 203.
69. C. Herman Pritchett, *Civil Liberties and the Vinson Court* (Chicago: The University of Chicago Press, 1954). See also Marquardt, "The Judicial Justice: Mr. Justice Burton and the Supreme Court," p. 217, and C. Herman Pritchett, "The Warren Court: Turn to Liberalism," *Nation*, July 14, 1956, pp. 32–34.
70. 328 U.S. 375 (1948).
71. 328 U.S. at 390.
72. 328 U.S. at 394.
73. 339 U.S. 816 (1950).
74. 49 U.S.C. 3(1), 49 U.S.C.A. 3(1).
75. 339 U.S. 629 (1950).
76. 339 U.S. at 636.
77. 339 U.S. 637 (1950).
78. 339 U.S. at 640.
79. 347 U.S. 483 (1954).

80. 163 U.S. 537 (1896).

81. Marquardt, "The Judicial Justice: Mr. Justice Burton and the Supreme Court," pp. 239–41.

82. Diary entry of May 5, 1946, book list on November page at end of 1956, Burton Papers, Manuscript Division, Library of Congress, Washington, D. C.:

Jurisdiction

1. *Curtis* - Jurisdiction of the U.S. Courts (2d ed.).
2. *Frankfurter* - Distribution of Jud. Power between U.S. & State Courts (1928) 13 Conn. L.Q. 499.
3. *Frankfurter & Landis* - Business of the Supreme Court.
4. *Supplements (Bond)* - Business of the Supreme Court.
5. *Frankfurter & Schulman* - Cases on Fed. Jurisdiction.

Procedure

Jurisdiction of the Sup. Ct. of the U.S. *Robertson & Kirkham*.

Constitutional Law

1. *Thayer*. Legal Essays Chapters: *Origin & Scope of Am. Doctrine of Const. Law* p. 1; *Legal Tender* p. 60; *Our New Possessions*, p. 153.
2. *Thayer*. Cases on Const. Law, (2 Vols.) Chap. III, IV, VII, X.
3. *Wambaugh*. Cases in Const. Law.
4. *Frankfurter*. Mr. Justice Holmes & the Court (1927) 41 HLR 121.
5. *Frankfurter*. Mr. Justice Brandeis & the Court (1931). 45 HLR 33.
6. *Frankfurter*. Mr. Justice Cardozo & Public Law (1939). 52 HLR 440.

83. Diary entry of February 26, 1954, Burton Papers, Manuscript Division, Library of Congress, Washington, D. C.

84. Berry, *Stability, Security and Continuity*, p. 226, n. 5.

85. Ibid., p. 231.

86. Benjamin N. Cardozo, "The Nature of the Judicial Process," Clarence Morris, ed., *The Great Legal Philosophers* (Philadelphia: University of Pennsylvania Press, 1959), p. 514.

87. Marquardt, "The Judicial Justice: Mr. Justice Burton and the Supreme Court," p. 70.

FOUR

VINSON'S TENURE ON THE COURT

Now that I am one of you, I want to tell you how happy your letter made me, and how much I welcomed your generous prophecy in regard to my conduct in the office of Chief Justice. I am looking forward to our association and know that it will be a happy and stimulating one.[1]
   Frederick Moore Vinson to Justice Felix Frankfurter, June 26, 1946

You are a sweet guy. With all the hundreds of things you had to do, to take time out to express felicitations for my birthday . . . was an expression of friendship that will never be forgotten. . . . It . . . clouded up my spectacles. It bedims my vision again today when I thank you again for such thoughtful friendship.[2]
   Chief Justice Vinson to Honorable Harry S. Truman, Independence, Missouri, January 23, 1953

BACKGROUND

Frederick Moore Vinson, thirteenth Chief Justice of the Supreme Court was born in Louisa, Kentucky on January 22, 1890, the fourth child born to Virginia Ferguson Vinson. His father, James Vinson, was a farmer, grocer and part-time jailer. Vinson received his B.A. from the Kentucky Normal School in Louisa in 1909, and an LL.B. in 1911 from Centre College in Danville, Kentucky where he compiled the highest academic average in the school's history.[3] During his college years, he excelled in mathematics and also developed a lifelong passion for baseball, serving as team captain during school terms and playing semi-professional ball during the summer.[4]

   Vinson engaged in the general practice of law from 1911 to 1923 in Louisa. In 1924, he won his first national political office in a special election to fill a vacancy in the House of Representatives. At the time of Vinson's election, he was Commonwealth Attorney charged with prosecution of county criminals. He had served previously in 1913–14 as City Attorney for the city of Louisa. During World War I, he spent three months in 1918 in Army Officers' Training School in Arkansas.[5] He served as Congressman from Kentucky from 1924 to 1929, and again from 1931 to 1937. His defeat in 1928 was probably the result of his active support for Al Smith for president. In 1928, he moved his practice to Ashland where it prospered until his appointment in 1937 to the Circuit Court of Appeals. He thus boasted two hometowns, retaining close ties with both during this period. He described his congressional district as Kentucky bluegrass country covering "nineteen counties, aggregating 5,499 square miles in area, with a population exceeding 272,725."[6] He maintained a lifelong interest in the people of Kentucky.[7]

His congressional career began when Calvin Coolidge was president and lasted into the fifth year of Roosevelt's presidency. He was an ardent New Dealer. He served on the most important committees including the Military Affairs Committee, the Appropriations Committee, and the Ways and Means Committee and its Tax subcommittee, of which he was the chairman. He was instrumental in drafting the Social Security Act of 1935 and the Revenue Act of 1937. He helped draft the first Guffey Coal Act of 1935, declared unconstitutional in *Carter v. Carter Coal Co.* (1936),[8] and the second Vinson-Guffey Coal Act of 1937, tailored to meet the Supreme Court objections which had invalidated the wage and hour provisions of the first act. Vinson vigorously supported legislation taxing undistributed corporation profits. Like Truman in the Senate, he worked in the House for Roosevelt's plan to reform the judiciary through "court packing." His only opposition to Roosevelt's legislative program came over veterans' benefits: he joined the overwhelming majority of his colleagues in opposing a reduction in veterans' pensions in 1933, and he voted to override Roosevelt's veto of the veteran's bonus bill in 1936.[9]

In 1937, Roosevelt appointed Vinson Judge of the Court of Appeals for the District of Columbia, a position he held for five years.[10] Sitting with distinguished jurists, including Wiley Rutledge, he heard a wide range of cases. The Court of Appeals for the District of Columbia was at once a "local appellate court for the District of Columbia, . . . a tribunal for review of a large number of federal administrative agencies and . . . a regular Circuit Court of Appeals."[11] Only three of Vinson's decisions from this Court were reversed on review by the Supreme Court.[12]

Chief Justice Stone appointed Vinson Chief Judge of the United States Emergency Court of Appeals in 1942. As Chief Judge, from March, 1942 until May, 1943, of this three-judge panel, Vinson reviewed price and rent control orders under the Emergency Price Control Act.[13] None of the four majority opinions he wrote was reversed, and his one dissenting opinion was adopted by the Supreme Court on review as the controlling opinion.[14] Judge Albert B. Maris who served with Vinson on the Emergency Court of Appeals described Vinson's work on that court: "He was not a Holmes or a Cardozo or a Brandeis. He was more of a judge of the type [that] some of the rest of us are, I guess, that carried on and met our problems as they ar[o]se without trying to write too much for the future."[15]

Following this six-year period in the federal judiciary, Vinson began a three-year trek through various administrative positions in the executive branch. On May 29, 1943 Roosevelt appointed him Director of Economic Stabilization, one of the most important of the wartime agencies, where he remained until March of 1945. He served briefly as Federal Loan Officer before becoming in April of that year Director of War Mobilization and Reconversion charged with formulating plans to convert from a wartime to a peacetime economy. Although he stayed for only three months, his performance in this job has been described as "little short of miraculous."[16] His rise continued under Truman who in July of 1945 appointed him Secretary of the Treasury, a post he held for eleven months before his appointment to the United States Supreme Court.[17]

The fact that Vinson's entire service in the executive branch occurred during emergency conditions undoubtedly reinforced his belief in a strong national government and emphasized as well the need for strong presidential leadership; both beliefs were ingrained by the time his Court of Appeals colleague Judge Lawrence Groner administered the oath to the new Chief Justice in a festive ceremony at the White House.[18] As Chief Justice, he would serve his president well. Richard Kirkendall, summarizing Vinson's achievements on the bench, concluded that "[he] had, in a sense, remained a part of the administration . . . Truman continued to admire Vinson's ability as an adviser and tapped it frequently, often in late-evening telephone conversations."[19]

As a congressman, Vinson had been intensely interested in economic and tax legislation, interests which continued after he became Chief Justice. His former law clerk on the Court of Appeals, Willard H. Pedrick, observed that "[u]nlike some judges, Vinson loved tax cases—the product of long service on the Ways and Means Committee."[20] But as John P. Frank pointed out in his annual reviews of the Court decisions, Vinson rarely wrote the majority opinion in tax cases. Frank credited Vinson with an "admirable" disinterestedness when assigning cases, noting that he "skimped himself in the distribution of the more interesting cases,"[21] which were "fairly passed around,"[22] and that there was "no hazing period of dull statutory and tax cases for the younger Justices, no playing of favorites."[23]

Vinson's few decisions in the tax area revealed his pro-government, pro-national orientation. Vinson's clerk, Howard J. Trienens, observed that in tax cases, Vinson wrote for the "Court and for the government," a bias expected from one with service in both the Treasury Department and on the Ways and Means Committee.[24] In one case, Vinson refused to return interest assessed against a taxpayer although a carryback credit erased the tax liability on which the interest was predicated.[25] To reach that conclusion, he argued that "[i]n the absence of a clear legislative expression to the contrary, the question of who properly should possess the right of use of the money owed the Government for the period it is owed must be answered in favor of the Government."[26] In another case, Vinson emphasized the need for unimpeded federal commerce by striking down a discriminatory state tax.[27] Although Vinson held for the taxpayer in his last tax case, *Healy v. Commissioner of Internal Revenue* (1953),[28] he based the decision on the need for an orderly system of revenue collection essentially favorable to the governmental authority.

JUDICIAL PERFORMANCE

During his tenure, Vinson averaged writing thirteen opinions per year. Of his total ninety-one opinions, twelve were dissenting and seventy-six were opinions for the Court. He dissented a total of sixty-seven times, fifty-five times without opinion.[29] The dissenting pattern on the Court under Vinson became more frequent and intense. Before 1935, approximately 85 percent of the cases were decided unanimously. The percentage of unanimous opinions for Vinson's first term was 36 percent, dropping to 26 percent in his third term and to a record low of 19 percent in 1952.[30]

A partial explanation of this increase can be seen in differing views about the value of multiple opinions. Vinson failed in his attempt to encourage Frankfurter to join the majority instead of writing a concurring opinion in *Kovacs v. Cooper* (1949).[31] He had persuaded Justice Reed to drop the language in the majority opinion to which Frankfurter objected and then asked Frankfurter to join. Frankfurter responded to Vinson's entreaties with a two-page exposition on the value of multiple opinions. Vinson caustically thanked Frankfurter for his "charming recitation" of the history of multiple opinions, but vigorously asserted that "any judge worth his salt" would be influenced only by "a conscientious resolution" of the issues before him.[32] Frankfurter, prompted by the opinion "to make some additional observations," wrote a separate concurrence.[33]

The two men had opposing views on the value of multiple opinions, which reflected conflicting views about the purpose of the Supreme Court. Vinson thought the Court's work should be primarily the resolution of disputes. Frankfurter emphasized the educational function of the Court. Vinson favored unanimity in the decisions because it provided a better guide for judges and lawyers interpreting the law.[34] He worked to provide this direction. Many have praised his ability to negotiate agreements among the justices. Justice Clark credited Vinson with having "an uncanny knack of placating opposing minds" and found him "persuasive at conference."[35] Frankfurter believed that division was "inherent in the functioning of the Court" and that "very little attention should be paid to the ephemeral griping of an uninformed laity... [or] an unlearned... narrowly preoccupied bar."[36]

In assessing dissent on the Vinson Court, Percival E. Jackson found that Black and Douglas, as liberals on a conservative court, were the main dissenters, followed by Frankfurter and Jackson as the conservative pair of dissenters.[37] The high incidence of dissent undercuts any assumption that Vinson was a "peacemaker" on the Court. Vinson was consistently unable to muster unanimous opinions.

The low number of cases decided by the Court during Vinson's tenure was a source of considerable speculation. John P. Frank reported the number of cases by term:

142 cases	1946–47
119 cases	1947–48
122 cases	1948–49
94 cases	1949–50
88 cases	1950–51
89 cases	1951–52
104 cases	1952–53[38]

Frank contrasted this low decision output with the pre-war average of two hundred. He expressed the opinion that the exercise of judicial deference of thirteen years duration might have been "shifting the solution of problems to branches closer to the electorate."[39] He strongly suggested that one reason for the case load reduction was the Court's use, and implied abuse, of discretion in hearing cases brought to them on *certiorari*. The number of cases denied hearing was so controversial that Frank listed some of them at the end of his 1950, 1951 and 1952 articles. Richard Kirkendall explained the low case load as a deliberate result of Vinson's administration. Vinson "reduced the burden on the court" because he believed the justices were overworked (witness Rutledge's untimely death) and because of his conception of the limited role the Court should play.[40] This view was also expressed in a collective article written by Vinson's law clerks, "In general, the Chief's philosophy regarding applications for review was that he couldn't run the world from his chair—a philosophy that made him much less anxious than some other justices to grant review of cases involving such matters as the administration by the states of their criminal procedures."[41]

Frankfurter's diary entry on October 19, 1946 after the first conference presided over by Chief Justice Vinson was a portent of Vinson's failure to coalesce the Court:

> First Conference in which argued cases were taken up. The way Vinson dealt with them gives further evidence that he is likely to deal with complicated matters on a surface basis. He is confident

and easy-going and sure and shallow... he seems to me to have the confident air of a man who does not see the complexities of problems and blithely hits the obvious points. He does it all in good temper and with dispatch.[42]

John P. Frank's later assessment of Vinson's tenure carried this theme further. He asserted that Vinson in his administrative position had the task of "the ultimate Yes or No, or the task of negotiating to some ultimate Yes or No."[43] He did not have the responsibility for detail:

> The jobs are too big to leave details to the leaders... And so we develop a breed of public men who... can delegate almost every aspect of their work except decision making. [O]ur society is filling the familiar reservoir of public officials from which we draw Supreme Court appointees with men who are equipped to handle broad responsibilities better than... great details; they are not quite cut out for the judicial job... Vinson... turned the once lonely job of Chief Justice of the United States into a staff operation.[44]

Richard Kirkendall reported that Vinson increased his number of law clerks from two to three and that "he relied heavily upon these aides for the task of writing opinions."[45] Justice Clark contended in 1973 that "... the law clerks were confined, when I was on the Court (and mine still does it) to writing memoranda and researching."[46] Karl R. Price, law clerk to Justice Vinson in 1946–47 who went with Vinson from the Treasury to the Court, recalled that Vinson did indeed use his law clerks for research, writing memoranda and also for writing the first drafts of the opinions. Vinson himself, however, wrote the final draft.[47] This perhaps contributed to Frank's characterization of Vinson's writing style:

> The most striking personality quality of Vinson's opinions [was] their odd lack of personality... [J]udicial personality is largely a matter of details; [It is evident in] the Holmes epigram, the Black way with facts, the Frankfurter vocabulary... There is, instead [of personality], an unevenness of quality in Vinson ['s opinions].[48]

USE OF JUDICIAL RESTRAINT

This unevenness did not, however, obscure the broad outlines of Vinson's judicial approach. His opinions were narrowly drawn, and he applied the judge-made rules in reaching decisions. Both of these tendencies were evident in the criminal procedure cases, the loyalty-security cases and the racial discrimination cases.

Criminal Procedure Cases

The case of *Harris v. United States* (1947)[49] and *Trupiano et al. v. United States* (1948)[50] involved the use of the exclusionary rule in search and seizure cases. Vinson wrote the majority opinion in the *Harris* case, from which Frankfurter strongly dissented. In the *Trupiano* case, Vinson dissented and was joined by Black, Reed and Burton. In both cases, Vinson favored allowing the evidence. *Harris v. United States* (1947) involved evidence obtained after a five-hour search of the defendant's four room apartment. The search was incident to a valid arrest warrant. The defendant was arrested for mail fraud and forgery. While the authorities were searching for evidence of this crime, they found draft cards illegally in the defendant's custody. They confiscated the evidence and charged him with illegal possession of the cards. The defendant sought to exclude the evidence alleging violation of the Fourth Amendment prohibitions against illegal searches and seizures. Vinson, in delivering the majority opinion, cited precedent for the proposition that each case stood on its own facts which in this case indicated to him that the search was not unreasonable. The entire apartment was under the immediate control of Harris, and the officers, following "basically reasonable" procedure, had discovered "property the possession of which [was] a crime."[51] Frankfurter's dissent was based on the opinion that the two cases cited as precedents for this decision, *United States v. Lefkowitz* (1932)[52] and *Go-Bart v. United States* (1931),[53] concerned situations that were "decisively different."[54] Frankfurter, in a thirteen-page memorandum circulated in April before the decision was handed down, argued that the general warrant with its historical implications violated the Fourth Amendment's guarantee against unreasonable searches and seizures. He argued that "the proposed opinion in the *Harris* case [went] way beyond prior decisions... it would allow rummaging throughout a house without a search warrant on the ostensible ground of looking for the instrument of a crime for which an arrest... had been authorized."[55]

In *Trupiano et al. v. United States* (1948), the majority, relying on the Fourth Amendment, disallowed evidence seized incident to a warrantless arrest, reasoning that the arrest was lawful but that the circumstances necessitated a search warrant. The *Harris* case was distinguished by the fact that the officers in *Trupiano* knew of the illegal operation long enough to have secured a valid search warrant. Vinson dissented, arguing that a reasonable search and seizure incident to a lawful arrest was valid procedure under the Fourth Amendment. He warned of the confusion likely to follow the majority holding, which he thought "inconsistent with judicial authority" and one not "adapted to conserve vital public and individual interests."[56] In these words, Vinson clearly enunciated his preference for upholding the rights of society against those of the individual.

In the two following cases, Vinson decided the issues on procedural technicalities. He deferred to the lower court, assuming that the court would act properly if given the chance or, at least, determining that the lower court must have the chance to act before the Supreme Court could address the issue. This application of judicial restraint was based on Vinson's understanding of the proper functioning of the judicial machinery.

In *Terminiello v. City of Chicago* (1949),[57] Vinson dissented, and separate dissents were written by Frankfurter and Jackson. Terminiello had given a provocative anti-Semitic speech which resulted in verbally violent disputes among the listeners. He was charged and found guilty of disturbing the peace. Douglas wrote the majority opinion overruling the state court decision by taking judicial notice of an error, thus invalidating the ordinance which prohibited provocative speech. Vinson wrote, "If the petitioner's counsel, who carefully made other constitutional objections throughout the proceeding below, had brought any issue here as to the constitutionality of the instruction, I would agree with the Court's decision."[58] The counsel's failure to object and raise the possibility of error to the lower court precluded the lower court's proper consideration of the issue and Vinson found that this was basically fair procedure. Insisting on the restraint tenet that the case be properly brought to the Court, Vinson invoked another tenet and refused to reach the question of First Amendment rights. Douglas reached the constitutional issue and considered the failure by counsel to make objection "immaterial."[59] Frankfurter wished to dispose of the writ for *certiorari* as "improvidently granted."[60]

Similarly, in *Stack v. Boyle* (1951),[61] Vinson relied on self-restraint. Petitioners were charged under the Smith Act for conspiracy and their bail had been set at amounts ranging from $2,500 to $100,000 They sought to contest the excessive bail by writ of habeas corpus under the Eighth Amendment. The District Court had granted habeas corpus, but Vinson found that the "petitioners' remedy [was] by motion to reduce bail, with the right of appeal to the Circuit Court of Appeals."[62] He accordingly remanded the case for the petitioners to seek the remedy through proper procedure. Vinson would not entertain the question of constitutionality because the case had been improperly brought before the Court. Justice Black had reservations about disposing of the case in such a technical manner. He encouraged Vinson to delete a paragraph which he felt might be read as condoning excessive bail. Black thought the opinion "not so strong a condemnation of what [had] been done and what [was] being done" as the "Court's expression should be."[63] Vinson agreed to delete the offensive paragraph and Black joined the more narrowly drawn opinion. Jackson's separate concurrence was joined by Frankfurter.

Loyalty-Security Cases

In cases involving loyalty-security issues, Vinson usually deferred to the investigatory power of Congress by upholding the power of contempt. In

United States v. Bryan (1950),⁶⁴ Helen R. Bryan, executive secretary of the Joint Anti-Fascist Refugee Committee, refused to produce records of the organization in her possession which had been subpoenaed by the House Committee on UnAmerican Activities. Her conviction for contempt of Congress was affirmed by Vinson's majority opinion. Vinson reasoned that the complainant failed to raise at the proper time the question of a quorum before the committee, and she, therefore, could not raise the question on appeal. He also found that the reading in the lower court of the testimony she gave before the committee, which was introduced as evidence of her failure to comply with the subpoena, did not violate the act which assured the Committee witness that no testimony would "be used as evidence in any criminal proceeding against [her] in court."⁶⁵ The immunity clause applied only to testimony concerning past criminal acts. He, therefore, upheld the enforcement of the subpoena.

In *United States v. Fleischman* (1950),⁶⁶ Vinson confirmed the conviction of a board member of the same organization for the same offense. He reasoned that although the materials subpoenaed were not in Fleischman's possession, she should have done everything in her power to produce them; she should have importuned the board to compel the production of the materials. Vinson expressed his concern that a court's failure to enforce the subpoena power of the Committee would "destroy the effective operation of all committees, which is the necessary result if they cannot compel the disclosure of facts."⁶⁷

Two other Vinson opinions demonstrated his zealous effort to maintain the authority of the national government. In *American Communications Association C.I.O. et al. v. Douds* (1950),⁶⁸ Vinson validated the provisions in the Taft-Hartley Act of 1947 which required labor organizations to file union officers' affidavits of loyalty as a prerequisite for using the services of the National Labor Relations Board. Vinson found the Congressional legislation reasonable and motivated by the fact that "interstate commerce must be protected from a continuing threat of strikes."⁶⁹ Reasoning that communists might cause strikes, Congress had acted to "prevent potential injury to the national economy."⁷⁰

In the 1951 case, *Dennis et al. v. United States* (1951),⁷¹ Vinson wrote the majority opinion, and his reasoning echoed the *Douds* rationale of the right of self-protection inherent in government. Vinson wrote for four of the justices who concurred with his reasoning that the First Amendment right of free speech was outweighed by the rights protected by the Smith Act which prohibited "willful advocacy of overthrow of Government by force or violence [and] conspiracy to advocate overthrow of Government by force or violence. . . ."⁷² In both cases, *Douds* and *Dennis*, Vinson appropriated the clear and present danger test for his purposes, and in *Dennis*, many commentators felt that he had replaced it with his own "perhaps and probable" test.⁷³

Frank argued that the Holmes-Brandeis position on the "clear and present danger test" formulated by Holmes in *Schenck v. United States* (1919)⁷⁴ required more facts in the record to establish the "gravity of the evil" than the test used by Judge Learned Hand in the Court of Appeals for the Second Circuit which Vinson adopted in *Dennis*. Holmes had written, "The question in every case is whether the words ... used are in such circumstances and are of such a nature to create a clear and present danger that they will bring about the substantive evils that Congress has a right to prevent. It is a question of proximity and degree."[75]

Vinson found Hand's interpretation of the rule "succinct and inclusive."[76] "In each case [courts] must ask whether the gravity of the 'evil,' discounted by its improbability, justifies such invasion of free speech as is necessary to avoid the danger."[77] From this test, Vinson deduced that the conspiracy itself created a sufficient danger to warrant government intervention.

Professor Chester James Antieau of Washburn University Law School found the danger posed by the defendants in the *Dennis* case an insufficient threat and denominated the restatement of the test by Hand a "perhaps and probable" test,[78] noting that the opinion rested on "a conspiracy amounting ... to a probable danger of an attempt at advocating bad ideas that would sometime break out into disquieting deeds."[79]

Vinson's reasoning indicated a readiness to find the legislation reasonable. He considered the danger posed by the defendant's conspiracy to organize the Communist party a sufficient threat under the circumstances and applied the rule of "clear and present danger" as modified by Hand.

Racial Discrimination Cases

Vinson used the Fourteenth Amendment for the benefit of the black citizen in the racial discrimination cases, although his approach was narrow. In *Shelley v. Kraemer* (1948),[80] a black couple in 1945 bought certain real property which was subject to restrictive covenants executed in 1911 with thirty of the thirty-nine owners of the area included in the covenants. The covenants forbade sale to or occupancy of any of the restricted property by "people of the Negro or Mongolian race."[81] Adjoining owners brought suit to enjoin the black couple from taking possession of the property and to have title to the land revested in the seller. Vinson decided the case on constitutional grounds, on the equal protection clause of the Fourteenth Amendment. He reasoned that state enforcement of the restrictive covenants denied "equal protection of the laws and that, therefore, the action of the state court [could not] stand."[82] He asserted, however, that the Amendment erected "no shield against merely private conduct, however discriminatory or wrongful" and would not reach the restrictive covenants standing alone.[83] Burton congratulated Vinson on the *Shelley* opinion adding, "If you can get unanimous action ... it will be a major contribution to the vitality of the Fourteenth Amendment, the Civil Rights Act, the general subject of interracial justice and the strength of the court as the 'living voice of the Constitution.' "[84]

This reasoning should be compared with Vinson's dissent in *Barrows et al. v. Jackson* (1953)[85] in which Minton delivered the opinion for the Court. A property owner claimed damages from a co-covenantor who sold his property in defiance of a racial covenant to a non-Caucasian. The California court awarded damages. Minton reasoned that the Court would not require "California to coerce [the party] to respond in damages for failure to observe a restrictive covenant that the Court would deny California the right to enforce in equity."[86] Minton held that the Constitution did not confer on any individual the right to demand action by a state which would result in a denial of equal protection to another. The state court award for damages was state action denying equal protection. The Court thus protected non-Caucasians who were not "identified but [were] identifiable."[87]

Vinson's dissent was a plea for judicial self-restraint. He reasoned that the *Shelley* case proscribed state enforcement of restrictive covenants and that the California award of damages should be allowed to stand because it did not involve state enforcement of the covenant, but the enforcement of a contract right of one party against another. He urged that the state of California should be allowed to enforce its own contract laws. Vinson argued that the constitutional issue could not be reached because *the party had no standing to raise the issue.*[88] Reasoning that only an injured non-Caucasian could argue that his constitutional rights were violated by the covenant, Vinson concluded, "I think that the absence of a direct injury to any identifiable non-Caucasian is decisive."[89]

Vinson acknowledged that his reasons were explicit tenets of judicial self-restraint: "So is every other jurisdictional limitation which depends, in the last analysis, solely upon this Court's willingness to govern its own exercise of power."[90] "We must set aside," he insisted, "predelictions on social policy and adhere to the settled rules which restrict the exercise of our power of judicial review."[91] This plea for restraint was a single voice. Frankfurter, the astute apostle of judicial self-restraint, did not find the tenets in this instance persuasive. He voted with the majority.

Vinson delivered the majority opinions in *Sweatt v. Painter et al.* (1950)[92] and *McLaurin v. Oklahoma State Regents for Higher Education et al.* (1950).[93] In both cases, however, Vinson approached the issues as narrowly as possible. He found that equal law school facilities were not, in fact, available to Sweatt and held that "the Equal Protection Clause of the Fourteenth Amendment required that the petitioner be admitted to the University of Texas Law School."[94] In *McLaurin*, Vinson, again speaking for a unanimous court, ruled that the equal protection clause of the Fourteenth Amendment required that students admitted to the same school be treated equally.

Although these two cases signaled a new direction, they were not broad endorsements of integration and they very carefully avoided overruling the

Plessy separate-but-equal doctrine. An approach of judicial restraint was integral to Vinson's method. Vinson narrowly decided each case. "As judge," Professor Francis A. Allen of Harvard Law School, former law clerk, wrote, "he ordinarily reacted suspiciously to the grand generalization."[95] Frankfurter offered minor suggestions in both *Sweatt* and *McLaurin* urging that "the more there is an appearance of unexcitement and inevitability about [the opinion], the better," and he expressed his hopes for an "all-but unanimous, if not a unanimous, Court."[96] In a long letter to Frankfurter, Vinson explained and defended his use of the material to which Frankfurter objected but he added, "I have always endeavored to meet the suggestions of my Brethren, and if the Court desires to delete the two sentences, they will be stricken."[97] Black's approval was unqualified: "This is written in beautiful style and I sincerely hope it can obtain a unanimous approval."[98]

Vinson's approach to the judicial function was enveloped by his belief in a strong federal government. His political work had been on a national level and his perspective was correspondingly national. He knew how the government worked and, as a justice, he sought to contribute to the functioning of government. This meant deferring to legislative and executive actions at all levels of government, but particularly at the federal level. Francis Allen pointed out that for Vinson, "the problems of liberty were the problems of men-in-society."[99] This perspective necessarily involved using the balancing-of-interest concept in judicial decision making. Vinson's predeliction was for a strong government in order to assure a society where legitimate interests could co-exist and where, if they clashed, the rights of each could be balanced appropriately.

USE OF JUDICIAL ACTIVISM

Vinson's rare use of judicial activism, augmented by this predeliction, was exemplified in his discretionary use of granting *certiorari*, and particularly in three cases reviewed under unusual procedure. Vinson's basic approach to granting review by writ of *certiorari* was conservative and restrained. His insistence on technical procedural regularity revealed another element of restraint, that of narrowly deciding cases. He was reluctant to grant *certiorari*, and when it was granted, he favored only a limited review. This sharply contrasted with Black's approach. Black voted regularly to grant *certiorari* and favored a full review of all questions presented in each case. Vinson's overall approach more closely paralleled that of Frankfurter, who voted most often to deny *certiorari*, insisted on narrow review and even developed the policy of refusing to vote in those cases in which he had voted to deny *certiorari*. Vinson's activism, however, surfaced in the use of the power to grant *certiorari* in cases pending in a court of appeal *before judgment*. Review in such a case required "a showing that the case [was] of such imperative public importance as to justify the deviation from normal appellate processes and to require immediate settlement."[100] Review was granted on this basis on two occasions during Vinson's seven-year tenure. Each case, *United States v. United Mine Workers* (1947)[101] and *Youngstown Sheet and Tube Company v. Sawyer* (1952),[102] involved government seizure of private property to control industrial disputes. Vinson disregarded procedural regularity on a third occasion when he called a special term of the full Court to review the stay of execution granted on June 17, 1953 by Justice Douglas in the Rosenberg case, *Rosenberg et ux. v. United States* (1953).[103]

Exercise of the power of *certiorari* in pending cases on appeal had been used once between 1937 and 1947. In 1942, the Court heard the case of seven German saboteurs in *Ex parte Quirin* (1942)[104] and denied the accused access to the civil courts from the military tribunal trying the accused. Prior to 1937, the Court under Chief Justice Hughes allowed *certiorari* in four cases pending appeal,[105] and in three of those cases struck down federal legislation enacted under the commerce clause. The court declared the Railroad Retirement Act unconstitutional in *Railroad Retirement Board v. Alton R. Co.* (1935)[106] and the Bituminous Coal Conservation Act of 1935 (Guffey Coal Act) unconstitutional in *Carter v. Carter Coal* (1936).[107] In the third case, *Rickert Rice Mills v. Fontenot* (1936),[108] the court restrained the collection of taxes authorized by the Agricultural Adjustment Act which had been declared unconstitutional in *United States v. Butler* (1936)[109] because the tax as well as the authorizing legislation was "regulation of agricultural production, a matter not within the power of Congress."[110] The judicial activism displayed in these three cases was aimed at legislation. While Vinson's use of judicial power in the two strike cases was equally defiant of legislative authority, he did not favor the rights of private property or the rights of individuals in these cases, as had the previous Court; he sought instead to augment executive power.

In *United States v. United Mine Workers* (1947),[111] Vinson's opinion upheld the injunctive relief granted the government against the striking mine workers, confirmed the fine against John L. Lewis and reduced the fine against the union. Vinson found that under the Norris-LaGuardia Anti-Injunction Act of 1932, proscriptions against injunctions did not apply to the government. The government by seizing an industry converted that industry into a public enterprise. Vinson reasoned that the War Labor Disputes Act of 1943 authorized seizure and found nothing in the legislative history which "constitute[d] an authoritative expression of Congress"[112] to withhold injunctive relief. Frankfurter concurred in the judgment but wrote a separate opinion which was in sharp contrast to this view of government power. He criticized Vinson's use of an "artificial canon of construction" which would exclude the government "from the operation of general statutes unless it [was] included by explicit language"[113] and found that Congress in the Norris-LaGuardia Act had been prompted to deny injunctive relief because of government use of the injunction. Frankfurter also relied heavily on the legislative history of the War Labor Disputes Act which authorized only criminal penalties for interference with the operation of seized industries. Congress had voted down the Connally amendment which would have allowed the government injunctive relief. He criticized the Vinson opinion for holding "that voting down the amendment had the same effect as voting it up."[114] The whole course of legislative history indicated to Frankfurter that Congress withheld the remedy of injunction. The remedy was not specifically authorized and it had been expressly voted down. By reasoning that government seizure of industry made the government a private employer, Frankfurter found the proscriptions of the Norris-LaGuardia Act applicable to the government. He concluded that in both Acts, Congress had effectively limited government power over seized industry. Injunctive relief was not authorized by the legislation authorizing seizure. The government, as a private employer, was bound by legislation regulating private employer-employee conduct.

In the *Steel Seizure Case* (1952),[115] which also reached the Court by unusual grant of *certiorari*, Vinson announced in his dissenting opinion judicial support for the president's inherent powers to seize industry in times of crisis. He berated the majority for failure to recognize the crisis while detailing the history of presidential power. Labeling the Court's interpretation of presidential authority as a "messenger-boy concept" emasculating the office, he found that the president's action was necessitated by the circumstances: the president was "faced with immediate national peril through stoppage in steel production on the one hand and faced with destruction of the wage and price legislation program on the other."[116]

Vinson's notes on the decision revealed that he was concerned about the "psychological effect on the world front" of curtailing the actions of the president. The decision, he felt, might be "construed as a limitation on existing power." He also noted, "My defense is not a defense of the present occupant. He will only be there a few more months. I speak for the power of the Chief Executive perhaps to save our country and civilization."[117]

In both cases dealing with seizure of private industry to further a war effort, Vinson found sufficient authority *outside legislation* to break strike efforts. In the *United Mine Workers* case, injunctive relief was available from the courts and in the *Steel Seizure Case*, presidential seizure should have provided the necessary relief. Neither action was authorized by legislation. Vinson ignored or explained away legislative impediments to the assertion of power. In both cases, he abandoned the judicial restraint tenet of deference to legislation and opted for strong executive power.

Vinson also defied the judicial restraint requirement that all remedies in the lower courts must be exhausted and all lower court procedures followed before review by the Supreme Court when he hastily called for a full court review of Douglas's stay of execution in the *Rosenberg* case (1953).[118] Indictment against the Rosenbergs had been returned in 1951 charging a conspiracy continuing from June 6, 1944 through July 16, 1950 with overt acts occurring in 1944–45. The government sought prosecution and obtained conviction under the Espionage Act of 1917 which gave the district judge sole authority in sentencing and in assessing penalties. Prior to the indictment, subsequent to the covert acts, but during the period of the continuing conspiracy, Congress passed the Atomic Energy Act of 1946 which withdrew from the district judge the authority to assess the death penalty. Under the terms of the new legislation, the death penalty had to be recommended by a jury. Douglas' stay of execution was predicated on the new argument presented by friends of counsel for the Rosenbergs. They argued that the penalty provisions of the later act controlled in the *Rosenberg* case. At the time of issuing the stay, Douglas (after twelve hours of deliberation) thought this substantial legal point needed to be determined before execution could proceed. He issued the stay on June 17, 1953. His dissenting opinion to the order vacating the stay contained his concern about the question of applicable penalty:

> [I]t is law too elemental for citation of authority that where two penal statutes may apply—one carrying death, the other imprisonment—the court has no choice but to impose the less harsh sentence... Here the trial court was without jurisdiction to impose the death penalty, since the jury had not recommended it.[119]

Frankfurter's dissent from the order vacating Douglas's stay of execution echoed his earlier prophecy of Vinson's judicial aptitude, "Neither counsel nor the Court, in the time available, were able to go below the surface of the question raised by the application for a stay which Mr. Justice Douglas granted."[120] Although Burton had voted with Frankfurter to allow oral argument, he voted with the majority to vacate the stay. Burton wrote a letter to the Chief Justice and a separate memorandum to the Court requesting that the record of his vote for a hearing be omitted unless the record would clearly show that he voted to deny the stay of execution, affirming "I do join explicitly in the denial of a stay."[121] Frankfurter would later refer to the *Rosenberg* case as "one of the least edifying episodes" in modern Court history.[122] Black's dissent pointed out the "unseemly haste" with which the Court moved to set aside Douglas's order, noting the lack of authority in statute, rule of court or precedent for such court action.[123]

The architect of this unprecedented court action, the Chief Justice, found sufficient power in the circumstances surrounding the case. Vinson found that the Court possessed power to decide the legal question raised by the new argument. Admitting that "ordinarily stays of individual Justices should stand until the grounds upon which they have issued can be reviewed through regular appellate processes," he reasoned that the Court's responsibility to supervise criminal justice in the federal courts included the duty to see that "punishments prescribed by the laws are enforced with a reasonable degree of promptness and certainty. The stay which had been issued promised many more months of litigation in a case which had otherwise run its full course."[124] After several hours of argument on June 18, the Court, having denied a rehearing, decided the legal point in question and held that the penalty provisions of the Espionage Act were applicable.

William W. Oliver, Vinson's clerk at the time, thought the decisive point for Vinson was that "there had to be a time at which you'd put an end to the consideration of a case."[125] But Frankfurter in a letter to Burton expressed his concern that the Douglas stay had put the "whole Court in a hole" and that "to wind up this case as quickly as possible" would place the Court "before the whole world" in the position of "refusing to hear the claims made by the lawyers" and of "being heedless to the pronouncement of a member of the Court."[126]

The execution of the Rosenbergs proceeded on schedule the day following the special Supreme Court term. On the morning of June 19, the Court decision was announced without opinion and in the evening of the same day, the penalty was imposed.[127]

ASSESSMENT

Vinson's approach to the judicial function was usually governed by judicial restraint, but, being enveloped by his belief in a strong federal government, his approach in the three pending cases was characterized by judicial activism. He abandoned his usual regard for the tenets of judicial restraint in the seizure cases and in the *Rosenberg* case to adopt an activist stance producing result-oriented opinions which revealed his personal preferences.

Usually, however, Vinson's opinions evinced a consistently restrained approach to decision making. He deferred to local government agencies, which led him to allow evidence obtained but not specified in the warrant. He also voted to allow evidence obtained without a warrant when there had been ample time to obtain one. He insisted that appeals be considered only on the points legally reserved for review and that cases be brought to the Court through the proper review structure. He deferred to Congressional investigatory methods and to legislation which required loyalty oaths and proscribed subversive activity. In racial discrimination cases, Vinson based his resort to the Constitution on narrow grounds and insisted that the person raising the constitutional issues have standing. This technical approach to decision making expressed a pragmatism informed by a belief that the primary function of the Court was not to make policy but to decide individual cases in a deliberative manner.

Administrative duties necessarily complicated Vinson's work, but minor differences among Court members especially plagued his term on the Court.

It was generally conceded that Vinson was an able conciliator but law clerk Willard H. Pedrick, later law professor at Arizona State University, insisted "there were some members of the Court with whom he just could not achieve a satisfactory working relationship."[128] Disagreements in opinions were intense, as were differences about the revised Rules of Civil Procedure submitted to the Attorney General in 1946–47,[129] about procedure for orders extending the time within which to file a petition for *certiorari*, or other review petitions to the Supreme Court,[130] and about modifications in the procedure for disposing of argued cases.[131] Vinson also presided over the Court when various members required special attention: Minton's health was a constant reason for his absence; Douglas suffered a fall from a horse which incapacitated him for months; and Jackson was away at Nuremburg for an extended period. Douglas's well-publicized divorce caused unfavorable comment to be addressed to the Chief Justice. Reed and Frankfurter were subpoenaed as character witnesses for Alger Hiss, arousing public consternation. Vinson's correspondence is full of adverse public sentiment expressed against the Court. Vinson himself became the focus for unfavorable criticism from church and right-wing groups who objected to a phrase he used in the *Dennis* case which indicated there were no absolutes.[132]

Although Vinson has been criticized for his stand on civil rights, his decisions in *Sweatt* and *McLaurin* paved the way for the abolition of the separate-but-equal doctrine. One of his former law clerks found that "an unfortunate twist of history" denied Vinson credit for making possible the *Brown* case and later civil rights opinions.[133] Burton's conference notes described cautious justices who first began to examine the issue of separate-but-equal facilities in the schools when the *Brown* case was argued before the Vinson Court. Burton recorded Vinson's statements to the Court, "When you face the complete abolition of public schools in some areas then it is most serious. Boldness is essential but wisdom indispensable."[134] That Vinson was not racist is borne out by the testimony of his contemporaries. All of those interviewed in the Vinson Oral History Project at the University of Kentucky insisted on his sense of fairness. W. E. Crutcher, who served as Vinson's office boy in Louisa, later editor of the *Morehead News*, noted that "Negro precincts always went overwhelmingly for Mr. Vinson."[135] Racism evidently did not prompt Vinson's narrow decisions on racial issues.

Fred Vinson, Jr., a Washington lawyer, perhaps best explained his father's approach, "He was not doctrinaire. He was not particularly 'cause' oriented . . . He was not a hairsplitter like Justice Frankfurter."[136] Willard H. Pedrick believed that "he was basically a pragmatist . . . he didn't go in for abstract philosophizing. He was a problem solver, a practical-minded man."[137] Frankfurter inadvertently paid Vinson a compliment in an undated, caustic note scribbled on a Friday in 1946, "You certainly don't have to assure me or I assure others—that nobody could 'pressure' you: 'right,' 'left' or 'center.' "[138]

NOTES

1. Letter, Vinson to Frankfurter, June 26, 1946, Frankfurter Papers, file "Vinson Correspondence," Manuscript Division, Library of Congress, Washington, D.C.

2. Letter, Vinson to Truman, January 23, 1953, Vinson Papers, file "Truman Correspondence," Special Collections of the Margaret I. King Library, University of Kentucky, Lexington, Kentucky.

3. Willard H. Pedrick, "From Congress to the Court of Appeals," 49 *Northwestern Law Review* 54, 58 (1954).

4. James J. Bolner, "Mr. Chief Justice Vinson," Ph.D. dissertation, University of Virginia, 1962, pp. 3–10.

5. Ibid., p. 5.

6. Ibid., p. 6.

7. Pedrick, "From Congress to the Court of Appeals," pp. 54–57.

8. 298 U.S. 238 (1936). William W. Oliver, "Vinson in Congress," 49 *Northwestern Law Review* 62, pp. 67–69 (1954).

9. Bolner, "Mr. Chief Justice Vinson," pp. 11–17. See also Oliver, "Vinson in Congress," pp. 67–73.

10. Pedrick, "From Congress to the Court of Appeals," p. 54.

11. Ibid., p. 58.

12. Bolner, "Mr. Chief Justice Vinson," p. 22.

13. Pedrick, "From Congress to the Court of Appeals," p. 60.

14. Bolner, "Mr. Chief Justice Vinson," p. 38.

15. Albert B. Maris, Oral History Interview, August 17, 1976, Vinson Papers, Special Collections of the Margaret I. King Library, University of Kentucky, Lexington, Kentucky.

16. Wilbur R. Lester, "Fred M. Vinson in the Executive Branch," 49 *Northwestern Law Review* 36, 49 (1954).

17. Ibid.

18. Bolner, "Mr. Chief Justice Vinson," p. 76.

19. Richard Kirkendall, "Mr. Fred Vinson," Leon Friedman and Fred L. Israel, eds. *The Justices of the Supreme Court, 1789–1969, Their Lives and Major Opinions*, vol. 4 (New York: Chelsea House, 1969), p. 2648.

20. Pedrick, "From Congress to the Court of Appeals," p. 59.

21. John P. Frank, "The United States Supreme Court: 1948–49," 17 *University of Chicago Law Review* 1, 46 (1949).

22. John P. Frank, "Fred Vinson and the Chief Justiceship," 21 *University of Chicago Law Review* 212, 241 (1954).

23. Ibid.

24. Howard J. Trienens, Oral History Interview, February 27, 1975, Vinson Papers, Special Collections of the Margaret I. King Library, University of Kentucky, Lexington, Kentucky.

25. *Manning, Collector of Internal Revenue, Fifth District of New Jersey v. Seely Tube and Box Co. of New Jersey*, 338 U.S. 561 (1950).

26. 338 U.S. at 566.

27. *Memphis Steam Laundry Cleaner, Inc. v. Stone, Chairman, State Tax Commission of Mississippi*, 342 U.S. 389 (1952).

28. 345 U.S. 278 (1953).

29. Albert P. Blaustein and Roy M. Mersky, *The First One Hundred Justices* (Hamden, Conn.: The Shoe String Press, Inc., 1978), pp. 146–49.

30. Kirkendall, "Fred M. Vinson," p. 2642.

31. 366 U.S. 77 (1949).

32. Letter, Vinson to Frankfurter, December 3, 1948, Vinson Papers, file "Frankfurter Correspondence," Special Collections of the Margaret I. King Library, University of Kentucky, Lexington, Kentucky.

33. Letter, Frankfurter to Vinson, December 2, 1948, Vinson Papers, file "Frankfurter Correspondence," Special Collections of the Margaret I. King Library, University of Kentucky, Lexington, Kentucky.

34. Letter, Vinson to Frankfurter, December 3, 1948, Vinson Papers, file "Frankfurter Correspondence," Special Collections of the Margaret I. King Library, University of Kentucky, Lexington, Kentucky.

35. Clark, Oral History Interview, Vinson Papers, August 20, 1973.

36. Letter, Frankfurter to Vinson, December 2, 1948, Vinson Papers, file "Frankfurter Correspondence," Special Collections of the Margaret I. King Library, University of Kentucky, Lexington, Kentucky.

37. Percival E. Jackson, *Dissent in the Supreme Court* (Norman: University of Oklahoma Press, 1969), pp. 497–99.

38. The yearly totals were reported in the articles summarizing the activity of the previous terms. John P. Frank, "The United States Supreme Court: 1946–47," 15 *University of Chicago Law Review* 1, 37–38 (1947); John P. Frank, "The United States Supreme Court: 1947–48," 16 *University of Chicago Law Review* 1, 34 (1948); John P. Frank, "The United States Supreme Court: 1948–49," 17 *University of Chicago Law Review* 1, 43 (1949); John P. Frank, "The United States Supreme Court: 1949–50," 18 *University of Chicago Law Review* 1, 49–50 (1950); John P. Frank, "The United States Supreme Court: 1950–51," 19 *University of Chicago Law Review* 165, 216 (1951); John P. Frank, "The United States Supreme Court: 1951–52," 20 *University of Chicago Law Review* 1, 57 (1952); and John P. Frank, "Fred Vinson and the Chief Justiceship," 21 *University of Chicago Law Review* 212, 218 (1954).

39. Frank, "The United States Supreme Court: 1948–49," pp. 54–55.

40. Kirkendall, "Fred M. Vinson," p. 2643.

41. Symposium, "Chief Justice Vinson and His Law Clerks," 49 *Northwestern Law Review* 26, 29 (1954).

42. Joseph P. Lash, ed., *From the Diaries of Felix Frankfurter* (New York: W. W. Norton & Co., Inc., 1974), p. 276.

43. Frank, "Fred Vinson and the Chief Justiceship," p. 244.
44. Ibid., pp. 245–46.
45. Kirkendall, "Fred M. Vinson," p. 2643.
46. Clark, Oral History Interview, Vinson Papers, August 20, 1973.
47. Telephone Interview with Karl R. Price, Attorney at Law, Washington, D.C., September 28, 1987.
48. Frank, "Fred Vinson and the Chief Justiceship," p. 244.
49. 331 U.S. 145 (1947).
50. 334 U.S. 699 (1948).
51. 331 U.S. at 155.
52. 285 U.S. 452 (1932).
53. 282 U.S. 344 (1931).
54. Memorandum to the Court, Frankfurter, April 1947, page 13, Vinson Papers, file "Supreme Court," Special Collections of the Margaret I. King Library, University of Kentucky, Lexington, Kentucky.
55. Ibid., p. 2.
56. 334 U.S. at 716.
57. 337 U.S. 1 (1949).
58. 337 U.S. at 8.
59. 337 U.S. at 5.
60. Memorandum, Frankfurter, April 9, 1949, Vinson Papers, file "Supreme Court," Special Collections of the Margaret I. King Library, University of Kentucky, Lexington, Kentucky.
61. 342 U.S. 1 (1951).
62. 342 U.S. at 7.
63. Memorandum, Black to Vinson, November 1, 1951, Vinson Papers, file "Supreme Court," Special Collections of the Margaret I. King Library, University of Kentucky, Lexington, Kentucky.
64. 339 U.S. 323 (1950).
65. 339 U.S. at 335.
66. 339 U.S. 349 (1950).
67. 339 U.S. at 365.
68. 339 U.S. 382 (1950).
69. 339 U.S. at 406.
70. 339 U.S. at 406.
71. 341 U.S. 494 (1951).
72. 341 U.S. at 495.
73. Frank, "Fred Vinson and the Chief Justiceship," p. 216.
74. 249 U.S. 47 (1919). Schenck published and distributed pamphlets advocating draft resistance and was convicted under the Espionage Act of June 15, 1917 for conspiring to obstruct the recruiting and training of draftees in World War I.
75. 249 U.S. at 52.
76. 341 U.S. at 510.

77. Hand quoted at 341 U.S. 510.

78. Chester James Antieau, "*Dennis v. United States*—Precedent, Principle or Perversion?" 5 *Vanderbilt Law Review*, 141, 143 (1952).

79. Ibid., p. 147.

80. 334 U.S. 1 (1948).

81. 334 U.S. at 5.

82. 334 U.S. at 20.

83. 334 U.S. at 13.

84. Memorandum, Burton to Vinson, April 24, 1948, Vinson Papers, file "Supreme Court," Special Collections of the Margaret I. King Library, University of Kentucky, Lexington, Kentucky.

85. 346 U.S. 249 (1953).

86. 346 U.S. at 258.

87. 346 U.S. at 249.

88. 346 U.S. at 266.

89. 346 U.S. at 267.

90. 346 U.S. at 266.

91. 346 U.S. at 269.

92. 339 U.S. 629 (1950).

93. 339 U.S. 637.

94. 339 U.S. at 636.

95. Francis A. Allen, "Chief Justice Vinson and the Theory of Constitutional Government: A Tentative Appraisal," 49 *Northwestern Law Review* 3, 4 (1954).

96. Memorandum, Frankfurter to Vinson, May 19, 1950, Vinson Papers, file "Chief Justice Opinions," Special Collections of the Margaret I. King Library, University of Kentucky, Lexington, Kentucky.

97. Letter, Vinson to Frankfurter, May 24, 1950, Vinson Papers, file "Chief Justice Opinions," Special Collections of the Margaret I. King Library, University of Kentucky, Lexington, Kentucky.

98. Memorandum, Black to Vinson, May 18, 1950, Vinson Papers, file "Chief Justice Opinions," Special Collections of the Margaret I. King Library, University of Kentucky, Lexington, Kentucky.

99. Allen, "Chief Justice Vinson and the Theory of Constitutional Government...," p. 7.

100. Robert L. Stern and Eugene Gressman, *Supreme Court Practice* (Washington, D. C.: BNA Incorporated, 1962), p. 545. See also pp. 151–93. See also Felix Frankfurter and James M. Landis, *The Business of the Supreme Court* (New York: The Macmillan Company, 1928), pp. 262–87.

101. 330 U.S. 258 (1947).

102. 343 U.S. 579 (1952).

103. 346 U.S. 273 (June 18 Special Term, 1953).

104. 317 U.S. 1 (1942).

105. *Carter v. Carter Coal Co.*, 298 U.S. 238 (1936); *Railroad Retirement*

Board v. Alton R. Co., 295 U.S. 330 (1935); *Rickert Rice Mills v. Fontenot*, 297 U.S. 110 (1936), and *United States v. Bankers Trust*, 294 U.S. 240 (1934).

106. 295 U.S. 330 (1935).
107. 298 U.S. 238 (1936).
108. 297 U.S. 110 (1936).
109. 297 U.S. 1.
110. 297 U.S. at 111.
111. 330 U.S. 258 (1947).
112. 330 U.S. at 284.
113. 330 U.S. at 313.
114. 330 U.S. at 326.
115. 343 U.S. 579 (1952).
116. 343 U.S. at 708. The *Steel Seizure Case* has elicited a substantial body of literature. Prominent works include: R. Alton Lee, *Truman and Taft-Hartley: A Question of Mandate* (Lexington: University of Kentucky Press, 1966); Maeva Marcus, *Truman and the Steel Seizure Case: The Limits of Presidential Power* (New York: Columbia University Press, 1977); Charles Sawyer, *Concerns of a Conservative Democrat* (Carbondale: Southern Illinois Press, 1968); Alan F. Westin, *The Anatomy of a Constitutional Law Case: Youngstown Sheet and Tube Co. v. Sawyer, The Steel Seizure Decision* (New York: Macmillan, 1958).

117. Conference notes by Vinson, Vinson Papers, file "Chief Justice Opinions," Special Collections of the Margaret I. King Library, University of Kentucky, Lexington, Kentucky.

118. *Rosenberg et ux. v. United States*, 346 U.S. 273 (June 18 Special Term, 1953). Explication of the controversial *Rosenberg* case has rarely been objective. The literature is immense and includes: Robert and Michael Meeropol, *We Are Your Sons: The Legacy of Julius and Ethel Rosenberg* (Boston: Houghton Mifflin, 1975); Louis Nizer, *The Implosion Conspiracy* (Garden City, N.Y.: Doubleday, 1973); Ronald Radosh and Joyce Milton, *The Rosenberg File: A Search for Truth* (New York: Holt, Rinehart and Winston, 1983); Malcolm Sharp, *Was Justice Done? The Rosenberg-Sobell Case* (New York: Monthly Review Press, 1956); Morton Sobell, *On Doing Time* (New York: Charles Scribner's Sons, 1974); John Wexley, *The Judgment of Julius and Ethel Rosenberg* (New York: Cameron and Kahn, 1955).

119. 346 U.S. at 312–13.
120. 346 U.S. at 308–9.

121. Memorandum to the Court by Burton, June 15, 1953, Letter to Vinson from Burton, Vinson Papers, file "Chief Justice Opinions," Special Collections of the Margaret I. King Library, University of Kentucky, Lexington, Kentucky.

122. Letter, Frankfurter to John Marshall Harlan, October 23, 1956, Burton Papers, file "Supreme Court," Manuscript Division, Library of Congress, Washington, D. C.

123. 346 U.S. at 296-97.
124. 346 U.S. at 287.
125. William W. Oliver, Oral History Interview, February 26, 1975, Vinson Papers, Special Collections of the Margaret I. King Library, University of Kentucky, Lexington, Kentucky.
126. Letter, Frankfurter to Burton, May 23, 1953, Burton Papers, file "Supreme Court," Manuscript Division, Library of Congress, Washington, D. C.
127. See generally Bernard Schwartz, *The Supreme Court, Constitutional Revolution in Retrospect* (New York: The Ronald Press Company, 1957), pp. 335-41.
128. Willard H. Pedrick, Oral History Interview, October 22, 1976, Vinson Papers, Special Collections of the Margaret I. King Library, University of Kentucky, Lexington, Kentucky.
129. Letter, Frankfurter to Vinson, December 27, 1946, Vinson Papers, Special Collections of the Margaret I. King Library, University of Kentucky, Lexington, Kentucky.
130. Memorandum, January 23, 1950, Frankfurter's Clerk; Letter, Frankfurter, January 24, 1950; Memorandum, Vinson, January 30, 1950; Memorandum, Frankfurter, February 1, 1950; Memorandum, Vinson, February 3, 1950 in which Vinson expressed his opinion that Frankfurter's proposals did not provide "ample protection" to the opposing party; Memorandum, Frankfurter, February 3, 1950 which was offered "not for the pleasure of arguing." Frankfurter defended his proposals, but added, "If the upshot of [my original memorandum] is to introduce the adversary proceeding in the granting of extension of time, I shall indeed rue the day I wrote that memorandum." Vinson Papers, file "Chief Justice Orders," Special Collections of the Margaret I. King Library, University of Kentucky, Lexington, Kentucky.
131. Memorandum, "Suggested Improvements for Disposition of Argued Cases," October 10, 1950, Vinson Papers, file "Chief Justice Orders," Special Collections of the Margaret I. King Library, University of Kentucky, Lexington, Kentucky. Memorandum, Frankfurter, June 1, 1951, and Letter, Frankfurter to Vinson, October 8, 1951 and Vinson's reply, October 11, 1951, Felix Frankfurter Papers, Manuscript Division, Harvard Law School Library, Cambridge, Massachusetts.
132. Letter, Father Wilfred Savard of Vaughn, New Mexico to Vinson, January 2, 1952 and Vinson's reply of January 8, 1952; Letter, Arthur Schlesinger, Jr., to Vinson, February 20 and 21, 1952 and Vinson's reply of March 5, 1952; Vinson Papers, file "Supreme Court Opinions," Special Collections of the Margaret I. King Library, University of Kentucky, Lexington, Kentucky. Religious leaders of both Catholic and Protestant churches were much alarmed by Vinson's words, and readily deduced that he denied the existence of God and of absolute laws for human behavior. Arthur Schlesinger, Jr.,

graciously defended Vinson against accusations made by a protestant leader in the South.

133. Howard J. Trienens, Oral History Interview, Vinson Papers.

134. Conference notes by Burton, Burton Papers, file "Supreme Court," Manuscript Division, Library of Congress, Washington, D. C.

135. W. E. Crutcher, Oral History Interview, January 8, 1975, Vinson Papers, Special Collections of the Margaret I. King Library, University of Kentucky, Lexington, Kentucky.

136. Fred Vinson, Jr., Oral History Interview, May 2, 1973, Vinson Papers, Special Collections of the Margaret I. King Library, University of Kentucky, Lexington, Kentucky.

137. Willard H. Pedrick, Oral History Interview, Vinson Papers.

138. Memorandum, Frankfurter to Vinson, undated, Friday of 1946, Vinson Papers, file "Frankfurter Correspondence," Special Collections of the Margaret I. King Library, University of Kentucky, Lexington, Kentucky.

FIVE

CLARK'S TENURE ON THE COURT

> I respect your conception of the Court's duty as to the disposition of its cases. Mine, which is entitled to like respect, as well as freedom from direct or circuitous pressures, is the opposite. As you say, the Court's judgment, like wine, 'requires seasoning.' But when old wine becomes *too* old, it goes sour. And so in my view it is one thing to give a case 'due deliberation' and quite another to confine it to the 'deep freeze' to be fed up at such later time as suits the whimsey.[1]
>
> Justice Clark to Justice Frankfurter, re: *Scales* dissent, February 8, 1960.

BACKGROUND

Thomas Campbell Clark was born September 23, 1899, in Dallas, Texas to Virginia Maxey Falls Clark and William Henry Clark. Both his father and grandfather had been prominent lawyers.[2] In 1896 his father had served as the fiftieth president of the Texas Bar Association. Clark, born into this heritage, combined pride in the profession with an intense personal dedication to his own work. Speaking to the Texas Bar in 1950, shortly after his appointment to the Supreme Court, he praised "the old-timers [who] were bold and strong in the performance of their duty—advocates who made the pursuit of the law a magnificent venture. It is our good fortune to have been nurtured by them in our profession."[3]

After graduating from high school in Dallas in 1917, Clark attended the Virginia Military Institute in the fall of 1917 for military training and joined the Texas National Guard in 1918, serving briefly in the 153rd Infantry as a sergeant. He enrolled at the University of Texas in 1919 and received his B.A. in 1921 and his LL.B. in 1922. He practiced with his father and brother in their Dallas firm until 1927 when he received his first public service appointment as head of the civil division of the office of District Attorney for Dallas County. He returned to the full-time private practice of law in 1933, but left Dallas in 1937 for Washington and the Justice Department, where he worked until he was appointed to the Supreme Court in 1949.[4] While his positions in government were all appointive, his service did span the legal spectrum: litigation, legislation, law enforcement and judicial.

Clark secured his initial job with the Justice Department as a special attorney under Attorney General Homer S. Cummings through the influence of powerful Texas Senator Tom Connally. Clark had barely arrived in Washington when he was asked to approach Connally about supporting the Roosevelt Court plan. When Clark refused, he was given no work until Chief Justice Hughes called up a backlog of war risk insurance cases and Clark was assigned to try them for the government.[5] Until he became Assistant Attorney General in 1943, Clark worked with cases involving war claims, anti-trust claims, evacuation of alien enemies from the Pacific coast and fraud in defense contracts. In 1942 he coordinated alien enemy control in the Western Defense Command and served as chief civilian officer assisting the Army in relocating Japanese-Americans living in the military zone on the Pacific Coast. Raymond Moley, chief Roosevelt advisor and former Assistant Secretary of State, who was in California at the time of Roosevelt's 1942 evacuation order, noted that Clark handled the relocation job with "firmness, as well as humaneness."[6]

In March of 1943, Clark was named Assistant Attorney General in charge of the Anti-Trust Division, where he served for only six months before being moved to the Criminal Division. As head of this division, he prosecuted those accused under the federal penal code and argued criminal cases for the government before the Supreme Court. Prosecutions against black marketeers, begun when he was in the Criminal Division, were expanded when he became Attorney General to include contractors accused of defrauding the government.[7] As Assistant Attorney General, he directed the work of the War Frauds Unit, working closely with the Truman Committee, often investigating charges prompted by the Committee's findings. Undoubtedly, this association influenced President Truman to appoint him Attorney General in June of 1945 to replace Francis Biddle.[8]

Under his direction as Attorney General, the Justice Department prosecuted 414 cases in the Supreme Court and won 314. Of these cases, 160 were in the anti-trust field.[9] Clark argued before the Vinson Court in the anti-trust case, *United States v. Paramount Pictures, Inc.* (1948)[10] as well as in the seizure case, *United States v. United Mine Workers of America* (1947).[11] He directed the perjury case against Alger Hiss, former State Department official, and the loyalty case against Eugene Dennis and others accused under the Smith Act in *Dennis v. United States* (1951).[12] He filed an historic *amicus curiae* brief in *Shelley v. Kraemer* (1948),[13] in which he detailed the history of the use of racial covenants in the various states and argued the government's position "that judicial enforcement of racially restrictive covenants on real property [was] incompatible with the spirit and the letter of the Constitution and laws of the United States."[14] The Committee on Civil Rights had recommended an increased attack on racially restrictive covenants and Truman had recommended to Clark that this be carried out.[15] Historian Richard Kirkendall called this action by the Justice Department "the beginning of the important part it would play in the civil rights movement in the years that lay ahead."[16]

In fact, the Executive Order creating the President's Committee on Civil Rights, signed by President Truman on December 5, 1946, was largely Clark's work, prepared in response to Truman's suggestion that the Justice Department's individual handling of the lynching cases then under investigation in Tennessee, Georgia and Louisiana was ineffective. Truman wrote Clark that it would "require the inauguration of some sort of policy to prevent such happenings."[17] Clark then drafted the Order setting up the committee, which was instructed to study not only mob violence but also the whole range of issues involving the violation of civil rights. The Committee report, submitted nine months later, on October 29, 1947, entitled *To Secure These Rights*, was, according to Truman's biographer Robert J. Donovan, "a political bombshell that catapulted the civil rights question to the forefront as never before in the twentieth century."[18]

Clark also drafted another historic Executive Order, number 9835, announced by Truman on March 21, 1947 which created a comprehensive and controversial federal loyalty program.[19] As part of this program, he compiled "the first Attorney General's list of dangerous political organizations,"[20] and he actively participated in the administration of other aspects of the loyalty-security program for federal employees. Clark's part in initiating the program prompted his abstention from consideration of loyalty cases heard by the Court during his first years on the bench, *Bailey v. Richardson* (1951)[21] and *Joint Anti-Fascist Refugee Committee v. McGrath* (1951).[22] Loyalty cases were only one group of cases from which Clark initially abstained because of his earlier involvement in the Attorney General's office. He abstained from sitting in 101 cases during his first term; fourteen were decided on the merits and several of the cases were affirmed by an evenly divided court, a fact he stated was "aggravating not only to [him] but to the Court."[23]

With this extensive legal background, Clark began his eighteen year term on the Supreme Court. He found the transition from Attorney General to Justice of the Supreme Court difficult, as had others before him. Justice Jackson thought it required five years to make the transition. Clark explained the difficulty as a result of the great differences in the routine of work of the two positions although he conceded the interrelationship of the jobs. The Justice Department handled government litigation which comprised approximately 34 percent of the Court's docket. Clark noted that the Attorney General and his assistants presented "51 percent of the argued cases."[24] When he resigned in 1967, he did so to facilitate the work of the

Court, as his son, Ramsey Clark, was appointed Attorney General on February 28, 1967. By resigning, he avoided the inherent conflict of interest of a father judging cases being prosecuted by his son.

Clark remained active after his retirement from the Supreme Court. He served on the Courts of Appeals and District Courts by assignment, sitting "on the courts of all eleven circuits, something no other judge ha[d] ever done."[25] The years from his retirement in 1967 until his death in 1977 were described by Chief Justice Warren Burger as filled with activities "aimed at improving justice."[26] Burger noted, among other contributions, Clark's part in creating the National College of the State Judiciary in Reno, Nevada, his work on the project to create Minimum Standards of Criminal Justice and his efforts on the American Bar Association's Committee on Evaluation of Disciplinary Enforcement.

Clark's tenure on the court has been described as a period of "growth."[27] He served only four Court terms under Chief Justice Vinson; the remaining fourteen were served under Chief Justice Earl Warren. He thus had two major adjustments to make, the transition from the Justice Department to the Court and the adjustment from one Chief Justice to another. Clark called the Attorney Generalship a stepping stone rather than a training ground for the Court.[28] When Warren became Chief Justice, the Court's philosophy changed from passive to active. Clark's adjustment continued and his independence increased. Whereas he and Chief Justice Vinson voted together more frequently than not, he and Warren frequently disagreed. Because Clark's tenure was longer than that served by the other Truman appointees, his opinions reflected the changing circumstances both on the Court and in society. University of Texas Professor of Law, Charles Allen Wright, speaking at the memorial services held for Clark by the Supreme Court, noted Clark's "important role in the controversial developments in constitutional law" in the areas of criminal procedure and race relations.[29] Clark often wrote vigorous dissents during the Warren period, although he stood with the majority in many of the epoch-making decisions, personally drafting the majority opinion in *Mapp* which extended the exclusionary rule to the states. Unlike the other Truman appointees, Clark's longer service gave him the opportunity to exercise the judicial approach of self-restraint on a Court which was predominantly judicially active.

JUDICIAL PERFORMANCE

Clark's opinion output included 214 majority opinions, 24 concurrences and 98 dissents.[30] Clark averaged writing 19.67 opinions per year, thus exceeding the average production of the three other Truman appointees: Burton's average of 12.77, Vinson's average of 13 and Minton's average of 15.57. Clark wrote an average of 11.89 majority opinions per year, comparing favorably with the 10.74 yearly average for Justice Frankfurter, and again exceeding the average for the other Truman appointees: Burton's of 7.38, Vinson's of 10.86 and Minton's of 9.43.[31]

Writing in June of 1965, Clark noted the "law explosion" facing the Court. "For example, the case load of the Supreme Court of the United States has increased over threefold since I took my seat there fifteen years ago."[32] Although there was an increase in overall Court productivity during the Warren years, the number of opinions do not support Clark's assertion. In 1949, during Clark's first year, the Court delivered 94 decisions. The figures for majority opinions on the Warren Court ranged from a low of 65 in 1953 to a high of 111 in 1963.[33]

During his tenure, Clark was dedicated to the work of judging, not to ideology. Years later, Ramsey Clark remembered his father as ". . . a wholly constructive human being, a man of giant and gentle strength; a man who work[ed] from morning to night—not for work, or an end in itself[,] [but] [m]eaningful work, well done."[34] A contemporary assessment of Clark's first term on the Court by Professor C. B. Dutton of the Indiana University School of Law found that Clark had "no strong liberal convictions, no anachronistic conservatism, no deep seated philosophy or idealism, no impracticable theories, no impressive scholarship, no flaming prose, no trenchant wit." On that basis he believed, "[T]here is much evidence that Tom Clark may prove to be a good working judge."[35]

In addition to his work on the Court, Clark was a constant advocate for effective judicial administration. John P. Frank, in reviewing his extra-judicial efforts, concluded that "Justice Clark set out to make American justice work better, and he has made it work better. No other single person has ever had so wide a consequence on the administration of justice among the various states."[36]

Clark expressed his concern for a workable legal system in his decisions as well as in his speeches. He conceived the work of the Court to comprehend four areas: (1) judicial review of state legislation; (2) judicial review of federal legislative and executive actions; (3) supervision over procedural problems in federal courts; and (4) protection of individual civil liberties against "encroachment by either federal or state governments."[37] He was aware of the delicate balance to be maintained by the Court vis-à-vis legislative and executive acts. He also regarded the supervisory function of the Court as an option which could be used to avoid reaching constitutional issues and, therefore, he favored basing decisions on procedural grounds.

Clark noted in 1970 that the Court's exercise of review of state legislation had resulted in the nullification of some 800 state laws and local ordinances whereas only 100 acts of Congress had been found unconstitutional. Clark, emphasizing both federalism and a workable system of triune powers, cautioned restraint. He felt that the Court would "indulge in usurpation of power if it allowed its own political, economic and social theories to invalidate appropriate action by the other branches of the federal government or the States." But he emphasized that the Constitution was "a living instrument which also must be construed in a manner to meet the practical necessities of the present" and cautioned that "[j]udicial abnegation must not be permitted to become judicial abdication."[38]

In assessing the Court's role as guardian of civil liberties, Clark recognized that the Constitution placed a check through the Fourteenth Amendment and the Bill of Rights upon the exercise of power by both federal and state governments. He wrote, approvingly, that the

> Fourteenth Amendment's due process clause afforded the Court an opportunity to incorporate the restrictions of some of the Bill of Rights against the States. Since [*Gitlow v. New York* (1952)],[39] the first eight amendments have just about been absorbed by the due process clause of the Fourteenth Amendment.[40]

Clark contributed, sometimes hesitantly, to the incorporation process.

USE OF JUDICIAL RESTRAINT

In his decisions, Clark demonstrated his adherence to a restrained role for the judiciary as well as his appreciation for proper judicial administration in state criminal procedure cases, federal criminal procedure cases, loyalty-security cases and alien rights cases. In these areas, Clark's work, prior to his Supreme Court appointment, obviously had been to further government interests. This emphasis would be carried over to the Court and translated into a philosophy of judicial restraint.

Criminal Procedure Cases

In cases involving state criminal procedure, Clark deferred to state rules of procedure if they reasonably could be sustained.

In *Michel v. State of Louisiana* (1955),[41] three blacks were accused and indicted for rape. The state of Louisiana had a procedural rule requiring that objections to the composition of the grand jury be made three judicial days following the end of the grand jury term. The evidence showed systematic exclusion of blacks from the grand jury panel, but Michel failed to object within the prescribed time. The grand jury term expired on March 2, experienced counsel was appointed March 5, and the motion to quash the indictment was filed on March 9, four days after counsel took the case. Clark, speaking for the majority, reasoned that experienced counsel could and should have contested within the statutorily prescribed time the composition of the jury, but noted, "We do not find that this requirement on its face raises an insuperable barrier to one making claim to federal rights."[42] Clark thought the circumstances supported the test of a reasonable opportunity to be heard. Frankfurter applauded Clark for incorporating his suggestions into the opinion and noted his agreement with the "basis for decision."[43]

In *Reece v. State of Georgia* (1955),[44] the Georgia rule of practice required that a challenge to the composition of the grand jury be made *before* indictment. Amos Reece, a "semi-illiterate Negro of low mentality,"[45] was sentenced to be electrocuted for the rape of a white woman. He had been arrested on October 20, 1953 and was indicted three days later by a grand jury that had been reconvened the day before his arrest pursuant to an "order which did not list him."[46] Local counsel was appointed on October 24 and, on October 30, before arraignment, the motion to quash the indictment was made. A hearing on the motion was held, the motion overruled, and the accused tried, convicted and sentenced on the same day.

Clark, in the majority opinion, ruled that under these circumstances the accused had not had a reasonable opportunity to object to the jury composition. Facts cited by the accused showed that no black had served on a grand jury panel for eighteen years, and that of the 534 names on the grand jury list drawn from an area with a large black population, only six were names of black people. Clark concluded: "This Court over the past fifty years has adhered to the view that valid grand jury selection is a constitutionally protected right."[47] Clark had originally based his decision not only on due process grounds, but also on "an immutable principle of justice."[48] Black conditioned his joining the opinion on the deletion of the latter phrase, asserting that it "sound[ed] too much like a reliance on 'natural law' which ... our constitution did not adopt."[49]

Clark issued a vigorous dissent in another Georgia case in which the accused had not challenged at the proper time the composition of the petit jury. In *Williams v. State of Georgia* (1955),[50] Frankfurter remanded the case of a black male accused and convicted of murder by an all white jury selected from slips colored differently according to race. The accused objected to the composition of the jury in his motion for a new trial. Under Georgia law, objections to the "array" had to be made before the beginning of the trial, "at the threshold," before the "jury is put upon the accused." Clark reasoned:

> While I, too, am not deaf to the condemned, I cannot ignore the long-established precedent of this Court. The proper course, as has always been followed here, is to recognize and honor reasonable state procedure as valid exercises of sovereign power.[51]

In *Edelman v. California* (1953),[52] the petitioner had been convicted under the California Penal Code for vagrancy. On appeal, he alleged the California statute was vague and, hence, unconstitutional. Clark refused to reach the issue of constitutionality, finding that the defense was not raised at trial as procedurally required. Clark found that the Court lacked jurisdiction to rule on requirements of "federal questions... not seasonably raised in accordance with requirements of state law."[53]

Clark registered a vigorous dissent in *Fay et al. v. Noia* (1963)[54] because of the procedural use of habeas corpus. The petitioner failed to perfect his appeal from a conviction of murder according to state procedural requirements. He later filed a petition for habeas corpus from prison. Clark reasoned that by allowing the petitioner to go free, the Court had made

> an abrupt break not only with the Constitution and with the statute, but also with its past decisions, disrupting the delicate balance of federalism, so foremost in the minds of the Founding Fathers and so uniquely important in the field of law enforcement.[55]

Clark feared that a spate of frivolous petitions would be encouraged by the ruling. He deplored the fact that the states' right to develop judicial procedures fell in the struggle for personal liberty and he reasoned that the "Constitution comprehends another struggle of equal importance... the struggle for law and order. [E]ach defeat in that struggle chips away inexorably at the base of that very personal liberty which it seeks to protect."[56] Clark then invoked legislation as the only means of

> restoring the writ of habeas corpus to its proper place in the judicial system. That place is one of great importance—a remedy against illegal restraint but it is not a substitution for or an alternative to appeal, nor is it a burial ground for valid state procedure.[57]

Clark showed a similar respect for Oregon's rule on burden of proof for insanity. Writing for the majority in *Leland v. State of Oregon* (1952),[58] he observed that Oregon was the only state requiring the defense of insanity to be proved beyond a reasonable doubt, a heavier burden than that required by other states or by the federal rules. Quoting Frankfurter's emphasis on "an alert deference to the judgment of the state court under review,"[59] Clark refused to rewrite or strike down the state's rule. Frankfurter, dissenting, mentioned the gulf between "deference to local legislation and complete disregard for the duty of judicial review,"[60] and found that the Oregon rule violated due process guarantees.

Clark deferred to the procedures of local police officers in two cases decided in 1958, and throughout his tenure, he consistently maintained this approach, eventually dissenting in the celebrated and seemingly definitive *Miranda v. Arizona* (1966).[61] In *Payne v. State of Arkansas* (1958),[62] a nineteen-year-old black was arrested with no warrant, denied a hearing, not advised of his right to remain silent or of his right to counsel, held incommunicado for three days, denied food and physically threatened. The majority found that his confession was coerced. Clark dissented, finding the confession voluntary, and relying on the belief that there was "sufficient other evidence of guilt to sustain the conviction."[63] Black's handwritten note to Clark about his dissent in the *Payne* case revealed the different concepts each held about the judicial role:

> You have strong grounds for your dissent on the *facts*—you also have strong *logical* grounds for your objections to consider the coercion point for failure of counsel to raise the constitutional objection below. But I venture to suggest that your dissent on this ground will give many people a wrong view of you—This defendant is sentenced to death. A majority of your Brethren think... he was convicted in a trial that violated his constitutional rights. If you *believed* that I think you would hesitate about letting him die solely because his lawyer failed properly to raise his constitutional point below.... I believe your procedural ground if published will do you a great injustice. I cannot help but believe that you agree that no appellate review rule is so *rigid* that it need not yield where its unbending application has to result in an unconstitutional execution.[64]

In *Crooker v. State of California* (1958),[65] Clark upheld the murder conviction of one who was refused counsel and not told of his right to remain silent. Clark reasoned that because the man was college-educated with one year of law school, the police tactics were not overreaching and the confession was voluntary.

When, eight years later, the majority found that Ernesto Miranda's confession after a two-hour interrogation was coerced,[66] Clark dissented, fearing a decrease in the number of convictions. But in 1971, he admitted that he had been wrong:

> The Court handed down *Miranda*, which set up four 'musts' that the police must afford one in custody before they can interrogate him.... Frankly, it looked as if there would be some troubles from *Miranda*. It might decrease the number of convictions [b]ut that conclusion has not proven true.... Today, because of *Miranda*, a police officer does not stop investigating when he obtains a confession. He knows that confessions are suspect.... Today... we have much better criminal detection than before *Miranda*.[67]

While on the bench, Clark, however, continued to defer to the criminal detection system. His interest in law enforcement developed before his tenure, continued during it and extended into his retirement. He deferred to reasonable state and local laws and procedures. His initial perception of the reasonableness of the *Miranda* rule was tempered by his law enforcement orientation.

Clark, nevertheless, showed a sensitivity to the assertions of unreasonable search and seizure advanced by the accused in state courts. Clark was in favor of applying the Fourth Amendment to the state as well as to the federal court systems. In federal cases, the exclusionary rule applied. In state cases, evidence illegally obtained could be introduced in court. In *Irvine v. California* (1954),[68] evidence obtained by an unreasonable search was allowed to support the conviction of the accused. Clark joined the majority, following the precedent of *Wolf v. Colorado* (1949),[69] which had confined the exclusionary rule to federal cases. He commented, "It is with reluctance that I follow *Wolf*. Perhaps strict adherence to the tenor of that decision may produce needed converts for its extinction."[70] In an uncirculated memorandum of February, 1954 shown only to Jackson, Clark argued against accepting "lawlessness on the part of the police as a solution to the lawlessness of the criminal."[71] He presented a sustained seven-page argument for extending the exclusionary rule to the states.[72]

In *Mapp v. Ohio* (1961),[73] police in Cleveland, searching for a fugitive, forcefully entered a house without a warrant. While there, they found obscene materials which led to the state court conviction of a Miss Mapp. Clark, seven years after his opinion in *Irvine*, delivered the majority opinion extending the exclusionary rule to the state courts. John Marshall Harlan objected to Clark's reasoning and would have decided the *Mapp* case on the rationale that the state law proscribing the obscene material was an attempt "at thought control" under the Fourteenth Amendment.[74] He concluded, "Your opinion comes perilously close to accepting 'incorporation' for the Fourth Amendment, and will doubtless encourage the 'incorporation' enthusiasts."[75] Clark, having redefined *Wolf*, described the "gist" of the opinion to Black, that "*Wolf* held the entire Fourth Amendment to be carried over against the states through the Fourteenth, and therefore the exclusionary rule which *Weeks* applied to federal cases must likewise be made applicable to state prosecutions."[76] In his opinion, Clark emphasized the enforcement problems:

> Under the double standard, federal prosecutors step[ped] across the street to the State's attorney with their unconstitutionally seized evidence. Prosecution on the basis of that evidence was then had in a state court in utter disregard of the enforceable Fourth Amendment.[77]

A similar dichotomy existed in the state and federal courts' acknowledgement of an indigent's right to counsel in capital and non-capital cases. Under *Johnson v. Zerbst* (1938),[78] the Sixth Amendment and Rule 44 of the Federal Rules of Criminal Procedure (adopted in 1946), this right existed in federal courts.[79] Clark voted with the majority in *Gideon v. Wainwright* (1963)[80] to make the same right to counsel available in state courts. Clarence Earl Gideon was convicted without benefit of counsel of breaking and entering with intent to commit a misdemeanor under a Florida state law which required appointment of counsel only in capital cases. The *Gideon* decision extended the protection of the Sixth Amendment to state defendants, erasing another double standard. Propounding that "[t]here is nothing more important in our system of government than the effective administration of criminal justice," Clark, in an address at St. John's University School of Law on April 2, 1966, discussed the difficulties posed by the *Gideon* ruling. "The assigned-counsel problem facing the courts is reaching insurmountable proportions, ... adequate representation of indigents is not presently afforded."[81]

Although Clark favored the use of the exclusionary rule in both state and federal courts, his tendency to find a violation of the Fourth Amendment was tempered by his appreciation for the problem of law enforcement. He described his approach in *United States v. Jeffers* (1951).[82] "[T]he mandate of the Amendment requires adherence to the judicial process. . . . [It] does not place an unduly oppressive weight on law enforcement officers but merely interposes an orderly procedure."[83] Clark reasoned that the evidence obtained without a warrant in this case should be suppressed as no exceptional circumstances existed to "abrogate the necessity" of obtaining a warrant.

In *Breithaupt v. Abram* (1956),[84] Clark spoke for the majority and allowed evidence, a blood sample disclosing 17 percent alcohol content which had been taken from an unconscious driver involved in an accident in which three people were killed. Clark applied the balancing test: "As against the right of an individual that his person be held inviolable . . . must be set the interests of society in the scientific determination of intoxication, one of the great causes of mortal hazards on the road."[85] The trio of Warren, Black and Douglas dissented, describing the police methods as repulsive. Clark's conclusions rested on his refusal to impute overreaching motives to the police and his observation that the sample was taken without violence or force. Both Frankfurter and Burton proposed sentences to be incorporated into Clark's opinion. Frankfurter offered to write a concurrence but preferred Clark to incorporate his ideas.[86] Frankfurter also encouraged Clark to refute Douglas's emphasis on the brutality of the procedure, "You should enlarge on the point I tried to make—namely the fair assumption that an obedient citizen would consent to have a blood test made as part of the sensible and civilized system of protecting him. . . . "[87]

In *Giordenello v. United States* (1958),[88] Clark expressed his view of the limited role of the court in cases on review. The majority excluded the heroin obtained during a warranted search because of a defect in the complaint signed by the officer pursuant to the issuance of the warrant. The officer had not stated that he had personal knowledge that heroin was being concealed; he merely stated the conclusion. The Court raised the issue of the sufficiency of the complaint *sua sponte*, on its own motion. Clark dissented: "I cannot agree to . . . free another narcotics peddler, this time on the ground that the complaint did not provide a sufficient basis upon which a finding of probable cause [for the search] could be made."[89] Clark reasoned that the arrest was valid under state law and deplored the Court's reliance for reversal on a point not raised on appeal by the petitioner. "Such purblindness may set the petitioner free, but it shackles law enforcement."[90]

Clark's deference to executive and legislative fact-finding procedures was expressed in three cases. In *Roviaro v. United States* (1957),[91] the majority through Burton held that the government's refusal to reveal the identity of an undercover agent was prejudicial error, noting that the privilege to withhold identity was limited by "fundamental requirements of fairness."[92] Clark's dissent lamented "the destructive effect which this conclusion [would] have on the enforcement of the narcotics laws."[93] He found that the record showed that the informant and the accused knew each other well and he considered the accused's objection a ruse:

> A casual reading of the record paints a picture of one vainly engaging in trial tactics rather than searching for real defenses—shadowboxing with the prosecution in a baseless attempt to get a name that he already had but in reality hoping to get a reversible error.... We should not encourage such tactics.[94]

In *Watkins v. United States* (1957),[95] the majority found that the petitioner, appealing from a conviction for contempt of Congress, could refuse to answer questions not deemed pertinent to the scope of the inquiry. John T. Watkins, appearing before a subcommittee of the House Committee on UnAmerican Activities, refused to answer questions concerning former communists, claiming that the matter was irrelevant to the Committee's work. Clark, believing the questions pertinent, expressed in dissent his dismay over the Court's

> mischievous curbing of the informing function of Congress.... So long as the object of a legislative inquiry is legitimate... the questions pertinent,... it is not for the courts to interfere with the committee system of inquiry.... The majority has substituted the judiciary as the grand inquisitor and supervisor of congressional investigations.[96]

In *Jencks v. United States* (1957),[97] Clark registered a dissent to Justice Brennan's majority ruling that the accused was entitled to access to the F.B.I. oral and written reports filed by two government witnesses who testified against him. He noted that the new rule of evidence pronounced by the Court would thwart the government's prosecution of criminal actions. His appeal to Congress for laws to prevent the effect of the holding was more than deference to legislation, it was deference to the legislature, and it was prompted by his belief that:

those intelligence agencies of our Government engaged in law enforcement may as well close up shop, for the Court has opened their files to the criminal and thus afforded him a Roman holiday for rummaging through confidential information as well as vital national secrets.[98]

C. Herman Pritchett discussed Clark's dissent as adding fuel in the last half of the decade of the fifties to the exaggerated charges being made against the Court. By its ruling, the Court had allowed Jencks, accused of perjury for falsely swearing he was not a communist, access to reports made to the F.B.I. by the two government witnesses who were Communist Party members paid by the F.B.I. to report on communist activities. Pritchett noted that the many requests for legislative action "failed in every case but one to stampede the Congress into an immediate legislative response," and that the Senate while considering the Jencks Bill parlayed the proddings of the Justice Department and "substantially modified the language which the Attorney General proposed."[99]

John P. Frank emphasized the significance of this Congressional modification.[100] He saw *Jencks* as a probable "bench mark" in the end of repression and the legislation as an outgrowth of a battle lost by "the forces of extreme reaction." He explained that, in the Senate, Senator Sam Ervin of North Carolina and Senator Frank O'Mahoney of Wyoming joined to endorse legislation to *preserve* the rule announced by the Court in *Jencks*. "Legislation, in support of the opinion and not against it, became law."[101]

Loyalty-Security Cases

Clark expressed the sentiment undergirding his decisions in the loyalty-security cases in *Rosenberg et ux. v. United States* (1953):[102]

> Our liberty is maintained only so long as justice is secure. To permit judicial processes to be used to obstruct the course of justice destroys our freedom. . . . Though the penalty is great and our responsibility heavy, our duty is clear.[103]

Clark agreed with the other three Truman appointees in the disposition of the *Rosenberg* case. He found significance in the fact that the case had been before the Court seven times, and he reasoned that "[w]here Congress by more than one statute proscribe[d] a private course of conduct, the Government may choose to invoke either applicable law"[104] unless the later act repealed the earlier one. The Atomic Energy Act, "instead of repealing the penalty provisions of the Espionage Act, in fact, preserve[d] them in undiminished force."[105] Clark reasoned further that the attempt to prosecute under the Atomic Energy Act would have been an attempt to apply an act *ex post facto*, as the defendant's alleged crimes occurred before Congress passed the 1947 Act.

Clark's participation in the preparation of the state's case prosecuting Dennis and other leaders of the Communist Party precluded his sitting in the case when it came before the Court, *Dennis v. United States* (1951).[106] In *Yates v. United States* (1957),[107] which effectively overruled *Dennis*, his dissent expressed his belief that the Court should have considered the *Dennis* holding controlling. Oleta O'Connor Yates, California State Secretary of the Communist Party, and thirteen others were accused of violating the Smith Act. The Court acquitted five of the accused and remanded for retrial the other nine. The majority reasoned that the Smith Act's proscription of advocacy to overthrow required not abstract argument (as held in *Dennis*) but overt action. Clark reasoned that the accused in *Yates* "served in the same army and were engaged in the same mission"[108] as those accused in *Dennis*. He chided the Court for "usurping the functions of the jury"[109] in its review and reassessment of the facts, thus emphasizing the judicial restraint maxim that cases are to be reviewed on the law only. Clark predicted that "The decision today prevents for all time any prosecution of Party members under [subparagraph 371 of] the Act."[110]

In *Uphaus v. Wyman* (1959),[111] the accused was prosecuted under the New Hampshire Subversives Act of 1951 for failure to furnish the list of guests attending the World Fellowship Camp. Clark, in the majority opinion sustaining the conviction, reasoned that the Smith Act superseded state sedition laws but did not preempt the field. States could still investigate and prosecute sedition against the state itself. Clark found "the governmental interest in self-preservation... sufficiently compelling to subordinate the interest in associational privacy of persons."[112] The state needed the list to determine "the presence of subversives in the state,"[113] and the facts indicated a nexus between the Attorney General's list and some persons known to have been at the camp.

Clark dissented when the Court refused on technical grounds to review a case on the merits brought under the Internal Security (McCarran) Act of 1950, *Communist Party of the United States v. Subversive Activities Control Board* (1955).[114] Frankfurter, exercising judicial restraint, remanded the case for consideration of the credentials of a witness, and was chided by Clark for refusing to decide the constitutional issues presented. Calling the Act "the bulwark of the Congressional program to combat the menace of world communism,"[115] Clark charged that the Court has disregarded its duty.

As Attorney General, Clark had endorsed the loyalty oath requirements of persons in federal employment. As a justice, he was to endorse the loyalty oaths required by other levels of government. In *Garner et al. v. Board of*

Public Works of Los Angeles (1951),[116] Clark upheld a loyalty oath required by the City of Los Angeles, reasoning that the loyalty of city employees might "prove relevant to their fitness and suitability for the public service. Past conduct may well relate to present fitness: past loyalty may have a reasonable relationship to present and future trust."[117] Failing to see the punishment inherent in a job qualification requirement, Clark reasoned that the sanction aspect of a bill of attainder was absent.

However, in *Slochower v. Board of Higher Education of the City of New York* (1956),[118] Clark struck down the dismissal of a German professor at Brooklyn College who had invoked the Fifth Amendment before a federal committee some twelve years before his discharge. Clark reasoned: "[W]e must condemn the practice of imputing a sinister meaning to the exercise of a person's constitutional right under the Fifth Amendment."[119] Frankfurter, who made numerous suggestions and corrections during the drafting of the *Slochower* decision, expressed his approval in March, writing Clark, "I think your *Slochower* opinion will have [a] very wholesome effect, without impairing the effective control by states of their servants."[120] Frankfurter, however, meticulously continued to make suggestions. In May, suspecting that the Court might be "open to a public attack," he suggested that a "controvertible, if not inaccurate" statement be deleted.[121] The carefully drawn opinion which Clark wrote did not deny the city's right to inquire into the loyalty of its employees, but found that the law "operate[d] to discharge every city employee who invoked the Fifth Amendment . . . " thereby making the invocation "equivalent either to a confession of guilt or a conclusive presumption of perjury."[122] Clark had shown a similar concern about imputed guilt earlier in *Weiman v. Updegraff* (1952)[123] when he struck down the loyalty oath required of faculty members in an Oklahoma state school because the oath did not require *scienter*, the defendant's guilty knowledge. He reasoned that under such an oath, "the fact of association alone determines disloyalty and disqualification; it matters not whether association existed innocently or knowingly."[124]

In *Cole v. Young* (1956),[125] the majority held that a federal employee could not be dismissed from his job as a food and drug inspector because of his membership in Nature Friends of America, an organization on the Attorney General's list, without showing that the employee's job was a sensitive one. The accused was convicted under Executive Order 10450 which amended the Executive Order 9835 drafted by Clark. Clark argued in his dissent that under such a test the government could become "honeycombed with subversive employees." Citing the legislative history of the Summary Suspension Act (1950),[126] and supporting the extension of presidential authority to remove disloyal employees in all federal government agencies, Clark reasoned that the Court's order struck "down the most effective weapon against subversive activities available to the Government."[127] He contended that the Court should defer to the legislation which gave the president discretion in the area of national security and not "intrude itself into presidential policy making."[128]

Alien Rights Cases

Clark's opinions dealing with the rights of aliens in deportation proceedings evidenced both a deference to the authority of the executive branch to act as provided by legislation and also a tendency to interpret the legislation as a grant of unlimited authority.

In *Marcello v. Bonds* (1955),[129] Clark for the majority ruled that the petitioner was not entitled to a hearing before deportation because the hearing provisions available under the Administrative Procedure Act were superseded by the subsequent Immigration and Naturalization Act of 1952. Exercising judicial restraint, he did not reach the constitutional issue of due process. The petitioner had been convicted for a marijuana violation which provided grounds for his deportation under the subsequent act. In their dissent, Justices Frankfurter, Black and Douglas reasoned that the subsequent act saved the hearing procedures of the earlier act. They emphasized that the petitioner, who had entered the United States at age eleven, had four children and a wife in the United States. "It is settled," they concluded, "that [the petitioner] cannot be deported without being accorded a fair hearing in accordance with the Due Process Clause of the Fifth Amendment."[130]

Clark delivered the majority opinion in *Shaughnessy v. United States ex rel. Mezei* (1953)[131] holding that Mezei could lawfully be excluded from the United States without a hearing under the emergency regulations promulgated pursuant to the Passport Act. Mezei, having lived in the United States some twenty-five years, left the country for nineteen months. When he sought to reenter the United States, he was "stopped at the border" and denied entry. Clark termed his being there "temporary harborage, an act of legislative grace... [which] bestow[ed] no additional rights."[132] Clark reasoned:

> [T]he times being what they are, Congress may well have felt that ... an alien in respondent's position is no more ours than [another country's];... [R]espondent's right to enter the United States depends on the Congressional will, and courts cannot substitute their judgment for the legislative mandate.[133]

Clark treated the question as a political one outside the purview of the judiciary. "Courts have long recognized the power to expel or exclude aliens as a fundamental sovereign attribute exercised by the Government's political departments, largely immune from judicial control."[134]

In *Heikkila v. Barber* (1953),[135] Clark wrote the majority opinion, with

Justices Black and Frankfurter dissenting. Heikkila sought to have the order of deportation reviewed and prayed for an injunction and declaratory relief. Clark reasoned that the Attorney General's decision for deportation under the Immigration Act was final and that judicial review was precluded by the statute. He buttressed his opinion with "a quarter of a century of consistent judicial interpretation."[136] "We are advised that the government has recommended legislation which would permit what Heikkila has tried here. But the choice is not ours."[137]

The only remedy available to contest the deportation order was habeas corpus, but this remedy was available only to aliens "within the country." Aliens stopped at the border or on parole awaiting determination of admissibility could not stop deportation proceedings. Clark wrote the majority opinions so holding in the two 1958 cases, *Leng May Ma v. Barber* (1958)[138] and *Rogers v. Quan* (1958).[139]

The Court reviewed a petition for habeas corpus in *United States ex rel. Accardi v. Shaughnessy* (1954).[140] The petition was denied by the district court. The alien had been ordered deported and appealed the decision to the Board of Immigration Appeals which affirmed the deportation order. Before the appeal hearing, the Attorney General had circulated a list of undesirable aliens whom he wished to have deported. Petitioner's name was on the list. Sending the case back for a hearing, Clark reasoned, "We think the petition for habeas corpus charges the Attorney General with precisely what the regulations forbid him to do: dictating the Board's decision."[141]

On remand, the District Court affirmed the Board's decision. Accardi appealed the District Court ruling and Clark, in the subsequent case (1955),[142] affirmed the deportation order on the basis that Accardi had not established the fact that the Board relied on the list.

ASSESSMENT

The assumption that Clark's long tenure on the Supreme Court allowed him to grow does not obscure the fact that his judicial approach remained the same. Clark continued to apply the various tenets of judicial restraint in different cases during his decision-making career. He decided the alien cases on statutory grounds, not reaching the constitutional issues. He deferred to legislative and executive actions when an issue could be considered political. He deferred to the wisdom of the legislature and tried not to substitute his opinion for the legislators'. He insisted that lower court remedies be exhausted and that points on appeal be made in a procedurally correct manner. He thought review of the facts not within the purview of the Court. He did not impute improper motives to the lawmakers or to the law enforcers.

Clark took one of the judicial restraint maxims and made it distinctively his own.[143] Abraham noted that "the Supreme Court of the United States has never held itself absolutely bound by its precedents."[144] Clark, basically a law and order man, rigidly followed precedent. When he wrote an opinion, such as *Mapp* which overruled precedent, he was motivated by a dedication to order. *Mapp* brought a more orderly administration of justice by synchronizing state and federal rules of practice. Clark dissented in cases such as *Miranda*, but when *Miranda* became the ruling case, the established precedent, Clark followed it.

Clark was aware of the inadequacies inherent in the judicial system. This is most evident in his later work urging reform. In *Breithaupt* (1956),[145] he had voted to uphold what the dissenters felt were unconstitutional police tactics to extract evidence from an unconscious inebriated driver. Later in 1972 Clark, urging reform of the criminal justice system, advocated medical care for criminals whose crimes were related to habitual alcoholism. He believed the solution to criminal justice problems rested with all three branches of government and he defended the Court's role in the process. He also disputed the correlation of the crime wave with Supreme Court decisions, noting the limited role played by the Court: "My extensive experience in the criminal field leads me to speculate that *Miranda* and *Mapp* have an effect on less than one-half of one percent of all crimes committed."[146]

His decisions revealed not only a keen sense of the limits of judicial power, but also a great respect for the law: "To perform the judicial function, the Founders created a human institution, the members of which are 'in endless error hurled.' "[147] Clark therefore participated in the deliberative process in an assertive manner. He was sufficiently firm in his convictions, but he also sought help from his colleagues. Charles Reed, Clark's law clerk in 1968, called him a "very effective judicial politician" with a keen sense of the collegial nature of the Court. Reed noted by 1968, Clark was able to forge opinions among the justices who were divided by emphasizing the points on which they agreed.[148]

Clark worked hard to accomplish judicially competent work. In 1952, Frankfurter responded to Clark's request for suggestions for reading material. He urged Clark to read the opinions of Holmes and Brandeis, the "one" essay by Thayer in the *Harvard Law Review*, the Fourteenth Amendment study by Charles Fairman in the *Stanford Law Review*, and other works by Paul Freund, M. W. Fuller, "etc. etc."[149] Frankfurter closed his homiletic epistle with some reflections on the *Steel Seizure Case*. For Frankfurter the "most significant thing" about the case was its meaning

> to thoughtful people who are fairly to be called "liberal"—New Dealers and Fair Dealers. [I]t vindicated and restored their faith in law. They feared our Court was just like Hitler's court, Stalin's court and Peron's court, merely a political agency of the government. And you, more than anyone else proved the Court's independence. From the point of view of wisdom, as against the shortsightedness of the

moment, [The Chief Justice], instead of making it hard for you, should have respected and admired your independence.[150]

Clark's Supreme Court career primarily reflected not growth but consistency—consistency in his dedication to finding the best workable solution to the problems presented in the case before him. Growth was consequently inevitable.

NOTES

1. Letter, Clark to Frankfurter, February 8, 1960, Clark Papers, file "Frankfurter Correspondence," Rare and Special Collections, Tarlton Law Library, University of Texas, Austin, Texas.

2. Anna Rothe, ed., *Current Biography, 1945* (New York: H. W. Wilson Co., 1946), p. 107. Clark used Tom exclusively as his first name. The Tarlton Law Library honors this practice.

3. Tom C. Clark, "Dynamic Process," 13 *Texas Bar Journal* 409 (1950).

4. Rothe, ed., *Current Biography*, p. 108.

5. Tom Clark, Oral History Interview, August, 1977, pp. 38–39; October 17, 1972; and February 8, 1973. Harry S. Truman Library. Independence, Missouri.

6. Raymond Moley, "New Faces in the Cabinet," *Newsweek*, June 4, 1945, p. 116, col. 2. Moley predicted that Clark's ability to work with people, to "gain the respect and liking of all parties to disputes," would serve the Truman administration well and improve relations between business and government.

7. Ibid., pp. 108–10.

8. Robert J. Donovan, *Conflict and Crisis, The Presidency of Harry S. Truman, 1945–1948* (New York: W. W. Norton and Company, 1977), p. 29.

9. *The National Cyclopaedea*, current series, vol. H, p. 21.

10. 334 U.S. 131 (1948).

11. 330 U.S. 258 (1947).

12. 341 U.S. 494 (1951). Richard Kirkendall, "Tom C. Clark," Leon Friedman and Fred L. Israel, eds. *The Justices of the Supreme Court, 1789–1969, Their Lives and Major Opinions*, vol. 4 (New York: Chelsea House, 1969), p. 2666.

13. 334 U.S. 1 (1948).

14. Tom C. Clark and Philip B. Perlman, *Prejudice and Property, An Historic Brief Against Racial Covenants* (Washington, D. C.: Public Affairs Press, 1948), p. 22. This brief illustrates the beginning of the Justice Department's participation in suits involving civil rights.

15. Robert J. Donovan, *The Tumultuous Years, The Presidency of Harry S Truman, 1949–1953* (New York: W.W. Norton and Company, 1982), p. 335 n. 9.

16. Kirkendall, "Tom C. Clark," p. 2666.

17. Truman to Clark, September 20, 1946, letter quoted in Robert J. Donovan, *Conflict and Crisis*, p. 245.

18. Donovan, *Conflict and Crisis*, p. 332. See generally pp. 332–37.

19. Paul L. Murphy, *The Constitution in Crisis Times* (Evanston: Harper and Row, 1972), p. 256.

20. Kirkendall, "Tom C. Clark," p. 2666.

21. 341 U.S. 918 (1951).

22. 341 U.S. 123 (1951).

23. Tom C. Clark, "Reminiscences of an Attorney General Turned Associate Justice," 6 *Houston Law Review* 623, 627 (1969).

24. Clark also listed other former Attorneys General named to the Court: Roger B. Taney (1835), Nathan Clifford (1848), Joseph McKenna (1898), William H. Moody (1906), James McReynolds (1914), Harlan Fiske Stone (1925), Frank Murphy (1940) and Robert Jackson (1941). Clark, "Reminiscences of an Attorney General," p. 626.

25. Chief Justice Burger and Ramsey Clark, "Tributes to Tom C. Clark," 63 *American Bar Association Journal* 1105, 1106 (1977).

26. Ibid., p. 1107.

27. Kirkendall, "Tom C. Clark," p. 2676.

28. Clark, "Reminiscences of an Attorney General," p. 626.

29. Charles Alan Wright, "Remarks," *In Memoriam: Honorable Tom C. Clark, Associate Justice: Supreme Court of the United States*, January 23, 1978, p. 18.

30. Albert P. Blaustein and Roy M. Mersky, *The First One Hundred Justices* (Hamden, Conn.: The Shoe String Press, Inc., 1978), p. 146.

31. Ibid., p. 149.

32. Tom C. Clark, "Citizens, Courts, and the Effective Administration of Justice," 49 *Journal of American Judicature Society* 6 (1965).

33. Blaustein and Mersky, *The First One Hundred Justices*, pp. 140–41.

34. Burger and Clark, "Tributes to Tom C. Clark," p. 1105.

35. C. B. Dutton, "Mr Justice Tom C. Clark," 26 *Indiana Law Journal* 169, 184 (1951).

36. John P. Frank, "Justice Tom Clark and Judicial Administration," 46 *Texas Law Review* 5, 56 (1967).

37. Tom C. Clark, "The Court and Its Function," 34 *Albany Law Review* 497, 500–501 (1970).

38. Ibid., p. 501.

39. 268 U.S. 652 (1925).

40. Clark, "The Court and Its Function," p. 501.

41. 350 U.S. 91 (1955).

42. 350 U.S. at 93.

43. Marginal note, Frankfurter on opinion circulated November 30, 1955, Clark Papers, file "Supreme Court Case," Rare and Special Collections, Tarlton Law Library, University of Texas, Austin, Texas.

44. 350 U.S. 85 (1955).
45. 350 U.S. at 89.
46. 350 U.S. at 89.
47. 350 U.S. at 87.
48. Opinion circulated November 25, 1955, p. 5, Clark Papers, file "Supreme Court Case," Rare and Special Collections, Tarlton Law Library, University of Texas, Austin, Texas.
49. Note, Black to Clark, December 1, 1955, requesting changes on pages 2 and 5, Clark Papers, file "Supreme Court Case," Rare and Special Collections, Tarlton Law Library, University of Texas, Austin, Texas.
50. 349 U.S. 375 (1955).
51. 349 U.S. at 393.
52. 344 U.S. at 357 (1953).
53. 344 U.S. at 358.
54. 372 U.S. 391 (1963).
55. 372 U.S. at 445.
56. 372 U.S. at 447.
57. 372 U.S. at 447.
58. 343 U.S. 790 (1952).
59. 343 U.S. at 799.
60. 343 U.S. at 807.
61. 384 U.S. 436 (1966).
62. 356 U.S. 560 (1958).
63. 356 U.S. at 569.
64. Memorandum (6 pages), Black to Clark, undated, Clark Papers, file "Supreme Court Case," Rare and Special Collections, Tarlton Law Library, University of Texas, Austin, Texas.
65. 357 U.S. 433 (1958).
66. 384 U.S. 436 (1966).
67. Tom C. Clark, "Justice Ye Shall Pursue," 38 *Tennessee Law Review* 481, 483–84 (1971).
68. 347 U.S. 128 (1954).
69. 338 U.S. 25 (1949).
70. 377 U.S. at 139. Frankfurter tried to convince Clark that *Wolf* did not control in the *Irvine* case, that there "was conduct by the police . . . which went way beyond not having a search warrant for the assailed evidence." Letter, Frankfurter to Clark, December 29, 1953, Felix Frankfurter Papers, file "Clark Correspondence," Manuscript Division, Library of Congress, Washington, D. C.
71. Memorandum (uncirculated), Clark to Court of February 1954, p. 1, Clark Papers, file "Supreme Court Case," Rare and Special Collections, Tarlton Law Library, University of Texas, Austin, Texas.
72. Memorandum (uncirculated), Clark to Court of February 1954.
73. 367 U.S. 643 (1961).

74. Letter, John Marshall Harlan to Clark, May 1, 1961, p. 1, Clark Papers, file "Supreme Court Case," Rare and Special Collections, Tarlton Law Library, Austin, Texas.

75. Ibid., p. 4.

76. Memorandum, Clark to Black, June 15, 1961, Clark Papers, file "Supreme Court Case," Rare and Special Collections, Tarlton Law Library, Austin, Texas. See also Letter, Black to Clark, June 15, 1961, in which Black insisted that the Fourth Amendment as a "whole" was to be held applicable against the states.

77. 367 U.S. at 658.

78. 304 U.S. 458 (1938).

79. See generally Tom C. Clark, "The Sixth Amendment and the Law of the Land," 8 *St. Louis University Law Journal* 1 (1963).

80. 372 U.S. 335 (1963).

81. Tom C. Clark, "Counsel for the Indigent Defendant," 41 *St. John's Law Review* 1, 2 (1972). This problem has not been solved. Asserting that "[t]he glorious trumpeting of equal justice through the right to counsel has been muted by insufficient funding," Chester Fairlie called attention to the national crisis in indigent defense in the article, "Gideon's Muted Trumpet," 69 *American Bar Association Journal* 172 (February 1983).

82. 342 U.S. 48 (1951).

83. 342 U.S. at 51.

84. 352 U.S. 432 (1956).

85. 352 U.S. at 439.

86. Frankfurter to Clark, February 14, 1957, Clark Papers, file "Supreme Court Case," Rare and Special Collections, Tarlton Law Library, University of Texas, Austin, Texas.

87. Frankfurter to Clark, February 6, 1957, Clark Papers, file "Supreme Court Case," Rare and Special Collections, Tarlton Law Library, University of Texas, Austin, Texas.

88. 357 U.S. 480 (1958).

89. 357 U.S. at 489.

90. 357 U.S. at 492.

91. 353 U.S. 53 (1957).

92. 353 U.S. at 60.

93. 353 U.S. at 66.

94. 353 U.S. at 67.

95. 354 U.S. 178 (1957).

96. 354 U.S. at 217.

97. 353 U.S. 657 (1957).

98. 353 U.S. at 681.

99. C. Herman Pritchett, *Congress Versus the Supreme Court, 1957–1960* (New York: Da Capo Press, 1973), pp. 120–21.

100. John P. Frank, *The Marble Palace* (New York: Alfred A. Knopf, 1972), pp. 192–95.
101. Ibid., p. 195.
102. 346 U.S. 273 (1953).
103. 346 U.S. at 296.
104. 346 U.S. at 294.
105. 346 U.S. at 294.
106. 341 U.S. 494 (1951).
107. 354 U.S. 298 (1957).
108. 354 U.S. at 345.
109. 354 U.S. at 346.
110. 354 U.S. at 349.
111. 360 U.S. 72 (1959).
112. 360 U.S. at 81.
113. 360 U.S. at 78.
114. 351 U.S. 115 (1955).
115. 351 U.S. at 127.
116. 341 U.S. 716 (1951).
117. 341 U.S. at 720.
118. 350 U.S. 551 (1956).
119. 350 U.S. at 557.
120. Marginal note, Frankfurter to Clark on opinion circulated March 28, 1956, Clark Papers, file "Supreme Court Case," Rare and Special Collections, Tarlton Law Library, University of Texas, Austin, Texas.
121. Letter, Frankfurter to Clark, May 21, 1956, Clark Papers, file "Supreme Court Case," Rare and Special Collections, Tarlton Law Library, University of Texas, Austin, Texas.
122. 350 U.S. at 557.
123. 344 U.S. 183 (1952).
124. 344 U.S. at 191.
125. 351 U.S. 536 (1956).
126. 64 Stat., 476 (1950).
127. 351 U.S. at 569.
128. 351 U.S. at 567.
129. 349 U.S. 302 (1955).
130. 349 U.S. at 315.
131. 345 U.S. at 206 (1953).
132. 345 U.S. at 215.
133. 345 U.S. at 216.
134. 345 U.S. at 210.
135. 345 U.S. 229 (1953).
136. 345 U.S. at 234.
137. 345 U.S. at 237.

138. 357 U.S. 185 (1958).
139. 357 U.S. 193 (1958).
140. 347 U.S. 260 (1954).
141. 347 U.S. at 267.
142. 349 U.S. 28 (1955).

143. Dennis Daniel Dorin called Clark's refusal to dissent after one term from an overruling case a "no subsequent dissent rule." Dennis Daniel Dorin, "Mr. Justice Clark and State Criminal Justice" (Ph.D. dissertation, University of Virginia, 1974), p. 4. The "rule" is a variation on a consistent theme, Clark's rigid adherence to precedent practiced throughout his Court term. This adherence applied to all precedents, including overruling ones (albeit after a waiting period). Dorin discussed three "precepts" which theoretically guided Clark's decisions: 1) refusal to dissent from an overruling precedent after the term in which it was announced, 2) dissent from precedent only if a majority could be mustered, 3) create a new precedent only in clear cases. Dennis D. Dorin, "Truman's 'Biggest Mistake': Tom Clark's Appointment to the Supreme Court," William F. Levantrosser, *Harry S. Truman, The Man From Independence*, (Westport, Conn.: Greenwood Press, 1986), p. 339.

144. Henry J. Abraham, *The Judicial Process* (New York: Oxford University Press, 1980), p. 384.

145. 352 U.S. 432 (1956).

146. Tom C. Clark, "The Courts, The Police and the Community," 46 *Southern California Law Review* 1, 4 (1972).

147. Clark, "The Court and Its Function," quoting Alexander Pope's *An Essay on Man*, p. 502.

148. Interview with Charles Reed, August 20, 1987, Washington, D. C.

149. Handwritten letter (8 pages), Frankfurter to Clark, July 5, 1952, Clark Papers, file "Frankfurter Correspondence," Rare and Special Collections, Tarlton Law Library, University of Texas, Austin, Texas.

150. Ibid.

SIX

MINTON'S TENURE ON THE COURT

Sherman Minton is among the greatest men Truman has been associated with in his forty years in public life.... In the Senate, Minton and Truman were together on every big issue....
When Truman became the President of the United States he appointed Sherman Minton to the Supreme Court, his top-notch appointment after the Chief Justice.
There never was a finer man or an abler public servant than the Honorable Sherman Minton.[1]
Harry S. Truman to Sherman Minton, July 19, 1961

My dear Hugo—
Congratulations on your conclusion of your 25th term on the Court—25 years of distinguished service unsurpassed in the history of the Court. One of my cherished memories is having served with you briefly in the Senate and on the Court. What a joy [it] was for your friends to vote for your confirmation and to see you go on after that dastardly attack on you to become one of the greatest justices and put to shame the lousy bastards that attacked you.[2]
Retired Justice Sherman Minton to Justice Hugo Black, June 29, 1962

BACKGROUND

Sherman Minton, Truman's last appointment to the Supreme Court, was born near Georgetown, Indiana on October 20, 1890, to Emma Lyvers Minton and John Evan Minton. The father, partially disabled, supplemented the family's meager income from his small farm by working as a day laborer for the railroad. After the death of his mother in 1901, the family moved to Ft. Worth, Texas in search of better times. Young Sherman, however, returned to Georgetown, where he lived with his grandmother until he finished school in nearby New Albany in 1911. He attended Indiana University from 1911 to 1915, graduating summa cum laude with an LL.B. In 1916, he received his master of law degree cum laude from Yale Law School. While serving in the United States Army in France, he studied law at the Sorbonne for several months before returning home in 1919. Although Minton excelled in academic work, he was also an outstanding athlete and student orator.[3] As platform manager for William Jennings Bryan in 1915, he had an opportunity to observe closely the greatest orator of his day as well as to see the country.

He was admitted to the Indiana bar in 1916 and practiced law in New Albany, Indiana until 1925, interrupted only by a two-year tour of duty in the infantry from 1917 to 1919. In 1925 he joined a law firm in Miami, Florida where he practiced for three years, returning to New Albany in 1928. He left New Albany in 1933 to accept the newly created job of Legal Advisor to the Public Service Commission of the state, a post to which he was appointed by his college classmate, the new Democratic governor, Paul V. McNutt.

Minton became active in the Democratic party in Indiana as soon as he finished law school. He waged unsuccessful campaigns for a seat in the United States House of Representatives in 1920 and 1930. In his brief fourteen months as Legal Advisor to the Indiana Public Service Commission, he "acquired [the] reputation for being at once a champion of the consumer and a nemesis of the utilities."[4] He supported McNutt's legislative program which attempted to solve the state's economic problems. Minton was elected to the United States Senate in 1934 on the campaign slogan "You can't offer a hungry man the Constitution."[5]

In the Senate, Minton was an ardent supporter of the Roosevelt administration.[6] He became assistant majority whip soon after arriving in Washington and majority whip in 1939. He succeeded Hugo Black in 1937 as chairman of the Senate Lobbying Committee. As a party leader in the Senate, he wholeheartedly supported New Deal legislative proposals and reacted with unrestrained anger when the Supreme Court in 1935–36 invalidated key parts of the Roosevelt recovery program. He endorsed without qualification the President's "court-packing" plan in 1937, attacking the Court publicly and privately. He also pushed his own brand of Court reform, a legislative proposal requiring the votes of seven justices to declare congressional acts unconstitutional.[7] Minton enthusiastically endorsed the Selective Service Act and the Smith Act. In 1940, he lost his bid for reelection to Raymond Willis when Indiana went solidly Republican behind native son Wendell Willkie for president. When Minton's term ended in January of 1941, Roosevelt appointed him one of five special administrative assistants to the president. During his four-month stint in the White House, Minton furthered the political fortunes of his friend, Senator Truman, by encouraging Roosevelt to support the Truman resolution calling for an investigation into waste and fraud in defense programs. Truman's chairmanship of this committee brought him the favorable national publicity[8] which was an important factor in his being chosen Roosevelt's running mate in 1944.

Minton's direct participation in party politics ended when Roosevelt appointed him in May of 1941 a judge of the United States Court of Appeals for the Seventh Court. However, his interest in politics never waned. In 1952 Truman, reporting to him on the success of his "barn-storming" tour in October on behalf of Adlai E. Stevenson, added in longhand that he knew Minton "must be itching to get into the fray."[9] In the 1956 campaign, the *New York Times* quoted Minton's public endorsement of Stevenson as well as his fear that Eisenhower's illness had left him handicapped, physically.[10] Truman assured him that he should not worry about the publicity because a jurist was "not to be muzzled any more than anyone else in this great country."[11] Minton's interest in politics continued. Eight months before his death, he wrote to fellow Democrat Black for his opinion of who would win in the Johnson-Goldwater race. Praising Black's "good political judgment," he expressed his lack of confidence in the polls and predicted Goldwater would carry Indiana.[12]

Minton served eight years on the Court of Appeals and wrote 196 majority opinions and 12 dissents.[13] His opinions would be consistent with those he wrote later on the Supreme Court. He upheld loyalty oaths, supported organized labor, and ruled in favor of administrative agencies and against monopolies.[14] While on the circuit bench, he also served in extra-judicial capacities. In 1945 Roosevelt appointed Minton to a five-man commission to review approximately one hundred court martial trial records,[15] and in 1948 Truman appointed him to a committee investigating the coal strike called by United Mine Workers' president John L. Lewis.

Minton and Black corresponded frequently when Minton was on the Circuit Court bench before he went to the Supreme Court. In 1949, Minton, "in the market for a clerk," wrote to Black expressing his hope that one of his sons, Hugo, Jr., or Sterling, might be available for the position.[16] Their letters encompassed political news, lengthy discussions of cases, birthday greetings, get-well condolences, family news and plans for shared vacations. The correspondence between these firm friends continued until Minton's death. He respected and admired Hugo Black and this high regard was mutual.

Although he had been an enthusiastic partisan and a Black admirer, when he became a justice, he practiced judicial self-restraint. As a politician, he had strongly supported the New Deal economic recovery measures, and on the Court, he consistently deferred to presidential and congressional actions. His support, however, should be viewed not merely as a continuation of his partisan preference, but rather as the application of previously held views on the proper role of the judiciary. In the mid–1930s, he based his criticism of the Supreme Court on his belief that a judicially active court was usurping the functions of Congress. Once on the Court, he put theory into practice by deferring to the legislative and executive branches.

Belief in a limited role for the judiciary was not the only factor influencing Minton's Supreme Court performance. Another was ill health. In 1943, two years after Minton's appointment to the federal appeals court, he learned that he had pernicious anemia, and in 1945 he suffered a heart attack which necessitated long-term hospitalization.[17] After his appointment to the Supreme Court in 1949, his daily schedule included an hour of rest after oral argument if work was to continue late in the day.[18] The year before his retirement in 1956, he began using a cane. He had trouble remembering oral arguments after returning to chambers. He described the condition as "depressing... My knees buckle and I lose my balance... Worst of all, it's gone to my brain."[19] In retirement, he was frustrated by his enforced physical inactivity and by his attempts to write his memoirs.[20] He died in 1965.

According to his son, Sherman A. Minton, a microbiologist at the University of Indiana Medical School, the diagnosis of pernicious anemia was not made until the spinal column had suffered permanent damage. Vitamin B_{12}, the best treatment, was not readily available at that time, but Dr. Minton did procure some for his father.[21] Clinical manifestations of the disease included *inter alia*, "stiffness, weakness, and spasticity, particularly in the lower extremities which [could] cripple the patient severely... Cerebral symptoms are common and include dullness, apathy, irritability [and] loss of concentration."[22] Minton's law clerks would testify to an ill temper. "Through the years," one said, "most of the law clerks regarded him as some sort of ogre and felt that we who worked for him were pitiful victims straight out of Dickens."[23] Following Minton's heart attack in 1945, he became virtually a "cardiac invalid for the rest of his life." The combination of pernicious anemia and cardiac disease slowed him down and his son suggested that it may have had also a depressing psychological effect.[24] Minton wrote to Truman in August of 1956:

> As I told you before, I feel compelled to accept retirement, which I will do in October. I assure you I would not take this step if I were not convinced that my condition of health compels it. It is not an easy thing to leave this attractive place where I have served a short time with such great satisfaction, and, again, my deepest appreciation to you for giving me this opportunity.[25]

Truman apparently knew when he appointed Minton to the Supreme Court that his health was not good. Burton's diary entry of September 19, 1949, asserted that Truman wanted to appoint Minton to the Murphy vacancy in July, but he did not because of Minton's health.[26] Two months later, Truman obviously had overcome his qualms about Minton's physical condition. The Senate Judiciary Committee had inquired into his health, but raised no objection. Truman, of course, did not regret his appointment as he considered Minton his second-best appointee.[27]

JUDICIAL PERFORMANCE

Minton served on the Court four years under Chief Justice Vinson and three years under Chief Justice Warren, spanning Truman's elected term and the first years of Eisenhower's presidency. Minton shared an ideological party and identification with both Vinson and Truman which he did not share with either Warren or Eisenhower. His quantitative output on the Supreme Court was not the lowest of the Truman appointees. His average of 9.43 majority opinions per year surpassed the Burton average of 7.38, but it compared less favorably with Vinson's average of 10.86 and Clark's average of 11.89. Minton's dissenting average of 5.00 per year exceeded that of Vinson (1.71) and Burton (3.85) and closely trailed Clark's (5.44). His total opinion average of 15.57 was lower than Clark's average of 19.67 and higher than Vinson's of 13.00 and Burton's of 12.77.[28]

Minton and Vinson each served seven years on the Court. Minton wrote ten fewer majority opinions (66) than did Vinson (76), but he wrote three times as many dissents (35 compared to Vinson's 12).[29] Minton wrote a total of eleven concurring opinions whereas Vinson wrote none. Minton's total opinion output for the seven years was one hundred and nine compared to Vinson's ninety-one.[30] One of Minton's former clerks on the Circuit Court concluded, "As a matter of sheer output, Mr. Minton can be well satisfied with his first year."[31] This output remained fairly constant.

The quality of Minton's opinion writing in the first term was described by his clerk, George Braden, as inconsistent. While he noted that "regardless of one's view of the result [in *Dennis v. United States* (1950)][32], the technique [was] eminently satisfactory."[33] He also pointed out the faults which affected much of Minton's writing: his tendency to "state the question for decision in such a way as to give the answer, thus apparently avoiding the necessity for setting forth any indication of the method by which he reached his conclusion," his tendency to emphasize precedent thereby avoiding the true issue of the case, and his confusing use of reasons for arriving at conclusions.[34] A later assessment of his style found it undistinguished and "colorless."[35] John P. Frank, on the other hand, examined Minton's opinions and, although he found that they often "assumed the point in issue" during the first term, 1949–50,[36] the following year "[t]hat mannerism was not evident,"[37] and Frank concluded that "[w]here close analysis is required, Minton's skill [was] very great."[38] Listing Minton's writing merits in the 1951–52 term as those of "brevity, clarity and candor," Frank noted that in at least one case, Minton's dissent was "better as a presentation of its views, than [was] the majority opinion."[39]

USE OF JUDICIAL RESTRAINT

As with Burton and Vinson, Minton's use of judicial restraint is readily seen in his opinions concerning procedure, loyalty-security and racial-discrimination.

Procedure Cases

Minton expressed his views on the limits of the judicial role in two cases involving the military courts. In *Burns et al. v. Wilson* (1953),[40] the petitioners had been convicted by court-martial of murder and rape. Awaiting death sentences, they petitioned for habeas corpus alleging their confessions were coerced and that they were denied counsel. The majority held that the district court had jurisdiction to determine whether the petitioners' rights were reviewed by the military court and that such a review had been exercised properly in this case.

In a separate opinion concurring with the result, Minton reasoned that the Supreme Court had "but one function, namely to see that the military court [had] jurisdiction, not whether it [had] committed error in the exercise of that jurisdiction."[41] Minton insisted that errors made in the military courts "must be corrected in the military hierarchy of courts provided by Congress,"[42] although he agreed with the majority decision which affirmed the district court's upholding of the military conviction.

In *United States ex rel. Toth v. Quarles* (1955),[43] Minton dissented from the majority opinion. Robert Toth, although honorably discharged, was subsequently arrested and convicted by a court-martial for killing a Korean citizen while serving in Korea. Under Article 3(a) of the Uniform Code of Military Justice, Congress sought to retain jurisdiction over ex-servicemen in the military courts for crimes committed while they were in service. For the majority, Black held that this provision which, in effect, extended military jurisdiction over civilians, was an encroachment on the jurisdiction of the federal courts, depriving citizens of their rights under the Constitution, and he declared that portion of the legislation unconstitutional. Abraham cited this case, the first of several cases invalidating portions of the Uniform Code of Military Justice Act of 1950, as illustrative of the restraint maxim requiring narrow decision. The declaration of unconstitutionality was confined to that portion of the statute specifically challenged.[44] Minton, dissenting, however, deferred to Congress' right to legislate in this area. He argued that by the legislation, Congress could imply "the continuing military status [of the separated servicemen] to warrant the [military] jurisdiction."[45] He reasoned that the petitioner was "still a soldier to answer in court martial for the crime he had committed as a soldier."[46]

Similarly, Minton took a narrow view of the Court's role in reviewing decisions made by the executive branch. In *Sicurella v. United States* (1955),[47] the majority overruled a Selective Service Board's decision denying conscientious objector status to a Jehovah's Witness. Minton vigorously dissented, arguing that

> the findings and classifications made by the Selective Service Board and Appeals Board are final. This Court... [is] not... a court of review... and... can only correct the Board's errors if they are so wanton, arbitrary and capricious as to destroy the Board's jurisdiction.[48]

Minton deferred to the Board's ruling as an "allowable judgment of reasonable men."[49]

In *United States v. Wunderlich et al.* (1951),[50] the Court through Minton upheld the arbitration clause (Article 15)[51] in a standard form government contract which gave the final decision in disputed claims to the head of the department. This dispute arose over a dam construction contract made with the Department of Interior. Minton concluded that the Interior official's arbitration was final and reviewable only for fraud, "conscious wrongdoing, an intention to cheat or be dishonest."[52] The dissent pointed to the dangers inherent in such a narrow review, especially when the final arbitrator was a party to the contract. The dissent also urged that an official's decision should be overturned when the official was "plainly out of bounds whether he [was] fraudulent, perverse, captious, incompetent or just palpably wrong."[53]

Minton insisted on procedural regularity, a major tenet of judicial restraint. As an appellate judge on the Seventh Circuit, he dealt constantly with review on technical procedural grounds. These technical considerations were often decisive for Minton in the cases before the Supreme Court.

In *Standard Vacuum Oil Co. v. United States* (1950),[54] the corporation sued for compensation for properties in the Philippine Islands which were requisitioned in 1941 and 1942 for military purposes. Minton emphasized that the Court of Claims, in dismissing claims barred by the statute of limitations, had "improperly considered facts not in the pleadings,"[55] as the plaintiff had alleged the taking but had pleaded no facts concerning the six intervening years. The Court could not review what was not in the record. Minton reasoned: "After all, pleadings and the making of a proper record have... a function to perform. This case points up that function. We will not review questions not clearly raised in the record."[56] Frankfurter circulated a three-page memorandum on December 8, 1949, while the case was being considered, in which he addressed the justification and limits for deciding cases simply on pleading technicalities.[57] And in a memorandum of March 21, 1950, he urged the Court to decide the case in the spirit of Rule 12(b) of the Federal Rules of Civil Procedure which allowed "matters outside the pleadings" to be received in evidence.[58] Minton's correspondence with Frankfurter indicated his willingness to negotiate the opinion. He acceded to Frankfurter's suggestions, expressing his hope that he had not done too much violence to Frankfurter's views.[59] Frankfurter and the Court joined Minton's opinion.

When an employee discharged from his job with the Veterans' Administration in New Orleans brought suit against the Regional Manager of the Veterans' Administration and the Civil Service Commission, *Blackmar v. Guerre* (1952),[60] Minton ruled that the Court was without jurisdiction. Blackmar had sued the Civil Service Commission directly. Under the Hatch Act (1939),[61] the plaintiff could transfer a contested ruling of the Civil Service Commission to the district court serving the area in which he resided. Minton held that this did not infer that Congress authorized direct suit in the district court but merely prescribed the proper route for judicial review. Minton reasoned that the Civil Service Commission was not a corporate entity to be sued independently and that Congress only authorized "one of its agencies to be sued *eo nomine*, in explicit language, or impliedly [when] the agency [was] the offspring of such a suable entity."[62]

In *Palmer v. Ashe* (1951),[63] Minton dissented from Frankfurter's holding that the petitioner in a habeas corpus proceeding was entitled to a judicial hearing on the merits. The petitioner was convicted eighteen years earlier of armed robbery. In his petition, he alleged that he had pleaded guilty to the charge of breaking and entering without counsel and that he was mentally incompetent. Minton emphasized the fact that the petitioner had not attempted to appeal by alleging "at the time of sentencing that he was mentally incompetent."[64] This initial procedural lapse combined with petitioner's record, which revealed repeated convictions over the years with no notice of mental disability, prompted Minton to defer to the lower Court's conclusion that the petitioner's allegations "were improbable in the light of the record . . . and that the necessity of a hearing was not indicated."[65]

In *United States v. Morgan* (1954),[66] a post conviction appeal for relief was brought by petitioner in the form of a writ of error *coram nobis*. *Coram nobis* is a common law writ used to correct errors of fact. The writ could be used, without regard to the statute of limitations, to introduce "facts that affect[ed] validity and regularity of judgment in both civil and criminal courts."[67] The majority allowed relief to the petitioner who sought to void a judgment under which he had served four years. He attempted to remove the conviction from his record because of its effect on sentencing in later prosecutions. As a second offender, he had been sentenced to a longer term under the New York Multiple Offender's Law. Minton dissented from the decision which "resurrect[ed] the ancient writ of error *coram nobis* from the limbo to which it presumably had been relegated by Rule 60(b) of the Federal Rules of Civil Procedure."[68] Minton argued that the writ had been superseded by Congressional enactment of provisions in Title 28 USC 2255 which provided "comprehensive procedure for collateral attacks on federal criminal judgments," and reasoned that Congress' failure to "extend the remedy there provided to persons not in federal custody" precluded him from doing so.[69] Minton insisted that limitations on the availability of the remedy were justified because "[t]he important principle that means for redressing deprivations of constitutional rights should be available often clashes with the also important principle that at some point a judgment should become final—that the litigation must eventually come to an end."[70]

Minton emphasized precedent in determining the jury issue in *Dennis v. United States* (1950).[71] This case was decided one year before the more famous case in which the defendant's conviction under the Smith Act was upheld. The accused challenged the composition of the jury which convicted him of failure to respond to a subpoena from the House Committee on Un-American Activities. Seven of the twelve jurors were government employees and he argued that, as a matter of law, a juror so employed was biased. Speaking for the majority, Minton reasoned that Congress had, through the 1935 act,[72] "intended to qualify Government employees as jurors."[73] He cited two cases, *United States v. Wood* (1936)[74] and *Frazier v. United States* (1948),[75] for the proposition that District of Columbia jurors could be challenged only for *actual* bias. Frankfurter, dissenting, argued that "[a]cquiescense in a precedent does not require its extension,"[76] and reasoned that in security cases, employees of the government should be presumed biased although they would not be disqualified in cases involving theft or drugs. Black's dissent emphasized that the precedents cited by Minton involved theft and dope-peddling and therefore were not controlling in a case in which "[g]overnment employees have reason to fear that an honest vote to acquit a Communist might be considered a 'disloyal' act which could easily cost them their jobs."[77]

Loyalty-Security Cases

Minton also adhered closely to precedent in a case involving alien rights. He vigorously dissented in *Shaughnessy v. Pedreiro* (1955)[78] when Black for the majority held that, under the 1952 Immigration and Naturalization Act, the Attorney General's deportation order was "final with respect to administrative procedure but not with respect to judicial review."[79] Judicial review, therefore, did not require habeas corpus proceedings but was available through the appeals process. Minton urged that the Court was bound by *Heikkila v. Barber* (1953),[80] decided two years previously, which held the Attorney General's decision "final" and reviewable only through the writ of habeas corpus.

In other cases involving aliens, Minton exercised deference to the executive branch and to the legislation authorizing its power. In *United States ex rel Knauff v. Shaughnessy* (1950),[81] the petitioner sought to enter the United States under the War Brides Act as the wife of an honorably discharged veteran. She was permanently excluded by an order of the Attorney General based on the recommendation of the Assistant Commissioner of Immigration and Naturalization that she be excluded "without a hearing on the grounds that the admission would be prejudicial to the interests of the United States."[82]

Minton, speaking for the majority, contended that Congress in prescribing procedures to facilitate or regulate the admission of aliens was "not dealing alone with a legislative power. It [was] implementing an inherent executive power... the power to control the foreign affairs of the nation."[83] He concluded that the president may delegate his power to an "executive officer of the sovereign, such as the Attorney General"[84] and that "[w]hatever the procedure authorized by Congress is, it is due process as far as an alien denied entry is concerned."[85] Minton found that the War Brides Act, which suspended quota requirements for war brides, did not "relax the security provisions of the immigration laws."[86] Frankfurter and Black joined Justice Jackson's dissent finding that the language of Congress was not "explicit enough" to find authorization for an "abrupt and brutal exclusion of a wife of an American citizen without a hearing."[87] Frankfurter, in a separate dissent, argued, "This is not the way to read such legislation. It is true also of Acts of Congress that '[t]he letter killeth.' "[88] He thought that the dominant concern of the War Brides Act was the well-being of the family and that the intent of the legislation dictated a different holding.

Minton used self-imposed restraint tenets to support his majority opinion in *Adler et al. v. Board of Education of the City of New York* (1952).[89] The suit was brought by Adler and others (some forty plaintiffs, of whom all but eight were dismissed) for a declaratory judgment that the New York Civil Service law, as implemented by the Feinberg Law requiring loyalty oaths of teachers, was unconstitutional. The petitioners sought to enjoin its implementation. To the argument that the use of the term "subversive" was vague, Minton answered:

> The question is not before us... Without raising in the complaint or in the proceedings of the lower courts the question of the constitutionality of 3021 of the Education Law of New York, appellants urge here for the first time that this section is unconstitutionally vague.[90]

To support his position, he reasoned that the "Court would not rule on the constitutionality of a state statute before the state courts have had an opportunity to do so."[91]

To answer the constitutional objections properly before the Court, Minton deferred to the reasonableness of the legislation:

> In the employment of officials and teachers of the school system, the state may properly inquire into the company they keep, and we

[know of] no rule, constitutional or otherwise, that prevents the state, when determining the fitness and loyalty of such persons, from considering the organizations and persons with whom they associate.[92]

To refute the First Amendment objections to the law, Minton inserted the rationale that for the employee "freedom of choice between membership in the organization and employment in the school system might be limited, but not his freedom of speech or assembly, except in the remote sense that limitation is inherent in every choice."[93] Minton justified this limitation by the state's police power "to defend its own existence."[94]

Minton and Frankfurter emphasized different restraint tenets to arrive at opposite conclusions. Frankfurter, dissenting, stressed two rules of judicial restraint:

> I think we should adhere to the teachings of this Court's history to avoid constitutional adjudication on merely abstract or speculative issues and to base [such adjudication] on the concreteness afforded by an actual . . . controversy . . . between adversaries [who are] immediately affected.[95]

Frankfurter's dissent grew out of his belief that the case should be dismissed on jurisdictional grounds. Frankfurter circulated his arguments for passing the case in a note to the Court on February 25, 1952, "Narrow decision on a serious question is always a matter of regret and therefore, if fairly avoidable, to be avoided. Therefore I venture to ask careful consideration of what I really believe to be the proper method of disposing of the case, however strong may be the convictions" on either side of the issue.[96] When his plea for dismissal was not successful, his dissent argued that the plaintiff's standing to contest the state law was based on the taxpayers' right to question local law and that this was not sufficient to establish standing to bring the suit under the Constitution. Further, he noted that no proceedings had been filed under the New York laws which had been on the books for thirty-two years and that no procedures for implementing the contested new law had been provided.

Racial Discrimination Cases

In three cases involving the rights of blacks, Minton utilized the restraint tenets of standing and justiciable issue. In *Barrows et al. v. Jackson* (1953),[97] Minton spoke for the majority to overturn the lower court's award of damages for breach of contract against a co-covenantor in a restrictive covenant agreement. "When . . . the parties cease to rely upon voluntary action to carry out the covenant and the State is asked to step in and give its sanction to the enforcement of the covenant,"[98] he held that a controversy under the Constitution had arisen and the state through such action had violated the equal protection clause of the Fourteenth Amendment.

Minton tackled the standing issue less rigidly. The complainant was being sued for damages for having sold her home to a non-Caucasian, but there was no non-Caucasian before the Court. "Ordinarily, one may not claim standing in this Court to vindicate the Constitutional rights of some third party,"[99] but Minton noted that the complainant would suffer a "direct pocketbook injury"[100] if the covenant were enforced and damages assessed against her. He found that the "reasons which underlie our rule denying standing to raise another's rights, which is only a rule of practice, are outweighed by the fundamental rights which would be denied by permitting the damage action to be maintained."[101] Referring to *Shelley v. Kraemer* (1948),[102] Minton held that the Court would not allow California to require damages to be paid by one in a private civil suit "for failure to observe a restrictive covenant that [the] Court would deny California the right to enforce in equity."[103] Minton's opinion won Frankfurter's approval. He wrote in the margin of the opinion circulated on May 16, 1953, "This is a true lawyer-like job. Greater praise is not in my vocabulary."[104] Burton also congratulated him on a "difficult constructive job, admirably done."[105]

In *Brotherhood of Railroad Trainmen et al. v. Howard et al.* (1952),[106] Minton filed a dissent based on his understanding that the parties to the dispute were not before the Court. The Brotherhood, an all-white union representing brakemen, and the employer signed an agreement whereby black brakemen (termed train-porters) lost their jobs as non-union workers and could not be rehired because they could not join the all-white brakemen's union. Black in the majority opinion ordered the district court to enjoin the enforcement of the contract because of its discriminatory effect.

Minton dissented, arguing that the dispute was between the employees over representation and was a question for the mediation board. Minton wrote, "I do not understand that private parties such as carriers and the Brotherhood . . . may not discriminate on the grounds of race."[107] He found no state or federal action and no law to proscribe discrimination among private parties. Minton therefore regarded the case as non-justiciable. He insisted that there be a definite controversy between bona fide adversaries to establish jurisdiction.

Minton emphasized that state action was necessary for violation of the Fourteenth and Fifteenth Amendments in discrimination cases. In *Terry v. Adams* (1953),[108] Minton was the lone dissenter. His dissent was based on the restraint maxim requiring bona fide adversaries to establish a justiciable issue. Black residents of Fort Bend County, Texas, brought suit to declare their rights to vote in the Jaybird Democratic primary. The Jaybird Democratic Association, an all-white party, through pre-primary elections, controlled the Democratic primary of the County. Black, for the majority, remanded the case to the district court to issue decrees and orders necessary "to afford Negro citizens of Fort Bend County" full protection of their voting rights, having determined that the Jaybirds effectively denied the franchise to black voters.[109]

Minton, dissenting, insisted, "I am not concerned in the least as to what happens to the Jaybirds and their unworthy scheme. I am concerned about what this Court says is state action within the meaning of the Fifteenth Amendment."[110] Minton summarized the answers given by Black, Frankfurter and Clark. Black's opinion which held the Court should "redress the wrong, even if it is individual action alone," he found praiseworthy but "not in accord with the Constitution."[111] Frankfurter found sufficient state action in the fact that a state official participated in the Jaybird primary. Clark found state action "in assumptions."[112] Minton emphasized that the Jaybirds were not a part of the Democratic Party and that "a political organization not using state machinery or depending upon state law to authorize what it does" was not "within the ban of the Fifteenth Amendment."[113] Minton considered the Jaybirds a successful pressure group whose actions were not covered by constitutional proscriptions.

ASSESSMENT

Minton's Supreme Court opinions were reasoned expositions employing the various tenets of judicial restraint to bolster his conclusions. They were the product of a skilled legal craftsman. He isolated the issue, discovered the facts, found the rule, applied the rule and rendered the judgment. His technical skill was used well in federal tax cases involving questions of lien priority which demanded such craftsmanship. His tendency to defer to legislative and executive action was a dominant and constant characteristic of his judicial approach.

Utilizing this aspect of his approach, he followed it to its logical conclusion in *Lewis v. United States* (1955).[114] The accused in *Lewis* was prosecuted for not paying an occupation tax, a 10 percent assessment imposed on gains realized by wagering. Wagering was by federal law a crime in Washington, D. C., and the accused asserted his Fourth and Fifth Amendment rights in a motion to dismiss the information.

Minton, speaking for the majority, held that the Gambler's Occupation Tax Act did not violate the constitutional rights of the accused, because "[t]he only compulsion under the Act [was] that requiring the decision which would-be gamblers must make at the threshold. They may have to give up gambling, but there is no constitutional right to gamble. If they elect to wager, though it be unlawful, they must pay the tax."[115] Frankfurter disagreed with the constitutional views in the case and with the "spurious use of the taxing power as a means of facilitating prosecution of federal offenses."[116] Black and Douglas registered their dissents and argued, "[I]f we remain faithful to the letter and spirit of the Bill of Rights, gamblers, like others, have a right to invoke [the Constitution's] safeguards."[117]

Minton seldom considered the application of the rules of practice judicially self-imposed should be "outweighed by... fundamental rights."[118] To do so would have required a more active role for the Court than he was willing to embrace. Minton's approach to review was consistently cautious and literal. Harry L. Wallace, Minton's former law clerk, noted that Minton was "extremely conscious of and insistent upon adhering to the constitutional and statutory limitations imposed on the Court's jurisdiction, regardless of resulting justice or injustice."[119]

Perhaps Minton's ill health and previous judicial experience contributed also to his narrow approach to judging. His work at the Court was more manageable because of its restricted nature. Not overly perturbed by the complex issues presented in the cases before the Court, Minton was able to maintain genial relationships with the members of the Court. In *Remmer v. United States* (1954),[120] Frankfurter agreed with Minton's opinion but disagreed with the use of the "word contact as a verb." Minton agreed to change the verb to "save printing costs" and Frankfurter commended the change as a "good illustration of [Minton's] sense of team work."[121] This bit of tongue-in-check reparteé illustrated Minton's willingness to agree with his colleagues on minor issues and to keep his efforts focused on the important issues before him. Not only did he maintain a long friendly correspondence with Black, but he also corresponded until his death with Frankfurter, who would tease him for being a "pathological" Democrat.[122] Emotionalism did not occupy a place in Minton's decisions. He approached the cases with studied concern, as a pragmatic problem-solver.

NOTES

1. Handwritten note, Truman to Minton, July 19, 1961, Truman Papers, file "Post Presidential," Harry S. Truman Library, Independence, Missouri.

2. Letter, Minton to Black, June 29, 1962, Black Papers, file "Minton Correspondence," Manuscript Division, Library of Congress, Washington, D. C.

3. John A. Garraty, ed., *Dictionary of American Biography, Supplement 7, 1961–65* (New York: Charles Scribner's Sons, 1981), p. 540.

4. Elizabeth Anne Hull, "Sherman Minton and the Cold War Front" (Ph.D. dissertation, New School for Social Research, 1977), p. 7.

5. Ibid., p. 12.

6. Ibid., p. 16.

7. Ibid., p. 20.

8. David Neal Atkinson reported that Minton enjoyed telling this incident to his law clerks, remarking, "That's the way Presidents are made.

And that's the way Justices are made," in David Neal Atkinson, "Mr. Justice Minton and the Supreme Court (1949–1956)" (Ph.D. dissertation, University of Iowa, 1969), p. 65.

9. Letter, Truman to Minton, October 15, 1952, file "Presidential Secretary's," Harry S. Truman Library, Independence, Missouri.

10. *New York Times*, August 21, 1956.

11. Letter, Truman to Minton, August 28, 1956, Truman Papers, file "Post Presidential," Harry S. Truman Library, Independence, Missouri.

12. Letter, Minton to Black, September 11, 1964, Black Papers, file "Minton Correspondence," Manuscript Division, Library of Congress, Washington, D. C.

13. Hull, "Sherman Minton and the Cold War Front," p. 38.

14. See *Inland Steel Workers of America v. N.L.R.B.*, 170 F.2d 247 (7th Cir. 1948), *United States v. New York Great Atlantic and Pacific Tea Co.*, 173 F.2d 79 (7th Cir. 1949), and *Standard Oil Co. v. Federal Trade Commission*, 173 F.2d 210 (7th Cir. 1949); Hull reported that Minton supported the worker in 70 percent of the cases. Hull, "Sherman Minton and the Cold War Front," p. 26.

15. Hull, "Sherman Minton and the Cold War Front," p. 36.

16. Letter, Minton to Black, May 5, 1949, Black Papers, file "Minton Correspondence," Manuscript Division, Library of Congress, Washington, D. C.

17. Richard Kirkendall, "Sherman Minton," Leon Friedman and Fred L. Israel, eds. *The Justices of the Supreme Court, 1789–1969, Their Lives and Major Opinions* (New York: Chelsea House, 1969), p. 2701.

18. Hull, "Sherman Minton and the Cold War Front," p. 37.

19. Atkinson, "Mr. Justice Minton," p. 114.

20. Atkinson, "Mr. Justice Minton," p. 120. See generally pp. 119–20.

21. Telephone interview, Sherman A. Minton, M.D., Professor of Microbiology, Indiana University School of Medicine, Indianapolis, Indiana, February 22, 1983.

22. James H. Jandl, "Pernicious Anemia," Paul B. Beeson, M.D. and Walsh McDermott, M.D., eds., *Cecil-Loeb Textbook of Medicine* (Philadelphia: W. B. Saunders Co., 1971), p. 1468.

23. Atkinson, "Mr. Justice Minton," p. 357.

24. Telephone interview, Sherman A. Minton M.D., February 22, 1983. David Neal Atkinson noted that Chief Justice Earl Warren issued invitations to Minton to attend football games with him in Washington but Minton was not well. "I'd have pushed his wheelchair, but I think he may have been sensitive about appearing in public in a wheelchair," Quoted by Atkinson, "Mr. Justice Minton," p. 161.

25. Letter, Minton to Truman, August 24, 1956, Truman Papers, file "Post Presidential," Harry S. Truman Library, Independence, Missouri.

26. Diary entry of Burton, September 19, 1949, Burton Papers, Manuscript Division, Library of Congress, Washington, D. C.

27. Handwritten note, Truman to Minton, July 19, 1961, Truman Papers, Harry S. Truman Library, Independence, Missouri.
28. Albert P. Blaustein and Roy M. Mersky, *The First One Hundred Justices* (Hamden, Conn.: The Shoe String Press, Inc., 1978), p. 149.
29. Ibid., p. 246. David N. Atkinson pointed out that 445 dissents were written during Minton's term, an average of forty-nine per justice. Minton's dissent rate was thus less than average. See Atkinson, "Mr. Justice Minton," pp. 137–153. See also David N. Atkinson, "Opinion Writing on the Supreme Court, 1949–1956: The Views of Justice Sherman Minton," 49 *Temple Law Quarterly* 105, 118 (1975). Atkinson's totals for opinions are taken from *Harvard Law Review* articles and differ from those reported by Blaustein and Mersky.
30. Blaustein and Mersky, *The First One Hundred Justices*, p. 146.
31. George D. Braden, "Mr. Justice Minton and the Truman Bloc," 26 *Indiana Law Journal* 153, 154 (1951).
32. 339 U.S. 162 (1950).
33. Braden, "Mr. Justice Minton and the Truman Bloc," p. 155.
34. Ibid., pp. 156–58.
35. Atkinson, "Mr. Justice Minton," p. 356.
36. John P. Frank, "The United States Supreme Court: 1949–50," 18 *University of Chicago Law Review* 1 (1950), p. 51.
37. John P. Frank, "The United States Supreme Court: 1950–51," 19 *University of Chicago Law Review* 165 (1951), p. 230.
38. Ibid., p. 229.
39. John P. Frank, "The United States Supreme Court: 1951–52," 20 *University of Chicago Law Review* 1 (1952), p. 67, citing *Standard Oil Co. v. Peck*, 342 U.S. 382 (1952).
40. 346 U.S. 137 (1953).
41. 346 U.S. at 147.
42. 346 U.S. at 147.
43. 350 U.S. 11 (1955).
44. Henry J. Abraham, *The Judicial Process* (New York: Oxford University Press, 1980), p. 374.
45. 350 U.S. at 45.
46. 350 U.S. at 44.
47. 348 U.S. 385 (1955).
48. 348 U.S. at 393.
49. 348 U.S. at 394.
50. 342 U.S. 98 (1951).
51. The Article is set forth in a footnote to opinion, 342 U.S. at 99.
52. 342 U.S. at 103.
53. 342 U.S. at 102.
54. 339 U.S. 157 (1950).
55. 339 U.S. at 157.
56. Ibid., 157.

57. Memorandum, Frankfurter to Court, December 8, 1949, Minton Papers, file "Supreme Court Case," Harry S. Truman Library, Independence, Missouri.
58. Memorandum, Frankfurter to Court, March 21, 1950, Minton Papers, file "Supreme Court Case," Harry S. Truman Library, Independence, Missouri.
59. Memorandum, Minton to Frankfurter, November 3, 1949, Minton Papers, file "Supreme Court Case," Harry S. Truman Library, Independence, Missouri.
60. 342 U.S. 512 (1952).
61. 5 U.S.C. 118(C) (1939).
62. 342 U.S. at 515.
63. 342 U.S. 134 (1951).
64. 342 U.S. at 139.
65. 342 U.S. at 141.
66. 346 U.S. 501 (1954).
67. 346 U.S. at 502.
68. 346 U.S. at 513.
69. 346 U.S. at 519.
70. 346 U.S. at 519–20.
71. 339 U.S. 162 (1950).
72. 49 Stat. 682 D.C. Code, 11–1420 (1940).
73. 339 U.S. at 166–67.
74. 229 U.S. 123 (1936).
75. 335 U.S. 497 (1948).
76. 339 U.S. at 175.
77. 339 U.S. at 180.
78. 349 U.S. 48 (1955).
79. 349 U.S. at 48.
80. 349 U.S. 229 (1953).
81. 338 U.S. 537 (1950). For a complete discussion and analysis of this case, see David N. Atkinson, "Justice Sherman Minton and the Balance of Liberty," 50 *Indiana Law Journal* 34, 48–55 (1974).
82. 338 U.S. at 539–40.
83. 338 U.S. at 542.
84. 338 U.S. at 543.
85. 338 U.S. at 544.
86. 338 U.S. at 547. For a complete discussion of the immediate reaction to this decision, see Frank, "The United States Supreme Court: 1949–50," 18 *University of Chicago Law Review* 1, 21–23 (1950).
87. 338 U.S. at 550.
88. 338 U.S. at 548.
89. 342 U.S. 485 (1952).
90. 342 U.S. at 496.
91. 342 U.S. at 496.

92. 342 U.S. at 493.//
93. 342 U.S. at 493.
94. 342 U.S. at 493.
95. 342 U.S. at 497–98.
96. Memorandum, Frankfurter to Court, February 25, 1952, Minton Papers, file "Supreme Court Case," Harry S. Truman Library, Independence, Missouri.
97. 346 U.S. 249 (1953). For a thorough discussion of the legal complexities presented in this case, see David N. Atkinson, "Justice Minton and the Protection of Minority Rights," 34 *Washington and Lee Law Review* 97 (1977).
98. 346 U.S. at 253.
99. 346 U.S. at 255.
100. 346 U.S. at 251.
101. 346 U.S. at 257.
102. 334 U.S. 1 (1948).
103. 346 U.S. at 258.
104. Marginal note, Frankfurter to Minton on opinion circulated May 16, 1953, Minton Papers, file "Supreme Court Case," Harry S. Truman Library, Independence, Missouri.
105. Note, Burton to Minton, May 18, 1953, Minton Papers, file "Supreme Court Case," Harry S. Truman Library, Independence, Missouri.
106. 343 U.S. 768 (1952).
107. 343 U.S. at 778.
108. 345 U.S. 461 (1953).
109. 345 U.S. at 470.
110. 345 U.S. at 484.
111. 345 U.S. at 485.
112. 345 U.S. at 485.
113. 345 U.S. at 490.
114. 348 U.S. at 419 (1955).
115. 348 U.S. at 422–23.
116. 348 U.S. at 423.
117. 348 U.S. at 425.
118. Minton, *Barrows et al. v. Jackson*, 346 U.S. 249, 257 (1953).
119. Harry L. Wallace, "Mr. Justice Minton—Hoosier Justice on the Supreme Court," 34 *Indiana Law Review* 145, 421 (1959).
120. 347 U.S. 227 (1954).
121. Notes, Minton to Frankfurter, Frankfurter to Minton, February 15, 1954, Minton Papers, file "Supreme Court Case," Harry S. Truman Library, Independence, Missouri.
122. Letter, Frankfurter to Minton, February 1, 1960, Felix Frankfurter Papers, file "Sherman Minton," Manuscript Division, Harvard Law School Library, Cambridge, Massachusetts.

SEVEN

CONCLUSION

The exercise of judicial self-restraint by the Truman appointees was an expression of their adherence to the limited role of the judiciary in the scheme of government. They disapproved of capricious judicial meddling with the law-making prerogatives of the legislative branches in both the state and national governments. They were particularly tolerant of governmental authority and emphasized the government's role in molding society. Each had broad political experience and brought to his position on the Court a pragmatic outlook. Each had been schooled, moreover, in the New Deal, and, as a result, had learned to be suspicious of the over-active judicial philosophy of the pre-Roosevelt Court.

None of the appointees was a legal scholar. None had a fully articulated or controlling philosophy of law. In this, they differed from their more articulate colleagues, Black and Frankfurter. They were, instead, practical lawyers who placed a premium on predictability and dependability in the law. While their performances on the Bench can be viewed primarily as a reaction to the pre–1937 Court's "exaltation of the judiciary as a buffer for property rights,"[1] they were also heirs of a continuing legal tradition. They belonged to the sociological school of jurisprudence which became "after 1937 the official doctrine of the Court."[2] Before *West Coast Hotel Co. v. Parrish et al.* (1937),[3] the Court had used actively the power of judicial review to thwart social legislative programs and to advance a philosophy of government that

> stressed the autonomy of private rights, especially the right to hold and use property free of governmental interference[,] . . . proclaimed the omniscience of law and the innate wisdom of its judicial interpreters; and . . . insisted that legislative encroachment on the affairs

of individual citizens and their corporate enterprises be kept to a minimum.[4]

Truman's appointees, responding to society's demands in their own period, allowed legislative experimentation in social problems by refusing to invoke actively the power of judicial review. The Roosevelt Court had allowed the legislation a deferential hearing. Like their immediate predecessors and unlike their counterparts on the pre–1937 Court, the Truman appointees deferred to legislation and only reluctantly "made law."

Although Truman's justices believed the judicial role should be a limited one, they used haphazardly and sporadically the self-imposed limitations on decision making. At times, they almost mechanically applied the rules. Whether they used the rules as excuses for particular results or as reasonable steps in reaching logical decisions was not always discernible. In *Irvine v. California* (1954),[5] for instance, Clark followed precedent, hoping thereby to initiate change by emphasizing the absurdity of the controlling law. In *Lewis v. United States* (1955),[6] Minton followed deference to the legislature to its logical conclusion, illustrating thereby the ambiguity of the legislation. Burton seemed to approach a case with an open mind, ready to apply the tenet logically, although in the bar admission cases, *Schware v. Board of Bar Examiners* (1957) and *Konigsberg v. State Bar* (1957), he refused to defer to the state authority. Vinson, particularly in the *Steel Seizure* decision, appeared to reason backward from the result and in some cases employed an activist approach. Schlesinger's comment that Black would "invoke deference to the legislature when it [did] something he [supported]"[7] described Black's constant practice. Black's ready tendency was to overrule legislation with which he disagreed. By contrast, the Truman appointees were more attuned to Frankfurter's rationale, and showed reluctance to engage in interested active judicial lawmaking.

Frankfurter, the apostle of Thayer, used the Court as a forum to expound the virtues of judicial self-restraint, and set the tone for the Vinson era. In an undated letter to Clark, he explained that "the highest exercise of judicial duty is to subordinate one's personal pulls and one's prior tendencies to the law...."[8] Welcoming Vinson to the Court, Frankfurter noted their shared devotion to the "application of reason and fair-play... as free from partisan or class bias as conscience and consciousness can attain it."[9]

The Truman appointees have been most strongly criticized for their votes on individual rights. Sociological jurisprudence, however, proclaimed that "law was as concerned with the collective social good as with the individual good, that the whole range of social interests, needs and wants came legitimately within its scope."[10] The Truman appointees, in this tradition, used law "not as a shield to safeguard personal liberties, but as a cooperative instrument to satisfy social needs."[11] Their conception of society's needs was shaped by their and the nation's recent past. The Great Depression and

World War II threatened the national community in fundamental ways. Their unanimous support of government regulation to meet these challenges frequently involved curtailing the rights of criminals, aliens and alleged subversives. In their votes, they gave priority to the rights of society over the rights of individuals. They also expressed their faith in government's ability to provide for the general welfare as well as the inherent right of government to protect itself. In the racial discrimination cases, perceiving no threat to the government, they voted, sometimes hesitantly and haltingly, to increase the rights of the black citizenry even when doing so involved a more active judicial role, at least as far as state laws were concerned.

While contemporary analysis of the Vinson Court focused on these civil liberties decisions, Professor Mark de Wolfe Howe of Harvard Law School questioned the quantitative analysis which assumed that a justice's vote by itself in a civil liberties case measured his "personal devotion" to liberty. Cases, Howe pointed out, are frequently not decided solely on the basis of the civil liberties question:

> [I]n every case involving civil liberties which comes to the Supreme Court there are issues of Federal jurisdiction and the relationship of the judicial power to the legislative and executive powers which are inescapable and which, in numerous instances, are of controlling importance.[12]

The opinions written by Truman's appointees verify Howe's assertion. The reasoning, buttressed by restraint rules, reveals *how* the decisions were made, and, perhaps more importantly, *what* was decided. It is patently erroneous as well as unfair to equate a justice's vote in a case which was decided by a procedural or jurisdictional issue or as a political question with the justice's personal belief in the substance of the litigant's cause. Some justices, admittedly, sit to mete out justice, but the Truman appointees, more often than not, made case by case decisions conscious of a framework of shared governmental power.

The process of Supreme Court opinion writing, as well as the judicial process itself, also qualifies the assumption that the justices always voted their personal preferences, and that their opinions were result-oriented. David N. Atkinson wrote that Minton's opinion-writing was based on his "general position" that the "opinion was a shorthand explanation of a group decision and not a proper vehicle for expressing personal views."[13] The concurrences of the Truman appointees further expressed this characteristic. While they served together on the Court, they often voted together (although not always), forming a bloc described by Professor Pritchett as "dominating the Court."[14] Their opinions, however, suggest that their agreement was an expression of their similar approaches to the judicial process and their shared belief in the place of the judiciary in the scheme of government rather than as a result of similar basic beliefs in human rights and individual causes.

Although the Truman appointees practiced self-restraint, criticism continues into the present over two notable decisions in which they have been criticized as judicial activists. Three of the appointees in 1954 voted with a unanimous Court to render the controversial decision overruling the *Plessy* separate-but-equal doctrine, *Brown v. Board of Education* (1954).[15] And one Truman appointee sitting on the Court in 1962 voted with the majority in the reapportionment case, *Baker v. Carr* (1962).[16] These decisions have been viewed by some scholars as prime examples of extreme judicial activism. Carl Swisher took issue with the leadership role played by the Court in *Brown*, arguing that the Court was not the proper branch for such a decision,[17] although Alexander H. Bickel, by emphasizing the Court's role in adapting the Constitution to current social needs and denouncing in the process the literalist's approach to constitutional construction, found that the *Brown* decision was in the tradition of judicial restraint. He argued for a Court which participates as a restrained partner in the government process, and he interpreted the *Brown* decision as one which had opened a colloquy with Congress.[18] Bickel also disagreed with Herbert Wechsler's thesis that the Supreme Court has a duty to decide all constitutional issues properly brought before it, arguing instead for the Court's discretion to decide not to decide.[19] Court of Appeals Judge Arthur Selwyn Miller, questioning the restraint urged by both Thayer and Bickel, endorsed the Court decisions in both cases and insisted that an affirmative jurisprudence which reads duties as well as limitations into the Constitution is consistent with the role and nature of government in the "positive state."[20] More recently, Raoul Berger criticized judicial legislation in both the *Brown* and *Baker* decisions, maintaining that the decisions were not dictated by a proper reading of the Constitution. Berger argued that the "intent" of the framers should have controlled and that segregation and suffrage were specifically excluded from the Fourteenth Amendment.[21]

The decades from 1937 to 1957 have been called a period of quiescence sandwiched between two activist courts, the earlier one politically conservative and the later one politically liberal.[22] As Schlesinger pointed out in 1947, the judicial restraint-judicial activist debate is not basically a conservative-liberal debate; it is a debate over the proper role the judiciary should play which is complicated by the fact that the judicial process is not a process of finding the law, but is rather a policy-making process. The Court, by interpreting and defining the law, is involved in making the law. The growing recognition expressed by Holmes in 1917 that "judges do and *must* legislate . . ."[23] has been followed by much concern about the extent of that legislative role. The complaints peaking in the 1930s against judicial activism came from those who disagreed with the results being promoted by the activism. Similarly, criticism beginning in the 1950s against the judicial activism of the Warren Court came from those who disagreed with the results promoted by that Court. J. Skelly Wright described the "obvious difference" by noting that the Nine Old Men in the 1930s "were trying to halt a revolution in the role of government as a social instrument" whereas the Warren Court was dedicated to "furthering that effort."[24] The critics preferred a sympathetic activism. Advocates of judicial restraint, however, have continued to emphasize that the proper role of the Court is not that of an active law-making body, and have accepted the position Thayer took in 1893:

> The checking and cutting down of legislative power, by numerous detailed prohibitions in the constitution, cannot be accomplished without making the government petty and incompetent.... Under no system can the power of courts go far to save a people from ruin; our chief protection lies elsewhere.[25]

Schlesinger continued in this same vein when he noted in 1947 that the

> larger interests of democracy in the United States require that the Court contract rather than expand its power, and that basic decisions on all questions save the fundamental rights of political agitation be entrusted as completely as possible to institutions directly responsive to popular control.[26]

Most important to Truman's appointees was Frankfurter's advocacy of the doctrine of judicial restraint. Writing to Reed in February of 1947, Frankfurter sought to clarify the term "judicial legislation":

> If "judicial legislation" is intended to mean that courts never add anything new or make something, but only "find" what is already in being, it is a fiction. If, however, it is used to convey that courts are very different law-makers from Congress or other legislatures, it states one of the basic postulates of our Government.... 'While the judicial function in construing legislation is not a mechanical process from which judgment is excluded, it is nevertheless very different from the legislative function. Construction is not legislation and must avoid that retrospective expansion of meaning which properly deserves the stigma of judicial legislation... To blur the distinctive functions of the legislative and judicial processes is not conducive to responsible legislation.'[27]

For a nonrepresentative body invested with great power, the various restraint maxims have served as objective standards for decision making, but because they are self-imposed and are applied, at times, subjectively, they have not contributed sure direction or certainty to the development of the law. Realizing that legislation alone had not proved to be a "sufficient agency of growth" for the law, Cardozo in 1921 called for a philosophy of law, "a theory of [law's] genesis, growth and aim" as a necessary ingredient for judicial reasoning.[28] Cardozo acknowledged and condoned the creative aspect inherent in judicial decision making:

> The adaptation of rule or principle to changing combinations of events demands the creative action of the judge. . . . The cycle is unending. Code is followed by commentary, and commentary by revision and thus the task is never done.[29]

The restraint maxims are, at best, only guides to be applied individually according to the wisdom and inclination of each justice. Participating fully in the debate over judicial function, Truman's appointees found the application of the maxims compatible with their concept of a limited judiciary and relegated the creative element to a lesser priority.

NOTES

1. G. Edward White, *The American Judicial Tradition, Profiles of Leading American Judges* (New York: Oxford University Press, 1976), p. 195.
2. Henry Steele Commager, *The American Mind, An Interpretation of American Thought and Character Since the 1880s* (New Haven, Conn.: Yale University Press, 1950), p. 381.
3. 300 U.S. 379 (1937).
4. White, *The American Judicial Tradition*, p. 189.
5. 347 U.S. 128 (1954).
6. 348 U.S. 419 (1955).
7. Arthur M. Schlesinger, Jr., "The Supreme Court: 1947," *Fortune* 35, no. 1 (January, 1947), p. 204.
8. Undated letter, Frankfurter to Clark from Dumbarton Avenue on a Sunday, Clark Papers, file "Frankfurter Correspondence," Rare and Special Collections, Tarlton Law Library, University of Texas, Austin, Texas.
9. Letter, Frankfurter to Vinson, June 6, 1946, Felix Frankfurter Papers, file "Vinson Correspondence," Manuscript Division, Harvard Law School Library, Cambridge, Massachusetts.
10. Commager, *The American Mind*, p. 380.
11. Ibid., p. 380.
12. In response to Irving Dillard's article, "Truman Reshapes the Supreme Court," *Atlantic Monthly*, January, 1950, p. 31, Mark de Wolfe Howe, in a companion article, questioned the value of his statistical approach in "Justice in a Democracy," *Atlantic Monthly*, January, 1950, p. 35. See C. Herman Pritchett, *Civil Liberties and the Vinson Court* (Chicago: The Univer-

sity of Chicago Press, 1954), for a discussion of the Vinson Court performance in civil liberties cases. Pritchett emphasized that both role perception and personal "sympathies" influenced the justices' votes in these cases.

13. David N. Atkinson, "Opinion Writing on the Supreme Court, 1949–1956: The Views of Justice Sherman Minton," 49 *Temple Law Quarterly*, 105, 112 (1975).

14. Pritchett, *Civil Liberties and the Vinson Court*, pp. 177–85.

15. 347 U.S. 483 (1954).

16. 369 U.S. 186 (1962).

17. Carl Swisher, "Dred Scott, 100 Years After," *Journal of Politics* 19 (1957): 183.

18. Alexander M. Bickel, *The Least Dangerous Branch* (New York: The Bobbs-Merrill Company, Inc., 1962), p. 254.

19. See Herbert Wechsler, "Toward Neutral Principles of Constitutional Law," 73 *Harvard Law Review* 1 (1959).

20. Arthur Selwyn Miller, "Toward a Concept of Constitutional Duty," *1968 Supreme Court Review* 199 (1968).

21. Raoul Berger, *Government by Judiciary, The Transformation of the 14th Amendment* (Cambridge, Mass.: Harvard University Press, 1977).

22. C. Herman Pritchett, "The Supreme Court Today: Constitutional Interpretation and Judicial Self-Restraint," 3 *South Dakota Law Review* 51 (1958).

23. *Southern Pacific Co. v. Jensen*, 244 U.S. 205, 221 (1917). The appointees sat on the Court during what Grant Gilmore has called an "Age of Anxiety," characterized by Cardozo's "hesitant confession that judges were, on rare occasions, more than simple automata, that they made law instead of declaring it." Grant Gilmore, *The Ages of American Law* (New Haven, Conn.: Yale University, 1977), pp. 74, 77.

24. J. Skelly Wright, "The Role of the Supreme Court in a Democratic Society—Judicial Activism or Restraint?" 54 *Cornell Law Review* 1, 2 (1968).

25. James B. Thayer, "The Origin and Scope of the American Doctrine of Constitutional Law," 7 *Harvard Law Review* 129, 156 (1893).

26. Schlesinger, "The Supreme Court: 1947," p. 208. Responding to rumors circulated on the Court indicating that he had seen Schlesinger's article before it was published, Frankfurter assured Justice Murphy in a note written January 6, 1947, that the rumor was an "unmitigated untruth." He admitted being interviewed by Schlesinger, but maintained that he did not "say a word about the Court's work or about any of its members." He maintained that Schlesinger, "[w]hen he left, . . . said that only one other member of the court was as tight-mouthed with him as I was." Note, Frankfurter to Murphy, January 6, 1947, Vinson Papers, file "Frankfurter" Special Collections of the Margaret I. King Library, University of Kentucky, Lexington, Kentucky.

27. Letter, Frankfurter to Reed, February 7, 1947, Vinson Papers, file "Supreme Court," Special Collections of the Margaret I. King Library, University of Kentucky, Lexington, Kentucky.

28. Benjamin N. Cardozo, *The Growth of the Law* (New Haven, Conn.: Yale University Press, 1924), p. 133.

29. Ibid., pp. 134–35.

BIBLIOGRAPHY

BOOKS

Abraham, Henry J. *The Judicial Process*. New York: Oxford University Press, 1980.

———. *Justices and Presidents, A Political History of Appointments to the Supreme Court*. 2d ed. New York: Oxford University Press, 1985.

Ackerman, Bruce A. *Private Property and the Constitution*. New Haven, Conn.: Yale University Press, 1977.

Adams, Raymond D., M.A., M.D., and Maurice Victor, M.D. *Principles of Neurology*, 2d ed. St. Louis, Mo.: McGraw-Hill Book Company, 1981.

Allen, Robert S. and William V. Shannon. *The Truman Merry-Go-Round*. New York: The Van Guard Press, Inc., 1950.

Baker, Leonard. *John Marshall, A Life in Law*. New York: Macmillan Publishing Company, Inc., 1974.

Bartholomew, Paul C. *Summaries of Leading Cases on the Constitution*. Totowa, N.J.: Littlefield, Adams and Co., 1977.

Berger, Raoul. *Government by Judiciary, The Transformation of the Fourteenth Amendment*. Cambridge, Mass.: Harvard University Press, 1977.

Berry, Mary Frances. *Stability, Security and Continuity, Mr. Justice Burton and Decision-Making in the Supreme Court (1945–1958)*. Westport, Conn.: Greenwood Press, 1978.

Beveridge, Albert J. *The Life of John Marshall*. Vol. 3. Dunwoody, Ga.: Norman S. Berg, Publisher, 1974.

Bickel, Alexander M. *The Least Dangerous Branch*. New York: The Bobbs-Merrill Company, Inc., 1962.

———. *The Supreme Court and the Idea of Progress*. New York: Harper and Row, 1970.

Bickel, Alexander M. and Benno C. Schmidt, Jr. *The Oliver Wendell Holmes Devise History of the United States Supreme Court, The Judiciary and Responsible Government*, 1910–1921. Vol. 9. New York: Macmillan Publishing Company, Inc., 1984.
Biddle, Francis. *Justice Holmes, Natural Law and the Supreme Court*. New York: Doubleday, 1961.
———. *Mr. Justice Holmes*. New York: Charles Scribner's Sons, 1942.
Black, Hugo. *A Constitutional Faith*. New York: Alfred A. Knopf, 1968.
Blaustein, Albert P. and Roy M. Mersky. *The First One Hundred Justices*. Hamden, Conn.: The Shoe String Press, Inc., 1978.
Bodenheimer, Edgar. *Jurisprudence, The Philosophy and Method of the Law*. Cambridge, Mass.: Harvard University Press, 1974.
Cahn, Edmond. *The Moral Decision*. Bloomington: Indiana University Press, 1955. New Midland Book Edition, 1981.
Cardozo, Benjamin N. *The Growth of the Law*. New Haven, Conn.: Yale University Press, 1924.
———. "The Nature of the Judicial Process." Clarence Morris, ed. *The Great Legal Philosophers*. Philadelphia: University of Pennsylvania Press, 1959.
Choper, Jesse H. *Judicial Review and the National Political Process, A Functional Reconsideration of the Role of the Supreme Court*. Chicago: The University of Chicago Press, 1980.
Clark, Tom C. and Philip B. Perlman. *Prejudice and Property, An Historic Brief Against Racial Covenants*. Washington, D. C.: Public Affairs Press, 1948.
Commager, Henry Steele. *The American Mind, An Interpretation of American Thought Since the 1880s*. New Haven, Conn.: Yale University Press, 1950.
Corwin, Edward S. *The Constitution and What It Means Today*. Princeton, N.J.: Princeton University Press, 1978.
———. *The "Higher Law" Background of American Constitutional Law*. Ithaca, N.Y.: Cornell University Press, 1955.
Curtis, Charles P., Jr. *Lions Under the Throne*. Boston: Houghton Mifflin Co., 1947.
Dawson, Nelson Lloyd. *Louis D. Brandeis, Felix Frankfurter and the New Deal*. Hamden, Conn.: The Shoe String Press, Inc., 1980.
Donovan, Robert J. *Conflict and Crisis, The Presidency of Harry S. Truman, 1945–1948*. New York: W. W. Norton and Company, 1977.
———. *The Tumultuous Years, The Presidency of Harry S Truman, 1949–1953*. New York: W. W. Norton and Company, 1982.
Douglas, William O. *The Court Years 1939–1975: The Autobiography of William O. Douglas*. New York: Random House, 1980.
Dunne, Gerald T. *Hugo Black and the Judicial Revolution*. New York: Simon and Schuster, 1977.

Ernst, Morris L. *The Great Reversals, Tales of the Supreme Court*. New York: Weybright and Talley, 1973.
Ferrell, Robert H., ed. *Harry S. Truman and the Modern American Presidency*. Boston: Little, Brown and Company, 1983.
———. *Off the Record, The Private Papers of Harry S. Truman*. New York: Harper and Row, 1980.
Frank, John P. *Mr. Justice Black, The Man and His Opinions*. Westport, Conn.: Greenwood Press, 1977.
———. *Justice Daniel Dissenting*. Cambridge, Mass.: Harvard University Press, 1964.
———. *The Marble Palace*. New York: Alfred A. Knopf, 1972.
Frankfurter, Felix and James M. Landis. *The Business of the Supreme Court*. New York: The Macmillan Company, 1928.
Friedman, Lawrence, M. *A History of American Law*. New York: Simon and Schuster, 1973.
Friedman, Leon and Fred L. Israel, ed. *The Justices of the Supreme Court, 1789–1969, Their Lives and Major Opinions*. Vols. 3, 4. New York: Chelsea House, 1969.
Fuller, Lon L. *The Morality of the Law*. New Haven, Conn.: Yale University Press, 1969.
Gilmore, Grant. *The Ages of American Law*. New Haven, Conn.: Yale University, 1977.
Golding, M. P., ed. *The Nature of Law*. New York: Random House, Inc., 1966.
Goodman, Walter. *The Committee, The Extraordinary Career of the House Committee on Un-American Activities*. New York: Farrar, Straus and Giroux, 1968.
Gosnell, Harold F. *Truman's Crises, A Political Biography of Harry S. Truman*. Westport, Conn.: Greenwood Press, 1980.
Hall, Jerome. *Foundations of Jurisprudence*. Kansas City, Mo.: The Bobbs-Merrill Company, Inc., 1973.
Hamby, Alonzo L. *Beyond the New Deal, Harry S. Truman and American Liberalism*. New York: Columbia University Press, 1973.
———. *The Imperial Years, The U.S. Since 1939*. New York: Longman, 1976.
Hart, H. L. A. *The Concept of Law*. Oxford: At the Clarendon Press, 1961.
Heller, Francis H., ed. *The Truman White House: The Administration of the Presidency, 1945–1953*. Lawrence: The Regents Press of Kansas, 1980.
Hirsch, H. N. *The Enigma of Felix Frankfurter*. New York: Basic Books, Inc., 1981.
Horwitz, Morton J. *The Transformation of American Law, 1780–1860*. Cambridge, Mass.: Harvard University Press, 1977.

Hudon, Edward G., ed. *The Occasional Papers of Mr. Justice Burton*. Portland, Me.: Anthoensen Press, 1969.

Hughes, Charles Evans. *The Supreme Court of the United States*. New York: Columbia University Press, 1966.

Jackson, Pervical E. *Dissent in the Supreme Court*. Norman: University of Oklahoma Press, 1969.

James, Joseph B. *The Framing of the Fourteenth Amendment*. Urbana: University of Illinois Press, 1965.

Jandl, James H. "Pernicious Anemia." In *Cecil-Loeb Textbook of Medicine*, 13th ed. edited by Paul B. Beeson, M.D., and Walsh McDermott, M.D. Philadelphia: W. B. Saunders Co., 1971.

Keeton, G. W. *The Elemental Principles of Jurisprudence*. London: Sir Isaac Pitman and Sons, Ltd., 1961.

Keeton, G. W. and Georg Schwarzenberger, eds. *Jeremy Bentham and the Law, A Symposium*. Westport, Conn.: Greenwood Press, 1970.

Kelly, Alfred H. and Winfred A. Harbison. *The American Constitution, Its Origin and Development*. New York: W. W. Norton and Company, Inc., 1963.

Konefsky, Samuel J., ed. *The Constitutional World of Mr. Justice Frankfurter*. New York: The Macmillan Company, 1949.

Krock, Arthur. *Memoirs, Sixty Years in the Firing Line*. New York: Funk and Wagnalls, 1968.

Kurland, Philip, ed. *Felix Frankfurter on the Supreme Court*. Cambridge, Mass.: The Belknap Press of Harvard University Press, 1970.

Kurland, Philip B. *Mr. Justice Frankfurter and The Constitution*. Chicago: The University of Chicago Press, 1971.

Lash, Joseph P., ed. *From the Diaries of Felix Frankfurter*. New York: W. W. Norton & Co., Inc., 1974.

Levantrosser, William F., ed. *Harry S. Truman, The Man From Independence*. Westport, Conn.: Greenwood Press, 1986.

Lewis, Anthony. *Gideon's Trumpet*. New York: Random House, 1967.

Lewis, Anthony. *The Supreme Court and How It Works*. New York: Random House, 1966.

Lusky, Louis. *By What Right*. Charlottesville, Va.: The Michie Company, 1975.

Magruder, Allan B. *John Marshall, American Statesman*. Cambridge: The Riverside Press, 1885.

Marcus, Maeva. *Truman and the Steel Seizure Case: The Limits of Presidential Power*. New York: Columbia University Press, 1977.

Mason, Alpheus Thomas. *The Supreme Court from Taft to Burger*. Baton Rouge: Louisiana State University Press, 1979.

McCune, Wesley. *The Nine Young Men*. New York: Harper and Row, 1947.

McCloskey, Robert G. *The American Supreme Court*. Chicago: University of Chicago Press, 1971.

Mendelson, Wallace. *Justices Black and Frankfurter: Conflict on the Court*. Chicago: University of Chicago Press, 1966.
Mersky, Roy M. and J. Myron Jacobstein. *The Supreme Court of the United States: Hearings and Reports on Successful and Unsuccessful Nominations of Supreme Court Justices by the Senate Judiciary Committee, 1916–1972*. Vols. 4 and 5. Buffalo, N.Y.: Wm. S. Hein and Company, 1975.
Miller, Charles A. *The Supreme Court and the Uses of History*. Cambridge, Mass.: Harvard University Press, 1969.
Miller, Merle. *Plain Speaking, An Oral Biography of Harry S. Truman*. New York: Berkeley Publishing Corporation, G. Putnam's Sons, 1974.
Mitchell, Broadus and Louise Pearson Mitchell. *A Biography of the Constitution of the United States*. New York: Oxford University Press, 1975.
Murphy, Bruce Allen. *The Brandeis-Frankfurter Connection*. New York: Oxford University Press, 1982.
Murphy, Paul L. *The Constitution in Crisis Times, 1918–1969*. Evanston, Ill.: Harper and Row, 1972.
Murphy, Cornelius F. *Modern Legal Philosophy*. Pittsburgh: Duquesne University Press, 1978.
Murphy, Walter F. *Congress and the Court*. Chicago: University of Chicago Press, 1962.
———. *Elements of Judicial Strategy*. Chicago: University of Chicago Press, 1964.
Murphy, Walter F. and C. Herman Pritchett. *Courts, Judges and Politics*. New York: Random House, 1961.
Parrish, Michael E. *Felix Frankfurter and His Times: The Reform Years*. New York: The Free Press, 1982.
Poen, Monte M. *Strictly Personal and Confidential, The Letters Harry Truman Never Mailed*. Boston: Little, Brown and Company, 1982.
Phillips, Harlan B., ed. *Felix Frankfurter Reminisces*. New York: Reynal and Company, 1960.
Prichard, E. F. and Archibald MacLeish, eds. *Law and Politics, Occasional Papers of Felix Frankfurter, 1913–1938*. New York: Capricorn Books, 1962.
Pritchett, C. Herman. *The American Constitution*. New York: McGraw-Hill Book Company, Inc., 1959.
———. *Civil Liberties and the Vinson Court*. Chicago: The University of Chicago Press, 1954.
———. *Congress Versus the Supreme Court, 1957–1960*. Minneapolis: University of Minnesota Press, 1961.
———. *The Roosevelt Court: A Study in Judicial Politics and Values (1937–1941)*. New York: The Macmillan Company, 1948.
Provine, Doris Marie. *Case Selection in the United States Supreme Court*. Chicago: The University of Chicago Press, 1980.

Pusey, Merlo J. *Charles Evans Hughes*. New York: Macmillan, 1951.
Rodell, Fred. *Nine Men, A Political History of the Supreme Court from 1790 to 1955*. New York: Random House, 1955.
Schubert, Glendon. *The Constitutional Polity*. Boston: Boston University Press, 1970.
———. *The Judicial Mind, the Attitudes and Ideologies of Supreme Court Justices, 1946–1963*. Evanston, Ill.: Northwestern University Press, 1965.
Schwartz, Bernard. *The Great Rights of Mankind*. New York: Oxford University Press, 1977.
———. *The Supreme Court, Constitutional Revolution in Retrospect*. New York: The Ronald Press Company, 1957.
Silverstein, Mark. *Constitutional Faiths: Felix Frankfurter, Hugo Black and the Process of Judicial Decision Making*. Ithaca, N.Y.: Cornell University Press, 1984.
Smith, Page. *The Constitution, A Documentary and Narrative History*. New York: Morrow Quill Paperbacks, 1980.
Stern, Robert L. and Eugene Gressman. *Supreme Court Practice*. Washington, D. C.: BNA Incorporated, 1962.
Strum, Phillippa. *The Supreme Court and "Political Questions," A Study in Judicial Evasion*. University: University of Alabama Press, 1974.
Swindler, William F. *Court and Constitution in the 20th Century, The New Legality, 1932–1968*. Kansas City, Mo.: Bobbs-Merrill Co. Inc., 1970.
Taylor, Telford. *Two Studies in Constitutional Interpretation*. Columbus: Ohio State University Press, 1969.
Thomas, Helen Shirley. *Felix Frankfurter, Scholar on the Bench*. Baltimore: The Johns Hopkins Press, 1960.
Truman, Harry S. *Memoirs*. Vols. 1 and 2. Garden City, N.Y.: Doubleday and Company, 1956.
———. *Truman Speaks*. New York: Columbia University Press, 1960.
White, G. Edward. *The American Judicial Tradition: Profiles of Leading American Judges*. New York: Oxford University Press, 1976.
Williams, Charlotte. *Hugo L. Black, A Study in the Judicial Process*. Baltimore: The Johns Hopkins University Press, 1950.
Williams, Jerre S. *The Supreme Court Speaks*. Austin: University of Texas Press, 1956.

ARTICLES

Abernathy, Glenn. "Expansion of the State Action Concept Under the Fourteenth Amendment." 43 *Cornell Law Quarterly* 375 (1958).
Allen, Francis A. "Chief Justice Vinson and the Theory of Constitutional Government: A Tentative Appraisal." 49 *Northwestern Law Review* 3 (1954).

Antieau, Chester James. *"Dennis v. United States*—Precedent, Principle or Perversion?" 5 *Vanderbilt Law Review* 141.

Atkinson, David N. "American Constitution Under Stress: Mr. Justice Burton's Response to National Security Issues." 9 *Houston Law Review* 271 (1971).

———. "From New Deal Liberal to Supreme Court Conservative: The Metamorphosis of Justice Sherman Minton." 1975 *Washington University Law Quarterly* 361.

———. "Justice Sherman Minton and the Balance of Liberty." 50 *Indiana Law Review* 34 (1974).

———. "Justice Sherman Minton and Behavior Patterns Inside the Supreme Court." 69 *Northwestern University Law Review* 716 (1974).

———. "Justice Sherman Minton and the Protection of Minority Rights." 34 *Washington and Lee Law Review* 97 (1977).

———. "Opinion Writing on the Supreme Court, 1949–1956: The Views of Justice Sherman Minton." 49 *Temple Law Quarterly* 105 (1975).

Barber, Kathleen L. "The Legal Status of the Communist Party: 1965." *Journal of Public Law* 94 (1966).

Becker, Theodore. "Inquiry Into a School of Thought in the Judicial Behaviour Movement." *Midwest Journal of Political Science.* 7 (1963): 254–66.

Berman, Daniel M. "Freedom and Mr. Justice Black: Record After Twenty Years." 25 *Missouri Law Review* 155 (1960).

Beth, Loren P. "The Wall of Separation and the Supreme Court." 38 *Minnesota Law Review* 215 (1954).

Black, Hugo. "The Bill of Rights." 35 *New York University Law Review* 865 (1960).

———. "Mr. Justice Frankfurter." 78 *Harvard Law Review* 1521 (1965).

———. "Reminiscences." 18 *University of Alabama Law Review* 3 (1963).

Braden, George D. "Mr. Justice Minton and the Truman Bloc." 26 *Indiana Law Journal* 53 (1951).

Brenner, Saul. "Fluidity on the United States Supreme Court: A Reexamination." *American Journal of Political Science* 24, no. 3 (August 1980): 526–35.

———. "Some Effects of Ideology and Threat Upon the Size of Opinion Coalitions of the U.S. Supreme Court." *American Journal of Political Science.* 8, no. 1 (1980), pp. 49–58.

Burger, Chief Justice and Ramsey Clark. "Tributes to Tom C. Clark." *ABA Journal* 63 (August 1977): 1105.

Burton, Harold H. "Cornerstone of Constitutional Law—Extraordinary Case of *Marbury v. Madison.*" *ABA Journal* 36 (October 1950): 805–8, 881–83.

———. "Independent Judiciary: The Keystone of Our Freedom." *ABA Journal* 39 (December 1953): 1067–70.

———. "Justice, the Guardian of Liberty: John Marshall at the Trial of Aaron Burr." *ABA Journal* 37 (October 1951): 735–38.
———. "Legal Tender Cases: A Celebrated Supreme Court Reversal." *ABA Journal* 37 (March 1956): 231–34.
———. "The Supreme Court." *ABA Journal* 33 (July 1947): 645–48.
———. "Two Significant Decisions: Ex Parte Milligan and Ex Parte McCardle." *ABA Journal* 31 (February 1955): 121–24, 176–77.
Burton, Harold H. and Waggamum, T. E. "The Story of the Place." 21 *George Washington Law Review* 253 (1953).
Cahill, F. V., Jr. "The United States Supreme Court, 1947–1948." 28 *Oregon Law Review* 26 (1948).
Cahn, Edmond. "Justice Black and First Amendment 'Absolutes': A Public Interview." 37 *New York University Law Review* 549 (1962).
Chase, Howard W. "The Libertarian Case for Making It a Crime to Be a Communist." 29 *Temple Law Quarterly* 121 (1956).
Clark, Tom C. "Citizens, Courts, and the Effective Administration of Justice." *Journal of the American Judicature Society* 49 (1965): 6.
———. "Counsel for the Indigent Defendant." 41 *St. John's Law Review* 1 (1966).
———. "The Court and Its Function." 34 *Albany Law Review* 497 (1970).
———. "The Courts, the Police and the Community." 46 *Southern California Law Review* 1 (1972).
———. "Dynamic Process." 13 *Texas Bar Journal* 409 (August 1950).
———. "Fair Play and Decency." 3 *San Diego Law Review* 1 (1966).
———. "Justice Ye Shall Pursue." 38 *Tennessee Law Review* 481 (1971).
———. "My Brother, Frankfurter." 51 *Virginia Law Review* 549 (1965).
———. "The Present State of Trial Advocacy." 12 *DePaul Law Review* 185 (1962).
———. "Reminiscences of an Attorney General Turned Associate Justice." 6 *Houston Law Review* 623 (1969).
———. "The Sixth Amendment and the Law of the Land." 8 *St. Louis University Law Journal* 1 (1963).
———. "Wiretapping and the Constitution." 5 *California Western Law Review* 1 (1968).
Corwin, Edward S. "The Steel Seizure Case: A Judicial Brick Without Straw." 53 *Columbia Law Review* 53 (1954).
Cushman, Robert F. "Incorporation: Due Process and the Bill of Rights." 51 *Cornell Law Quarterly* 467 (1966).
Danelski, David J. "Values as Variables in Judicial Decision Making: Notes Toward a Theory." 19 *Vanderbilt Law Review* 721 (1966).
Danzig, Richard. "How Questions Begot Answers in Felix Frankfurter's First Flag Salute Opinion." 1977 *Supreme Court Review* 257 (1977).
Dillard, Irving. "Truman Reshapes the Supreme Court." *Atlantic Monthly*, January, 1950.

Dodd, E. Merrick. "The Supreme Court and Organized Labor, 1941–1945." 58 *Harvard Law Review* 1018 (1945).

Dunne, Gerald T. "Justice Hugo Black and Robert Jackson, The Great Feud." 19 *St. Louis University Law Journal* 465 (1975).

Dutton, C. B. "Mr. Justice Tom C. Clark." 26 *Indiana Law Journal* 169 (1951).

Elman, Philip, "The Solicitor General's Office, Justice Frankfurter, and Civil Rights Litigation." 100 *Harvard Law Review* 817 (1987).

Fairlie, Chester, "Gideon's Muted Trumpet." 69 *ABA Journal* 69 (February 1983): 172.

Fairman, Charles. "Does the Fourteenth Amendment Incorporate the Bill of Rights? The Original Understanding." 2 *Stanford Law Review* 5 (1949).

———. "The Supreme Court and the Constitutional Limitations on State Governmental Authority." 27 *University of Chicago Law Review* 40 (1953).

———. "What Makes a Great Justice? Mr. Justice Bradley and the Supreme Court." 30 *Boston University Law Review* 49 (1950).

Fraenkel, Osmond K. "The Supreme Court and Civil Rights: 1946 Term." 47 *Columbia Law Review* 953 (1947).

Frank, John P. "The Appointment of Supreme Court Justices: Prestige, Principles and Politics." 2 *Wisconsin Law Review* 172 (1941).

———. "The Appointment of Supreme Court Justices: III." 4 *Wisconsin Law Review* 461 (1941).

———. "Hugo L. Black: Free Speech and the Declaration of Independence," 2 *Law Forum* 577 (1977).

———. "Justice Tom Clark and Judicial Administration." 46 *Texas Law Review* 5 (1967).

———. "Supreme Court Justice Appointments: II." 3 *Wisconsin Law Review* 343 (1941).

———. "The United States Supreme Court: 1946–47." 15 *University of Chicago Law Review* 1 (1947).

———. "The United States Supreme Court: 1947–48." 16 *University of Chicago Law Review* 1 (1948).

———. "The United States Supreme Court: 1948–49." 17 *University of Chicago Law Review* 1 (1949).

———. "The United States Supreme Court: 1949–50." 18 *University of Chicago Law Review* 1 (1950).

———. "The United States Supreme Court: 1950–51." 19 *University of Chicago Law Review* 165 (1951).

———. "The United States Supreme Court: 1951–52." 20 *University of Chicago Law Review* 1 (1952).

———. "Fred Vinson and the Chief Justiceship." 21 *University of Chicago Law Review* 212 (1954).

BIBLIOGRAPHY

Frankfurter, Felix. "Memorandum on 'Incorporation' of the Bill of Rights into the Due Process Clause of the Fourteenth Amendment." 78 *Harvard Law Review* 746 (1965).

———. "Some Reflections on the Reading of Statutes." 47 *Columbia Law Review* 527 (1947).

———. "The Supreme Court in the Mirror of Justices." 105 *University of Pennsylvania Law Review* 781 (1957).

Forrester, Ray. "Mr. Justice Burton and the Supreme Court." 20 *Tulane Law Review* 1 (1945).

Freund, Paul A. "Storm Over the American Supreme Court." 21 *Modern Law Review* 345 (1958).

———. "The Supreme Court and Civil Liberties." 4 *Vanderbilt Law Review* 533 (1951).

Fox, Edward J. "Judges and Politics." 27 *Temple Law Quarterly* 1 (1953).

Grossman, Joel. "Role-Playing and the Analysis of Judicial Behavior: The Case of Mr. Justice Frankfurter." 11 *Journal of Public Law* 285 (1962).

———. "Social Science Approaches to the Judicial Process." 79 *Harvard Law Review* 1551 (1967).

Gunther, Gerald. "The Subtle Vices of the 'Passive Virtues'—A Commentary on Principle and Expediency in Judicial Review." 64 *Columbia Law Review* 1 (1964).

Hamilton, Walton. "Preview of a Justice." 48 *Yale Law Journal* 819 (1939).

Handler, Emmerich. "The Fourth Amendment, Federalism, and Mr. Justice Frankfurter." 8 *Syracuse Law Review* 166 (1957).

Harper, Fowler V. and Alan S. Rosenthal. "What the Supreme Court Did Not Do in the 1949 Term—An Appraisal of *Certiorari*." 99 *University of Pennsylvania Law Review* 293 (1950).

Hart, H. L. A. "Holmes' Positivism—An Addendum." 64 *Harvard Law Review* 929 (1951).

———. "Positivism and the Separation of Law and Morals." 71 *Harvard Law Review* 593 (1958).

Henkin, Louis. "Selective Incorporation of the Fourteenth Amendment." 73 *Yale Law Journal* 74 (1963).

Howard, A. E. Dick. "From Warren to Burger: Activism and Restraint." *The Wilson Quarterly* (Spring 1977): 109.

Howe, Mark de Wolfe. "Justice in a Democracy." *Atlantic Monthly*. January 1950.

———. "The Positivism of Mr. Justice Holmes." 64 *Harvard Law Review* 529 (1951).

Kellogg, Frederic R. "Learned Hand and the Great Train Ride." *The American Scholar* (Autumn 1987).

Kennedy, Randall. "Colloquy, A Reply to Phillip Elman." 100 *Harvard Law Review* 1938 (1987).

Knowlton, Robert E. "The Supreme Court, *Mapp v. Ohio* and Due Process of Law." 49 *Iowa Law Review* 14 (1963).
Krislov, Samuel. "Mr. Justice Black Reopens the Free Speech Debate." 11 *U.C.L.A. Law Review* 189 (1963).
Kurland, Philip B. "Personal Thoughts About Some Problems of Judicial Biography." 36 *Notre Dame Lawyer* 490 (1961).
Lefberg, Irving F. "Chief Justice Vinson and the Politics of Desegregation." 24 *Emory Law Journal* 243 (1975).
Lester, Wilbur R. "Fred M. Vinson in the Executive Branch." 49 *Northwestern Law Review* 36 (1954).
Leuchtenberg, William E. "The Origins of Franklin D. Roosevelt's 'Court-Packing' Plan." 1966 *Supreme Court Review* 347.
Levinson, Sanford V. "The Democratic Faith of Felix Frankfurter." 25 *Stanford Law Review* 430 (1973).
Lucey, Francis E. "Natural Law and American Legal Realism: Their Respective Contributions to a Theory of Law in a Democratic Society." 30 *The Georgetown Law Journal* 493 (1942).
MacLeish, Archibald. "Felix Frankfurter: A Lesson in Faith," 1966 *Supreme Court Review* 1 (1966).
McCloskey, Robert G. "The Supreme Court Finds a Role: Civil Liberties in the 1955 Term." 42 *Virginia Law Review* 735 (1956).
Mason, Alpheus T. "The Supreme Court, Free Government's Balance Wheel." *The Wilson Quarterly* (Spring 1977): 93.
Meiklejohn, Alexander. "The First Amendment Is An Absolute." 1961 *Supreme Court Review* 245 (1961).
Mendelson, Wallace. "Mr. Justice Frankfurter and the Process of Judicial Review." 103 *University of Pennsylvania Law Review* 295 (1954).
Miller, Arthur Selwyn. "Toward a Concept of Constitutional Duty." 1968 *The Supreme Court Review* 199 (1968).
Minton, Sherman. Book Review of John P. Frank's *Mr. Justice Black: The Man and His Opinions*, 24 *Indiana Law Journal* 299 (1949).
Murphy, Walter F. "Courts as Small Groups." 79 *Harvard Law Review* 1565 (1966).
Notes: "The Mootness Doctrine in the Supreme Court." 88 *Harvard Law Review* 373 (1974).
Oliver, William W. "Vinson in Congress." 49 *Northwestern Law Review* 62 (1954).
Paulsen, Conrad G. "The Persistence of Substantive Due Process in the States." 34 *Minnesota Law Review* 91 (1950).
Pedrick, Willard H. "From Congress to the Court of Appeal." 49 *Northwestern Law Review* 54 (1954).
Peters, Roger Paul. "The Supreme Court and the Spirit of 1957." 7 *Buffalo Law Review* 30 (1957).

Pollitt, Basil H. "What is Wrong With the Supreme Court of the United States." 25 *Florida Law Journal* 233 (1951).
Porter, Mary Cornelia. "That Commerce Shall Be Free: A New Look at the Old Laissez-Faire Court." 1976 *The Supreme Court Review* 135 (1976).
Pound, Roscoe. "Mechanical Jurisprudence." 8 *Columbia Law Review* 605 (1908).
Pound, Roscoe. "The Theory of Judicial Decision." 37 *Harvard Law Review* 802 (1924).
Pritchett, C. Herman. "The Supreme Court Today: Constitutional Interpretation and Judicial Self-Restraint." 3 *South Dakota Law Review* 51 (1958).
Redlich, Norman. "Are There Certain Rights Retained by the People?" 37 *New York Law Review* 787 (1962).
Reich, Charles A. "Mr. Justice Black and the Living Constitution." 76 *Harvard Law Review* 673 (1963).
Rogat, Yosal. "Mr. Justice Holmes: A Dissenting Opinion." 15 *Stanford Law Review* 254 (1963).
Rostow, Eugene V. "The Democratic Character of Judicial Review." 66 *Harvard Law Review* 193 (1952).
Schlesinger, Arthur M. "The Supreme Court: 1947." *Fortune* 35, no. 1 (January 1947).
Schmidhauser, John R. "*Stare Decisis*, Dissent and the Background of the Justices of the Supreme Court," 14 *University of Toronto Law Journal* 194 (1962).
Slotnick, Elliot E. "The Equality Principle and Majority Opinion Assignment on the U.S. Supreme Court." *Polity* 12, no. 2 (Winter 1979): 318–32.
Smith, Russell A. "The Supreme Court and Labor." 8 *Southwestern Law Journal* 1 (1954).
Spaeth, Harold J. "The Judicial Restraint of Mr. Justice Frankfurter: Myth or Reality," *Midwest Journal of Politics* 8 (1964): 22.
Strong, Frank R. "Fifty Years of Clear and Present Danger: From Schenck to Brandenburg, and Beyond." 1969 *Supreme Court Review* 41 (1969).
Stumpf, Samuel E. "The Moral Element in Supreme Court Decisions." 6 *Vanderbilt Law Review* 41 (1952).
Swindler, William F. "The Chief Justice and Law Reform 1921–1971." 1971 *Supreme Court Review* 241 (1971).
Swisher, Carl. "Dred Scott, 100 Years After." *Journal of Political Science* 19 (1957): 183.
Symposium. "Chief Justice Vinson and His Law Clerks." 49 *Northwestern Law Review* 26 (1954).
Symposium. "Controversy Over the Supreme Court." 10 *Syracuse Law Review* 242 (1959).

Symposium. "The Writing of Judicial Biography." 24 *Indiana Law Journal* 363 (1949).

Symposium. "Social Science Approaches to the Judicial Process." 79 *Harvard Law Review* 1551 (1966).

Thayer, James B. "The Origin and Scope of the American Doctrine of Constitutional Law." 7 *Harvard Law Review* 129 (1893).

Vinson, Fred. "The Enduring Constitution." 6 *Washington & Lee Law Review* 1 (1949).

Wallace, Harry L. "Mr. Justice Minton—Hoosier Justice on the Supreme Court. Part I." 34 *Indiana Law Journal* 145 (Winter 1959).

———. "Mr. Justice Minton—Hoosier Justice on the Supreme Court. Part II." 34 *Indiana Law Journal* 377 (Spring 1960).

Warren, Earl. "Mr. Justice Black: Thirty Years in Retrospect." 15 *U.C.L.A. Law Review* 397 et seq. (1967).

Wechsler, Herbert. "Toward Neutral Principles of Constitutional Law." 73 *Harvard Law Review* 1 (1959).

White, G. Edward. "The Rise and Fall of Justice Holmes." 39 *University of Chicago Law Review* 51 (1971).

Wright, J. Skelly. "Professor Bickel, The Scholarly Tradition and the Supreme Court." 84 *Harvard Law Review* 769 (1971).

———. "The Role of the Supreme Court in a Democratic Society—Judicial Activism or Restraint?" 54 *Cornell Law Review* 1 (1968).

Yarbrough, Tinsley. "Mr. Justice Black and Legal Positivism." 57 *Virginia Law Review* 375 (1971).

———. "Litigant Access Doctrine and the Burger Court." 31 *Vanderbilt Law Review* 33 (1978).

CASES

Adair v. United States, 208 U.S. 161 (1908).

Adler et al. v. Board of Education of the City of New York, 342 U.S. 485 (1952).

American Communications Association C.I.O. et al. v. Douds, 339 U.S. 382 (1950).

Ashdown v. State of Utah, 357 U.S. 426 (1958).

Ashwander et al. v. Tennessee Valley Authority et al., 297 U.S. 288 (1936).

Bailey v. Richardson, 341 U.S. 918 (1951).

Baker v. Carr, 369 U.S. 186 (1962).

Ballard v. United States, 329 U.S. 187 (1946).

Barrows et al. v. Jackson, 346 U.S. 249 (1953).

Beilan v. Board of Education, School District of Philadelphia, 357 U.S. 399 (1958).

Blackmar v. Guerre, 342 U.S. 512 (1952).

Briethaupt v. Abrams, 352 U.S. 432 (1957).

Brotherhood of Railroad Trainmen et al. v. Howard et al, 343 U.S. 768 (1952).
Brown v. Board of Education, 347 U.S. 483 (1954).
Burns et al. v. Wilson, 346 U.S. 137 (1953).
Bute v. People of State of Illinois, 333 U.S. 640 (1948).
Carter v. Carter Coal, 298 U.S. 238 (1936).
Chisholm v. Georgia, 2 Dallas 419 (1793).
Cole v. Young, 351 U.S. 536 (1956).
Commissioner of Internal Revenue v. Estate of Louis Sternberger, 348 U.S. 187 (1955).
Commissioner of Internal Revenue v. Wilcox et al., 327 U.S. 404 (1946).
Commissioner of Internal Revenue v. Wodehouse, 337 U.S. 369 (1949).
Communist Party of the United States v. Subversives Activities Control Board, 351 U.S. 115 (1956).
Crooker v. State of California, 357 U.S. 433 (1958).
Davis v. Mann, 377 U.S. 678 (1964).
Dennis v. United States, 339 U.S. 162 (1950).
Dennis et al. v. United States, 341 U.S. 494 (1951).
Dred Scott v. Sanford, 19 Howard 393 (1857).
Edelman v. California, 344 U.S. 357 (1953).
Ex parte Quirin, 317 U.S. 1 (1942).
Fay et al. v. Noia, 372 U.S. 391 (1963).
Fletcher v. Peck, 6 Cranch 87 (1810).
Frazier v. United States, 335 U.S. 497 (1948).
Garner et al. v. Board of Public Works of Los Angeles, 341 U.S. 716 (1951).
Gayla v. Browder, 352 U.S. 903 (1956).
Gideon v. Wainwright, 372 U.S. 335 (1963).
Giordenello v. United States, 357 U.S. 480 (1958).
Goldman v. United States, 316 U.S. 129 (1942).
Goldstein et al. v. United States, 316 U.S. 114 (1942).
Gray v. Sanders, 372 U.S. 368 (1963).
Griffin v. Illinois, 351 U.S. 12 (1956).
Harris v. United States, 331 U.S. 145 (1947).
Healy v. Commissioner of Internal Revenue, 345 U.S. 278 (1953).
Heikkila v. Barber, 345 U.S. 229 (1953).
Helvering v. Davis, 301 U.S. 619 (1937).
Henderson v. United States et al., 339 U.S. 816 (1950).
Hipolite Egg Co. v. United States, 220 U.S. 45 (1911).
Hoke v. United States, 227 U.S. 308 (1913).
Holmes v. City of Atlanta, 350 U.S. 879 (1955).
Hylton v. United States, 3 Dallas 171 (1796).
Inland Steel Workers of America v. N.L.R.B., 170 F.2d 247 (7th Cir. 1948).
Irvine v. California, 347 U.S. 128 (1954).
Jencks v. United States, 353 U.S. 657 (1957).
Johnson v. Virginia, 373 U.S. 61 (1963).

Johnson v. Zerbst, 304 U.S. 458 (1938).
Joint Anti-Fascist Refugee Comm. v. McGrath, 341 U.S. 123 (1951).
Konigsberg v. State Bar, 353 U.S. 252 (1957).
Leland v. State of Oregon, 343 U.S. 790 (1952).
Leng May Ma v. Barber, 357 U.S. 185 (1958).
Lewis v. United States, 348 U.S. 419 (1955).
Little et al. v. Barreme et al., 2 Cranch 170 (1804).
Lochner v. New York, 198 U.S. 45 (1905).
Louisville Joint Stock Land Bank v. Radford, 295 U.S. 555 (1935).
Lucas v. Forty-Fourth Gen'l Ass'y., 377 U.S. 713 (1964).
McDonald et al. v. United States, 335 U.S. 451 (1948).
McLaurin v. Oklahoma State Regents for High Education et al., 339 U.S. 637 (1950).
Manning, Collector of Internal Revenue, Fifth District of New Jersey v. Seeley Tube and Box Co. of New Jersey, 338 U.S. 561 (1950).
Mapp v. Ohio, 367 U.S. 643 (1961).
Marbury v. Madison, 1 Cranch 137 (1803).
Marcello v. Bonds, 349 U.S. 302 (1955).
Maryland Comm. for Fair Representation v. Tawes, 377 U.S. 656 (1964).
Mayor of Baltimore v. Dawson, 350 U.S. 877 (1955).
Memphis Steam Laundry Cleaner, Inc., v. Stone, Chairman, State Tax Commission of Mississippi, 342 U.S. 389 (1952).
Michel v. State of Louisiana, 350 U.S. 91 (1955).
Minnesota Rate Cases, 230 U.S. 352 (1913).
Miranda v. Arizona, 384 U.S. 436 (1966).
Morgan v. Commonwealth of Virginia, 328 U.S. 375 (1946).
Muir v. Louisville Park Theatrical Ass'n., 347 U.S. 971 (1954).
New York Times Co. v. Sullivan, 376 U.S. 254 (1964).
NLRB v. Jones and Laughlin Steel Corporation, 301 U.S. 1 (1937).
On Lee v. United States, 343 U.S. 747 (1952).
Palmer v. Ashe, 342 U.S. 134 (1951).
Panama Refining Co. v. Ryan, 293 U.S. 388 (1935).
Payne v. State of Arkansas, 356 U.S. 560 (1958).
Plessy v. Ferguson, 163 U.S. 537 (1896).
Pollock v. Farmers' Loan & Trust Co., 158 U.S. 601 (1895).
Railroad Retirement Board v. Alton R. Company, 295 U.S. 330 (1935).
Reece v. State of Georgia, 350 U.S. 85 (1955).
Remmer v. United States, 347 U.S. 227 (1954).
Reynolds v. Sims, 377 U.S. 533 (1964).
Rickert Rice Mills v. Fontenot, 297 U.S. 110 (1935).
Rogers v. Quan, 375 U.S. 193 (1958).
Roman v. Sincock, 337 U.S. 695 (1964).
Rosenberg et ux v. United States, 346 U.S. 273 (June 18 Special Term, 1953).
Roviaro v. United States, 353 U.S. 53 (1957).

Rutkin v. United States, 343 U.S. 130 (1952).
Schechter Poultry Corp. v. United States, 295 U.S. 495 (1935).
Schenck v. United States, 249 U.S. 47 (1919).
Schware v. Board of Bar Examiners, 353 U.S. 252 (1957).
Shaughnessy v. Pedreiro, 349 U.S. 48 (1955).
Shaughnessy v. United States ex rel. Mexei, 345 U.S. 206 (1953).
Shelley v. Kraemer et ux, 334 U.S. 1 (1948).
Shreveport Rate Cases, 234 U.S. 342 (1914).
Sicurella v. United States, 348 U.S. 385 (1955).
Slochower v. Board of Higher Education of the City of New York, 350 U.S. 551 (1956).
Sonzinsky v. United States, 300 U.S. 506 (1937).
Stack v. Boyle, 342 U.S. 1 (1951).
Standard Oil Co. v. Federal Trade Commission, 173 F.2d 210 (7th Cir. 1949).
Standard Oil Co. v. Peck, 342 U.S. 382 (1952).
Standard Vacuum Oil Co. v. United States, 339 U.S. 157 (1950).
State Athl. Comm'n. v. Dorsey, 359 U.S. 533 (1959).
State of Louisiana ex rel. Francis v. Resweber, Sheriff et al., 329 U.S. 459 (1947).
Stewart Machine Co. v. Davis, 301 U.S. 548 (1937).
Sweatt v. Painter et al., 339 U.S. 629 (1950).
Terminiello v. City of Chicago, 337 U.S. 1 (1949).
Terry v. Adams, 345 U.S. 461 (1953).
Trupiano et al. v. United States, 334 U.S. 699 (1948).
United States v. Bankers Trust, 294 U.S. 240 (1934).
United States v. Bryan, 339 U.S. 323 (1950).
United States v. Butler, 297 U.S. 1 (1936).
United States v. E. C. Knight Co., 156 U.S. 1 (1895).
United States v. Fleischman, 339 U.S. 349 (1950).
United States v. Jeffers, 342 U.S. 48 (1951).
United States v. Morgan, 346 U.S. 502 (1954).
United States v. New York Great Atlantic and Pacific Tea Co., 173 F.2d 79 (7th Cir. 1949).
United States v. Paramount Pictures, Inc., 334 U.S. 131 (1948).
United States ex rel. Accardi v. Shaughnessy, 347 U.S. 260 (1954).
United States ex rel. Accardi v. Shaughnessy, 349 U.S. 280 (1955).
United States ex rel. Knauff v. Shaughnessy, 338 U.S. 537 (1950).
United States ex rel. Toth v. Quarles, 350 U.S. 11 (1955).
United States v. United Mine Workers, 330 U.S. 258 (1947).
United States v. Wood, 299 U.S. 123 (1936).
United States v. Wunderlich et al., 342 U.S. 98 (1951).
Uphaus v. Wyman, 360 U.S. 72 (1959).
Virginia Railroad Co. v. System Federation, 330 U.S. 515 (1937).
Ware v. Hylton, 3 Dallas 199 (1796).
Watkins v. United States, 354 U.S. 178 (1957).

Weiman v. Updegraff, 344 U.S. 183 (1952).
Wesberry v. Sanders, 376 U.S. 1 (1964).
West Coast Hotel Co. v. Parrish et al., 300 U.S. 379 (1937).
Williams v. State of Georgia, 349 U.S. 375 (1955).
WMCA, Inc. v. Lomenzo, 377 U.S. 633 (1964).
Wolf v. Colorado, 338 U.S. 25 (1949).
Wright v. Vinton Branch, 300 U.S. 440 (1937).
Yates v. United States, 354 U.S. 298 (1957).
Youngstown Sheet and Tube Company v. Sawyer, 343 U.S. 579 (1952).

DISSERTATIONS

Atkinson, David Neal. "Mr. Justice Minton and the Supreme Court (1949–1956)." Ph.D. dissertation, University of Iowa, 1969.
Berman, David M. "The Political Philosophy of Hugo L. Black." Ph.D. dissertation, Rutgers University, 1957.
Bolner, James J. "Mr. Chief Justice Vinson." Ph.D. dissertation, University of Virginia, 1962.
Dorin, Dennis Daniel. "Mr. Justice Clark and State Criminal Justice." Ph.D. dissertation, University of Virginia, 1974.
Gilkey, Royal Clarence. "Mr. Justice Frankfurter and Civil Liberties as Manifested in and Suggested by the Compulsory Flag Salute Controversy: A Study of Fifteen Years of Supreme Court Opinions (1939–1953)." Ph.D. dissertation, University of Minnesota, 1957.
Hull, Elizabeth Anne. "Sherman Minton and the Cold War Front." Ph.D. dissertation, New School for Social Research, 1977.
Marquardt, Ronald Gene. "The Judicial Justice: Mr. Justice Burton and the Supreme Court." Ph.D. dissertation, University of Missouri, 1973.

MISCELLANEOUS

Dictionary of American Biography, Supplement 7, 1961–65. New York: Charles Scribner's Sons, 1981.
New York Times (February, 1937; June, 1951; June 1952; October 1947; October, 1948; and June 1977).
Newsweek, June 4, 1945.
Richmond Times Dispatch, September 13, 1987.
Personal Interview with Rufus Burrus, Attorney at Law, personal attorney to Harry S. Truman. Independence, Missouri, September 21, 1987.
Personal Interview with John P. Frank, Attorney at Law, Historian, Author, Professor, former law clerk to Hugo L. Black. Phoenix, Arizona. January 28, 1983.

Telephone Interview with Charles Reed, Attorney at Law, former law clerk to Tom C. Clark, Washington, D. C., August 20, 1987.
Telephone Interview with James R. Ryan, Attorney at Law, former law clerk to Harold Burton. Tulsa, Oklahoma, September 11, 1982.
Telephone Interview with Sherman A. Minton, M.D., Professor of Microbiology, Indiana University School of Medicine, Indianapolis, Indiana. February 22, 1983.
Telephone Interview with Karl R. Price, Attorney at Law, former law clerk to Frederick Moore Vinson, Washington, D. C., September 28, 1987.
The National Cyclopaedia of American Biography. 1892–1972. Current Vol. H.
U.S. Congressional Record, 78th Cong., 1st Session, vol. 89, Part 2, A 3786.
U.S. Reports. Volumes 326 through 388, inclusive.
Washington Post. June 23, 1947.

SPECIAL COLLECTIONS

Harold Hitz Burton Papers, Manuscript Division, Library of Congress, Washington, D. C.
Hugo La Fayette Black Papers, Manuscript Division, Library of Congress, Washington, D. C.
Tom C. Clark Papers, Rare and Special Collection, Tarlton Law Library, University of Texas, Austin, Texas.
Felix Frankfurter Papers, Manuscript Division of the Library of Congress, Washington, D. C.
Felix Frankfurter Papers, Manuscript Division, Harvard Law School Library, Cambridge, Massachusetts.
Sherman Minton Papers, Harry S. Truman Library, Independence, Missouri.
Truman Papers, Harry S. Truman Library, Independence, Missouri.
Frederick Moore Vinson Papers, Special Collections of the Margaret I. King Library, University of Kentucky, Lexington, Kentucky.

INDEX

Abraham, Henry J.: restraint tenets, 2–3; selection criteria, 25, 57, 103, 116
Adamson v. California (1948), 38
Adler et al.v. Board of Education of the City of New York (1952), 120
Administrative Procedures Act, 102
Agriculture Adjustment Act (1933), xvi, 75
Allen, Francis A., 74
American Civil Liberties Union, 10
American Communications Association C. I. O. et al.v. Douds (1950), 71
American Heritage Foundation, 41 n.49
American Law Institute, 50
Antieau, Chester James, 72
Ashdown v. State of Utah (1958), 51
Ashland College, 4
Atkinson, David Neal, 124–25 n.8, 125 n.24, 126 n.29, 127 n.81, 128 n.97, 131
Atomic Energy Act (1946), 99–100
Attorneys General, 106 n.24
Austin, John, 9

Bailey v. Richardson(1951), 89
Baker v. Carr (1962), xxi n.22, 132
Bakeshop law, New York, xvi
Ball, Senator Joseph H., 46
Ballard v. United States (1946), 52
Ball-Burton-Hill-Hatch resolution (B2H2), 46–47

Barrows et al.v. Jackson (1953), 73, 121–22
Beilan, Herman A., 54
Beilan v. Board of Education, School District of Philadelphia (1958), 54
Bentham, Jeremy, 9
Berger, Raoul, 132
Berry, Mary Frances, 48–49, 54, 55; on restraint, 57
Bickel, Alexander M., 3, 21 n.65, 132
Biddle, Francis, 88
Black, Hugo La Fayette: on balancing, 6; on Bill of Rights, 6, 7; on absolutism of First Amendment, 6, 19–20 n.34; incorporation under Fourteenth Amendment, 38; re Jackson, 22 n.96, 27; as judicial activist, xv, xvii, xix, 8, 14–17, 129–34; as legal positivist, 8–9; literalism, 6, 8, 20 n.47; as member of Court with Burton, 46, 47, 50, 51, 54, 56, with Clark, 95, 97, 102, 103, with Minton, 111, 112, 113, 116, 119–20, 122; and with Vinson, 67, 68, 69, 70, 74, 77; philosophy, 6–9, 19 n.2; political career, 4–6; re Robert's letter, 26; as Roosevelt appointee, xv, xvii, xix, xxi n.17; under Truman, 28, 31, 34
Black, Hugo La Fayette, Jr., 113
Black, Martha Toland, 4

Black, Sterling, 113
Black, William La Fayette, 4
Blackmar v. Guerre (1952), 118
Blaustein, Albert P., 49
Bowdoin College, 46
Braden, George D., 115
Brandeis, Louis Dembitz: appointment, xxi n.17; influence on Frankfurter, 9–13, 21 n.55, 52, 104; on judicial activism, 3; Truman's opinion of, xviii; compared with Vinson, 64–65
Breithaupt v. Abram (1956), 97, 104
Brennan, William J., 98
Brotherhood of Railroad Trainmen et al. v. Howard et al. (1952), 122
Brown v. Board of Education (1954), 35–36, 56, 79, 132
Bryan, William Jennings, 112
Burger, Warren E., 90
Burns et al. v. Wilson (1953), 116
Burrus, Rufus, 33
Burton, Alfred Edgar, 46
Burton, Gertrude Hitz, 46
Burton, Harold Hitz: appointment, xviii, 17, 25, 27–28, 31–32; on *Brown v. Board of Education*, 35; confirmation, 33; evaluated, 36–38, 47–49, 56–58, 129, 130, 132, 134; use of judicial restraint, 50–56; as member of Court, 36–38, 69, 72, 77, 79, 90, 97, 122; re Milton's health, 114; re opinions on criminal procedure, 50–53, on loyalty security, 53–55, and on racial discrimination, 55–56; pre-Court career, 45–47; retirement, 45; on *Steel Seizure Case*, 32
Bute v. People of State of Illinois, (1948), 50
Butler, Pierce, xxi n.17
Byrnes, James Francis, xxi

Cardozo, Benjamin N., xvii, 9, 52, 57, 64, 134, 135 n.2
Carter v. Carter Coal Co. (1936), 64, 75
Centre College, 65
Certiorari, writ of: effect on Court, 35, 49, 59 n.24, 67, 79; use in judicial activism, 15–16, 74–76; use in judicial restraint, 35, 49, 70, 74; Rule of Four, 22, 35, 49
Chisholm v. Georgia (1937), 1
Civil Rights Act, 72
Civil Rights Committee, President's, 89
Clark, Ramsey, 90, 91
Clark, Thomas Campbell: appointment, xviii, 29–30; confirmation, 34; evaluation, 36–38, 49, 90, 103–5, 110 n.143, 115, 129–34; use of judicial restraint, 92–103; as member of Court, 4, 17, 36–38; opinions on alien rights, 102–3, on criminal procedure, 92–99, 107 n.70, and on loyalty security, 99–102; pre-Court career, 87–90; re *Steel Seizure Case*, 32–33, 41 n.45, 104–5; friendship with Truman, 29–30, 32–33, 41–42 n.49, 42 nn.50, 55; on Truman's Court appointments, 25–26, 27–28, 40 n.27; on Vinson, 29, 66, 68
Clark, Virginia Maxey Falls, 87
Clear and present danger test, 16, 71–72, 82 n.74
Cold War, 37
Cole v. Young (1956), 101
Commissioner of Internal Revenue v. Estate of Louis Sternberger (1955), 47
Commissioner of Internal Revenue v. P. G. Wodehouse (1949), 47
Commissioner of Internal Revenue v. Wilcox et al. (1946), 47–48
Committee to Investigate the National Defense Program (the Truman Committee), 27–30, 47, 88, 112–13
Communist Party of the United States v. Subversive Activites Control Board (1955), 100
Connally, Thomas Terry (Tom), 29, 47, 88
Connally Amendment, 76
Constitution: as construed by Burton, 50–56, by Black, 14–17, by Clark, 92–103, by Frankfurter, 14–17, by Minton, 116–24, and by Vinson, 69–74; flexibleness of, 12; four corners of,

9, 13, 20 n.47; judicial review under, 1–2; literalness of, 6; restraint tenets for interpretation of, 2–3; value of: Black on, 6–8, Brandeis on, 12, Frankfurter on, 11–14, Holmes on, 12–13, and Marshall on, 11
Coolidge, Calvin, 64
Coram nobis writ of, 118
Court-packing plan, Roosevelt's, xvii, 3–4, 21, 34, 55, 64, 88, 112
Crooker v. State of California (1958), 95
Crutcher, W. E., 79
Cummings, Homer S., 88
Curtis, Benjamin R., 49

Dennis et al. v. United States (1951), 14, 16, 49, 53, 71, 88, 100
Dennis v. United States (1950), 115, 119
Donovan, Robert J., 89
Dorin, Dennis Daniel, 110
Douglas, William Orville: appointed, xxi n.17; in dissent, 34, 38, 47, 50, 51, 56, 97, 123; majority opinion, 70; Minton's opinion of, 28; re Roberts' letter, 26; re *Rosenberg* Case, 77–79; re *Steel Seizure Case*, 32
Dred Scott v. Sandford, 2, 11, 33
Due process, substantive, 53
Duncan, Richard M., 32
Dunne, Gerald T., 22
Dutton, C. B., 91

Edelman v. California (1953), 93
Eighth Amendment, 53, 70
Eisenhower, Dwight D., xix, 45, 115
Elman, Philip, 36, 43 n.76
Emergency Court of Appeals, 40 n.27, 64
Ervin, Sam, 99
Espionage Act (1917), 77, 78, 100
Ex parte Quirin (1942), 75
Executive Order no. 9835, 89, 101
Executive Order no. 10340, 14, 15, 32
Executive Order no. 10450, 101

Fair Labor Standards Act (1938), 19 n.23
Fairlie, Charles, 108 n.81

Fairman, Charles, 104
Fay et al. v. Noia (1963), 94
Ferrell, Robert H., 37
Fifteenth Amendment, 122–23
Fifth Amendment, 16, 54, 101, 102, 123
First Amendment, 7, 16, 17, 19, 54, 70, 71, 121
Fletcher v. Peck (1810), 2
Fortune, 34
Fourteenth Amendment, 7, 11–19, 38, 50, 54, 56, 72, 73, 92, 96, 104, 122
Fourth Amendment, 52, 69, 90, 96, 97, 123
Francis, Willie, 52–53
Frank, John P.: on Burton, 47, 48; on Clark, 91; on Court, 36, 67; on Minton, 115; on Vinson, 35, 65, 68
Frankfurter, Emma, 10
Frankfurter, Felix: compared with Black, 4–17, 22–23 n.97; on Brandeis, 10, 11–12, 20–21 nn.51, 55; on Holmes, 12–13; on judicial function, 11–14, 133; use of judicial restraint, 14–17, 129–33, 134; on Marshall, 11; as member of Court, 27, 34, 35, 38, with Burton, 46, 47, 48, 49, 51, 52, 53, 56–57, 61 n.82, with Vinson, 61, 67, 68, 69, 70, 71–72, 78, 79, 88 n.130, with Clark, 87, 90, 94, 97, 100, 102, 103, 104–5, 107, and with Minton, 117–22, 124; philosophy, 11–14, 17; political activities, 10–11; pre-Court career, 9–11; re Roberts' letter, 26; as Roosevelt's appointee, xv, xix n.17, 4, 9; on Thayer, 13–14; conflict with Vinson, 35–36, 43 n.76, 64
Frankfurter, Leopold, 10
Frazier-Lempke Federal Farm Bankruptcy Act (1934), xvi, xx–xxi n.12
Frazier v. United States (1948), 119
Freund, Paul, 104
Fuller, M. W., 104
Fuller Court, xvi

Gambler's Occupation Tax Act (1951), 123

Garner et al. v. Board of Public Works of Los Angeles (1951), 101
Gideon, Clarence Earl, 96
Gideon v. Wainwright (1963), 96–97, 108
Gilmore, Grant, 135 n.23
Giordenello v. United States (1958), 97
Gitlow v. New York (1925), 92
Goldwater, Barry, 113
Griswold v. Connecticut (1965), 20 n.47
Groner, Lawrence, 65
Guffey Coal Act (Bituminous Coal Conservation Act, 1935), 64, 75

Habeas corpus, 94, 103, 116, 118
Hand, Learned, 72
Harlan, John Marshall, 53, 96
Harris v. United States (1947), 69
Harvard Law School, 9–10, 46, 131
Hatch Act (1939), 118
Healy v. Commissioner of Internal Revenue (1953), 66
Heflin, Tom, 5
Heikkila v. Barber (1953), 102–3, 119
Helvering v. Davis (1937), xx
Henderson v. United States et al. (1950), 55
Hepburn Act (1906), xvi, xx
Hill-Burton Hospital Act (1948), 47
Hiss, Alger, 79, 88
Holmes, Oliver Wendell, Jr.: clear and present danger test, 16, 71–72; in dissent, 3; influence on Frankfurter, 9, 12–13, 52, 104; on judicial legislation, 132; Truman on, xviii; compared with Vinson, 64, 68
Holt, Ivan Lee, 41
House Committee on UnAmerican Activities, 54, 71, 98
Howe, Mark de Wolfe, 131, 134
Hughes, Charles Evans, xvi, xvii, 4, 26, 29, 75, 88
Hull, Elizabeth Anne, 125
Hylton v. United States (1796), 2

I Am sect, 52
Idaho Power and Light Company, 46
Immigration and Naturalization Act (1952), 102, 119

Internal Revenue Code, 47–48
Internal Security Act (McCarran Act) (1950), 100
Interstate Commerce Act (1887), xvi
Irvine v. California (1954), 96, 107, 130

Jackson, Percival E., 67
Jackson, Robert Houghwout: appointed, xxi; as Attorney General, 89, 106 n.24; feud with Black, 22 n.96, 27, 34, 42 n.61; as possible Chief Justice, 27, 29, 34, 42 n.61; as member of Court, 38, 67, 70, 96, 120; at Nuremburg, 27, 79
Japanese-Americans, 88
Jay, John, 15
Jaybird Democratic Association, 122–23
Jencks v. United States (1957), 98–99
Jewell Ridge Coal Corp. v. United Mine Workers (1945), 27
Johnson, Lyndon Baines, 113
Johnson v. Zerbst (1938), 50, 96
Joint Anti-Fascist Refugee Committee, 71
Joint Anti-Fascist Refugee Committee v. McGrath (1951), 54, 89
Judicial activism, 1–4; Black's use of, xv, xvii, xix, 8, 14–17, 129–34; Burton's use of, 54–55; dichotomy on the Court, 4–17, 129–34; Vinson's use of, 74–78
Judicial legislation: Brandeis on, 3; Frankfurter on, 133; Holmes on, 3, 132; Truman's conception, 31–32
Judicial self-restraint: Frankfurter on, 11–14, 15, 35; history of, 1–4; tenets, 2–3; use of, *see under individual justices*; use of, generally, on the Vinson Court, 129–34; use of specific tenets: requirement of case or controversy, 18, 78, 121, limiting *certiorari*, 15, 16, 22, 35, 49, 59, 67, 70, 74–75, 76, 79, avoiding constitutional issue— non essential to merits of case, 12, 15, 21, 54, 56, 70, 100, 103, 116, 121, deference to executive or legislative entities, 51, 52, 55, 70, 74, 78, 91, 93, 94–95, 98, 101, 102, 103,

117, 118, fact-finding left to the jury, 7, 100, 103, reliance on precedent, 26, 103–4, 110, 119, proper procedure required, 70, 74, 78, 91, 95, 98, 103, 117, 118, and requiring standing, 73, 78, 122
Jurisprudence, sociological, 8, 14, 129–31
Jury selection, 22, 92, 93

Kelley, Edward J., 46
Keynes, John Maynard, 10
Kirkendall, Richard, 65, 67, 68, 89
Konigsberg v. State Bar (1957), 54, 130
Kovacs v. Cooper (1949), 66
Ku Klux Klan, 5

LaFollette, Robert M., xvi, 10
La Guardia, Fiorello, 46
Leland v. State of Oregon (1952), 94
Leng May Ma v. Barber (1958), 103
Lewis, John L., 75, 113
Lewis v. United States (1955), 123, 130
Leysin, Switzerland, 46
Liberalism: New Deal "liberal," 11, 104; "process," 17; "substantive," 17
Little v. Barreme (1804), viii
Louisville Joint Stock Lead Bank v. Radford, xx
Lynching, 89

McCune, Wesley, 28
McDonald et al. v. United States (1948), 51
McLaurin v. Oklahoma State Regents for Higher Education et al. (1950), 56, 73, 79
McNutt, Paul V., 112
McReynolds, James Clark, xxi, 43 n.76
Mann Act (1910), xvi
Mapp v. Ohio (1961), 96, 104
Marbury v. Madison (1803), 2
Marcello v. Bonds (1955), 102
Maris, Albert B., 64
Marshall, John, 1, 11–12; judicial restraint, 18 n.4
Mason, Alpheus T., 3
Meiklejohn, Alexander, 19 n.34

Merskey, Roy M., 49
Michel v. State of Louisiana (1955), 92
Miller, Arthur Selwyn, 132
Miller, Merle, 32–33
Minnesota Rate Cases (1913), xx, 8
Minow, Newton N., 35
Minton, Emma Lyvers, 111
Minton, John Evan, 111
Minton, Sherman: appointment, xviii, 17, 25, 30–31; friendship with Black, 6, 28, 31, 110–14, 124; confirmation, 34; as Democrat, 112–13, 124; evaluated, 36–38, 49, 90, 115, 126 n.29, 129–34; illness, 114–15, 124, 125 n.24; use of judicial restraint, 116–24; as member of Court, 32, 73, 124; opinions on procedure, 116–19, on loyalty security, 119–21, on racial discrimination, 73, 121–23, on nomination of Burton, 28, and of Vinson, 31–32; pre-Court career, 111–14; retirement, 114; on *Steel Seizure Case*, 32; friendship with Truman, 31, 111, 114, 124 n.8
Minton, Sherman A., 114
Miranda, Ernesto, 95
Miranda v. Arizona (1966), 95, 104
Moley, Raymond, 88, 105 n.6
Moore, E. H., 34
Morehead News, 79
Morgan v. Commonwealth of Virginia (1948), 55
Murphy, Frank, xxii n.17, 29, 135 n.26
Murphy, Paul L., xvi
Muscles Shoals Dam, 5

National Association for the Advancement of Colored People, 10
National College of the State Judiciary, 90
National Conference on Citizenship, 41 n.49
National Industrial Recovery Act (1933), xvi, xx n.12
National Labor Relations Act (Wagner-Connery 1935), xvii, xx n.13, 20
New Deal: fate of legislation, xvi–xvii; second New Deal, 9, 20–21 n.51, 35;

support of Black, 5, Brandeis-Frankfurter, 10–11, 21 n.55, as a Court, xvii, 129, Minton, 112–13, and Vinson, 64
New Hampshire Subversives Act (1951), 100
New York Times, 34
N. L. R. B. v. Jones and Laughlin Steel Corporation, xx n.13
Norris-LaGuardia Anti-Injunction Act (1932), 75–76
Nuremburg trials, 27, 79

Oliver, William W., 35, 78
O'Mahoney, Frank, 99
On Lee v. United States (1952), 51–52

Palmer v. Ashe (1951), 118
Panama Refining Co. v. Ryan (1935), xx n.12
Patterson, Robert P., 27
Payne v. State of Arkansas (1958), 94–95
Pearson, Drew, 48
Pedrick, Willard H., 79
"Perhaps and probable" test, 71–72
Phi Beta Kappa, 46
Plessy v. Ferguson (1896), 56, 74, 132
Pollock v. Farmer's Loan & Trust Co. (1895), xx
Portal-to-portal pay, 27
Price, Karl R., 68
Prichard, Edward F., Jr., 35–36, 37
Pritchett, C. Herman, 55, 99, 131, 134–35 n.12
Progressive Party, xvi
Prohibition, 5, 18 n.19
Provine, Doris Marie, 49
Public Utilities Holding Act (1935), 10
Pure Food and Drug Act (1906), xvi
Pusey, Merlo, 29

Racial covenants, 88–89
Racial discrimination, 30; cases, 55–56, 72–74, 121–23; Vinson on, 36, 79
Railroad Retirement Board v. Alton R. Co. (1935), 75
Rayburn, Sam, 29
Recall, judicial, xvi

Reece, Amos, 93
Reece v. State of Georgia (1955), 93
Reed, Charles, 104
Reed, Stanley Forman: appointed, xvii, xxi n.17; as member of Court, 36, 47, 66, 69, 79, 133
Rehnquist, William H., 20 n.47
Remmer v. United States (1934), 124
Republican Party, 10, 45, 46
Revenue Act (1937), 64
Richards-Gebaur Air Base, 41–42 n.49
Rickert Rice Mills v. Fontenot (1936), 75
Roberts, Owen Josephus, 3, 20, 26, 27
Robinson, Joseph Taylor, 8 n.15
Rodell, Fred, 34, 48
Rogers, William P., 45
Rogers v. Quan (1958), 103
Roosevelt, Franklin Delano: appointments, xxi n.17, 4, 9, 18 n.15, 25; associations with Burton, 46, Clark, 88, Minton, 30, 34, 112–13, and Vinson, 64, 65; Court-packing plan, xvii, 3, 21 n.55, 34, 64, 88, 112; Roosevelt Court (1937–1946), xv–xviii, 129–30
Roosevelt, Theodore, 10
Rosenberg et ux v. United States (1953), 75, 76, 77–78, 84, 99
Roviaro v. United States (1957), 98
Rule of Four, 22, 35, 49
Rutkin v. United States (1952), 48
Rutledge, Wiley Blount, xxi n.17, 29, 64, 67

Sacco and Vanzetti, 10
St. Louis Globe-Democrat, 34
Santayana, 13
Scales, 87
Schechter Poultry Corp. v. United States (1935), xx
Schenck v. United States (1919), 16, 71–72, 82 n.74
Schlesinger, Arthur M., Jr.: on Black, 130; Court furor over article, 135 n.26; on judicial restraint-activist dichotomy, xv, xix, 38, 132; on necessity for restraint, 133; on Vinson's

appointment, 34; in Vinson's defense, 85–86 n.132
Schware v. Board of Bar Examiners (1957), 54–55, 130
Schwellenbach, Lewis B., 31
Securities Act (1933), 10
Selective Service Act (1940), 112
Senate Special Committee to Investigate Lobbying Activities, 5–6, 30, 112
Shaughnessy v. Pedreiro (1955), 119
Shaughnessy v. United States ex rel. Mezei (1953), 102
Shelley v. Kraemer (1948), 72–73, 88, 122
Sherman Anti-Trust Act (1890), xvi, xix–xx n.3
Shreveport Rate Cases (1914), xx n.8
Sicurella v. United States (1955), 116–17
Silverstein, Mark, 23
Slochower v. Board of Higher Education of the City of New York (1956), 101
Smith, Alfred E., 10, 64
Smith Act (1940), 16, 53, 71, 100, 112, 119
Social Security Act (1935), xvii, 21, 64
Soil Conservation Act (1935), 20
Sozinsky v. United States (1937), xx–xxi n.14
Stack v. Boyle (1951), 70
Standard Vacuum Oil Co. v. United States (1950), 117
State of Louisiana ex rel. Francis v. Resweber, Sheriff et al. (1947), 52–53
Steel Seizure Case (Youngstown Sheet and Tube Company v. Sawyer, 1952), 14, 15, 30, 32, 33, 75, 76, 84 n.116, 104, 130. *See also individual justices*
Stevenson, Adlai Ewing, 113
Stewart Machine Co. v. Davis (1937), xx n.13
Stimson, Henry L., 10
Stone, Harlan Fiske, xvii, xxi n.17, 3, 4, 17, 26, 27, 45, 64
Stone Court, 27, 29
Summary Suspension Act (1950), 101
Sutherland, George, xxi

Sweatt v. Painter et al. (1950), 56, 73, 79

Taft-Hartley Act (1947), xiii, 14, 71
Terminiello v. City of Chicago (1949), 70
Terry v. Adams (1953), 122
Thayer, James Bradley, xvi, xix, 13, 57, 61 n.82, 104, 130, 132, 133
To Secure These Rights, 89
Trienens, Howard J., 36, 65
Truman, Harry S.: appointees, 4, 17; re Burton, 27, 31, 32, 33, 45; re Clark, 25–26, 29–30, 32–33, 34, 41–42 nn.45, 49, 88–89, 90; on Court, xviii–xix; Court assessed, 35–38, 129–134; on Court packing, xviii; Executive Order 9835—89, 101; Executive Order 10340—14, 15, 32; Executive Order 10450—101; re Minton, 30–31, 32, 34, 111–12, 114, 115; re Vinson, 17, 25, 28–29, 30–32, 39 n.19, 40 n.27, 63, 65; on *Steel Seizure Case*, 14, 32–33

United Nations, 46–47
United States Code of Military Justice (1950), 116
United States ex rel. Accardi v. Shaughnessy (1954), 103
United States ex rel. Knauff v. Shaughnessy (1950), 119
United States ex rel. Toth v. Quarles (1955), 116
United States v. Bryan (1950), 71
United States v. Butler (1936), xx n.12, 75
United States v. E. C. Knight, Co. (1895), xx n.3
United States v. Fleishman (1950), 71
United States v. Francis I. Dupont de Nemours and Co. (1957), 49
United States v. Jeffers (1951), 97
United States v. Lefkowitz (1932), 69
United States v. Morgan (1954), 118
United States v. Paramount Pictures, Inc. (1948), 88
United States v. United Mine Workers (1947), 75, 76, 88, 113

United States v. Wood (1936), 119
United States v. Wunderlich et al. (1951), 117
Uphaus v. Wyman (1959), 100

Van Devanter, Willis, xxi n.17
Vinson, Frederick Moore: appointment, xv, xviii, xix, 17, 25, 28–29, 34, 65; on *Brown v. Board of Education*, 35–36; confirmation, 33–34; conflict with Frankfurter, 35–36, 85 n.130; death, 29; re *Dennis et al. v. United States* (1951), 71–72, 79, 85–86 n.132; evaluated, 4, 35–38, 49, 66–68, 78–79, 90, 115–16, 129–34; use of judicial activism, 74–78; use of judicial restraint, 68–74; as member of Court, 49, 56, 90, 115–16; opinions on criminal procedure, 69–70, on loyalty security, 70–72, and on racial discrimination, 56, 72–74; "perhaps and probable" test, 71–72; pre-Court career, 63–66; racism, 79; re *Rosenberg* case, 76–78; re *Steel Seizure Case*, 32, 76; Truman on, 28–29, 30, 39 n.19
Vinson, Frederick Moore, Jr., 79
Vinson, James, 63
Vinson, Virginia Ferguson, 63
Vinson Court: case load, 67; decisions, 50–56, 66–78, 92–103, 115–23; evaluated, 31–33, 35–38, 129–34; nature of, xix; productivity, 49; Truman's appointments, 25–31, 33–34
Vinson-Guffey Coal Act (1937), 64
Virginia Railroad Co. v. Systems Federation (1937), xx–xxi n.14

Wallace, Harry L., 124
Wallace, Henry A., 30
War Brides Act (1945), 119–20
Ware v. Hylton (1796), 1
War Labor Disputes Act (1943), 75–76
Warren, Earl, xix, 4, 90, 97, 115, 125
Warren Court, xvi, 35, 91, 132–33
Washington, George, 15
Washington Star, 27, 34
Watkins, John T., 98
Watkins v. United States (1957), 98
Ways and Means Committee (House), 65
Wechsler, Herbert, xix, 132
Weiman v. Updegraff (1952), 101
West Coast Hotel Co. v. Parrish et al. (1937), xx n.14, 3, 129
Western Reserve University, 46
White, G. Edward, 17
Wilbur, Rollin A., 46
"Williamsburg" yacht, 30
Williams v. State of Georgia (1955), 93
Willis, Raymond, 112
Willkie, Wendell, 112
Wiretapping, 20 n.40, 51–52
Wodehouse, P. G., 47
Wolf v. Colorado (1949), 96, 107 n.70
Works Progress Administration, 20–21 n.51
World Fellowship Camp, 100
Wright, Charles Allen, 90
Wright, J. Skelly, 133
Wright v. Vinton Branch (1937), xx–xxi n.14

About the Author

FRANCES HOWELL RUDKO, an attorney in private practice for 15 years, was recently appointed to the position of Law Clerk to Chief Judge Franklin Waters, Western District Federal Court of Arkansas. Her interests extend equally into the fields of law and history and she is currently working on the Supreme Court and international law in the early nineteenth century.